A Servant of God

Selected Writings of Fulton J. Sheen

A Servant of God

Selected Writings of Fulton J. Sheen

Vol II

The Seven Last Words
The Cross & the Beatitudes
Victory Over Vice
The Way to Happiness
The Way to Inner Peace

Copyright © 2021 Mockingbird Press

All rights reserved. The original works are in the public domain to the best of publisher's knowledge. The publisher makes no claim to the original writings. However, the compilation, construction, cover design, trademarks, derivations, foreword, descriptions, added work, etc., of this edition are copyrighted and may not be reproduced, distributed, or transmitted in any form or by any means, including photocopying, recording, or other electronic or mechanical methods, without the prior written permission of the publisher, except in the case of brief quotations embodied in critical reviews and certain other non-commercial uses permitted by copyright law, or where content is specifically noted as being reproduced under a Creative Commons license.

Cover, "An Orange and Yellow Tulip with a Butterfly," by Dutch School, c. 1700
Cover Design by Jenny Frank, Copyright © 2021 Mockingbird Press, LLC
Foreword by Rachael Underhill, Copyright © 2021 Mockingbird Press, LLC
Interior Design by Maria Johnson

Publisher's Cataloging-In-Publication Data

Sheen, Fulton, author; Underhill, Rachael, foreword by
Servant of God : Selected Writings of Fulton J. Sheen : Volume II : The Seven Last Words, The Cross and the Beatitudes, Victory Over Vice, The Way to Happiness & The Way to Inner Peace / Fulton Sheen with Rachael Underhill

Paperback	ISBN-13: 978-1-68493-003-6
Hardback	ISBN-13: 978-1-68493-004-3
Ebook	ISBN-13: 978-1-68493-005-0

1. Religion—Christianity—Catholic. 2. Philosophy & Religion—Religion & Beliefs—Christianity, I. Fulton Sheen. II. Rachael Underhill. III. Servant of God : Selected Writings of Fulton J. Sheen. IV. Title: Volume II : The Seven Last Words, The Cross and the Beatitudes, Victory Over Vice, The Way to Happiness & The Way to Inner Peace

REL010000 / APY

Type Set in Schoolbook / **Franklin Gothic Demi**

Mockingbird Press, Augusta, GA
info@mockingbirdpress.com

Contents

Foreword 1

The Seven Last Words 3
    Introduction 7
    The First Word 9
    The Second Word 12
    The Third Word 15
    The Fourth Word 18
    The Fifth Word 21
    The Sixth Word 24
    The Seventh Word 27

The Cross and the Beatitudes 31
    Introduction 33
    The First Word 34
    The Second Word 40
    The Third Word 46
    The Fourth Word 51
    The Fifth Word 57
    The Sixth Word 62
    The Seventh Word 67

Victory Over Vice 73
    Introduction 77
    The First Word: Anger 78
    The Second Word: Envy 84
    The Third Word: Lust 91
    The Fourth Word: Pride 98
    The Fifth Word: Gluttony 105
    The Sixth Word: Sloth 113
    The Seventh Word: Covetousness 121

Way To Happiness 129
    Introduction 131
    Plan And Purpose 131
    Chapter 1: Contentment 133
    Chapter 2: Reducing Ego to Zero 135
    Chapter 3: Joy 137
    Chapter 4: Is Modern Man Far From Peace? 139
    Chapter 5: Joy From The Inside 142

Chapter 6: Love Is Infinite 145
Chapter 7: The Philosophy Of Pleasure 147
Chapter 8: Work 149
Chapter 9: Repose 152
Chapter 10: The Idle in The Marketplace 154
Chapter 11: The Three Causes Of Love 156
Chapter 12: When Lovers Fail There Is Love 159
Chapter 13: True Love 161
Chapter 14: The Effects Of Want Of Love 163
Chapter 15: Reflections On Love 165
Chapter 16: The Mystery Of Love 167
Chapter 17: Love And Ecstasy 169
Chapter 18: Motherhood 171
Chapter 19: Parents And Children 173
Chapter 20: Blood, Sweat And Tears 175
Chapter 21: The Teen-Agers 178
Chapter 22: More About Teen-Agers 181
Chapter 23: The Loves Of Youth 183
Chapter 24: "Getting Away With It" 185
Chapter 25: Self-Discipline 187
Chapter 26: Kindness 189
Chapter 27: Fear And Ethics 191
Chapter 28: Rest And Mediation 193
Chapter 29: Better To Give Than Receive 195
Chapter 30: The Spirit Of Service 197
Chapter 31: How To Give 199
Chapter 32: Progress 201
Chapter 33: The Mass-Man 203
Chapter 34: A Recall To The Inner Life 205
Chapter 35: Why We Are Not Better 207
Chapter 36: Revolution Starts With Man 209
Chapter 37: There Is Hope 211

Way to Inner Peace 213
Part 1: Inner Peace 215
Part 2: Goodness 227
Part 3: Happiness 239
Part 4: Virtue 251
Part 5: Learning 261
Part 6: Wisdom 271
Part 7: You 285
Part 8: Faith 299

Foreword

THE selected works in this volume seek to educate both the new follower of Christ and the lifelong devotee on their place in the world and their responsibilities to God and their fellow human beings. These works provide a better understanding of Jesus Christ and guidance for living a life of serenity and inner joy.

Archbishop Fulton J. Sheen (b. 1895 – d. 1979) was a Catholic priest, writer, educator, and television and media personality. After becoming a priest in 1919, it wasn't long before he was sharing his views on scripture and philosophy with others. He wrote his first book in 1925, and taught philosophy at the Catholic University of America in Washington, DC from the 1920s until 1950.

In 1930, he began The Catholic Hour, a widely popular Sunday night radio program. After 20 successful years, he switched mediums and began the television show Life is Worth Living in 1952. The show was a hit, and Archbishop Sheen earned an Emmy for the program in 1953.

While appearing in the media, writing his books, teaching, and seeing to his duties as a bishop (consecrated in 1951), Sheen also found the time to lead the Society for the Propagation of the Faith, raising millions of dollars for charity and missionary work.

The books in this collection represent a span of 21 years of Archbishop Sheen's priestly life. Three of them share a similar theme—the examination of Christ's Seven Last Words.

The Seven Last Words are the sayings of Jesus Christ upon the cross. In The Seven Last Words, Archbishop Sheen explains the content of this final sermon. Recorded in the gospels of Mark, Matthew, John, and Luke, these short yet profound phrases guide us through the death of the Saviour while providing a better understanding of the depths of His Divine Love. Beginning with forgiveness for His tormentors and ending by turning His face toward His Heavenly Father, Christ's final words show His teachings in action, just as He did throughout His life.

The Cross and the Beatitudes explores the Seven Last Words from another angle. In this work, Archbishop Sheen draws a parallel between the eight Beatitudes from the Sermon on the Mount and these final sayings. These Beatitudes, or blessings, offer guidance to the listener, arguing for love and humility rather than strength and pride. While there are eight beatitudes, Archbishop Sheen considers the final to be an overarching blessing that includes the seven preceding it. By connecting seven beatitudes to the Seven Last Words, he unites the beginning of Christ's spiritual teachings with their completion upon Calvary.

In Victory Over Vice, he approaches the Seven Last Words in yet a different way. This work examines the seven cardinal sins through the lens of the Last Words of Christ. While these sins in others led to the crucifixion, Jesus Christ's response to them gives us a blueprint for how to face them in ourselves and in those around us.

The two remaining works in this collection are general guides to a life of peace and tranquility. Way to Happiness makes the argument that inner joy comes from fulfilling our primary purpose—to overflow with "...Pure Life, Pure Truth and Pure Love—and that is the definition of God." To this end, Archbishop Sheen has provided short essays on the themes of happiness, work, love, children, youth, inner peace, giving, and man. These essays help the reader to apply Biblical principles to their everyday lives.

Similarly, Way to Inner Peace explores the power of humility and virtue to bring us the tranquility that we seek. This work, in particular, has value to the religious and the secular alike. It argues that we reflect what we seek out. When we pursue comparisons with others and submerge ourselves in scandal and drama, we will always rob ourselves of life's serenity.

The Seven Last Words

[1933]

Compassionate Queen of the Seven Swords in
Hearts where Christ thy Son is King,
I give thee Seven Words.
Lovingly accept for what is best in them,
Dropped from a cross and the lips of God.

Introduction

THREE ELEMENTS conspire in the making of every great message: a pulpit, an audience, and a truth. These three were present in the two most notable messages in the life of Our Blessed Saviour, the first and the last which He delivered to mankind. The pulpit of His first message was the mountainside; His audience, unlettered Galileans; His truth, the Beatitudes. The last message He delivered had for its pulpit the Cross; for its audience, Scribes and Pharisees who blasphemed, temple priests who ridiculed, Roman soldiers who gambled, timid disciples who feared, Magdalen who wept, John who loved, and Mary who grieved as only a mother can grieve. Magdalen, John, and Mary—penitence, priesthood, and innocence—the three types of souls to be found forever beneath the Cross of Christ. The sermon that audience heard from the pulpit of the Cross was the Seven Last Words, the dying sayings of a Saviour Who, by dying, slew death.

In the four thousand years of Jewish history, the dying words of only three are recorded: Israel, Moses, and Stephen. The reason perhaps is that no others are found so significant and representative as these three. Israel was the first of the Israelites; Moses, the first of the legal dispensation; Stephen, the first martyr. The dying words of each begin something sublime in the history of God's dealings with men. Not even the last words of Peter or Paul or John have been our legacy, for no spirit ever guided a pen to reveal the secrets of their dying lips. And yet the human heart is always anxious to hear of the state of a mind at that very common and yet very mysterious moment called death.

In His goodness, Our Blessed Lord has left us His thoughts on dying, for He more than Israel, more than Moses, more than Stephen is representative of all humanity. In this sublime hour, therefore, He calls all His children to the pulpit of the Cross, and every word He says to them is set down for the purpose of an eternal publication and an undying consolation. There was never a preacher like the dying Christ. There was never a congregation like that which gathered about the pulpit of the Cross. There was never a sermon like the Seven Last Words.

Those seven words, unlike the words of dying men, never died. They were caught up in the ears of that vast audience and then echoed down over the hillside of Jerusalem and through the labyrinth of men's minds, waking even the dead from their graves. Now even in this hour they are caught up by our own poor hearts that must decide, once more, if they will be tempted by the love of that Saviour. Calvary is the new mountain of temptation, and it is not now Satan tempting Christ, but Christ tempting us—tempting us to love the Love we fall just short of in all love.

THE FIRST WORD

*Father, Forgive Them For
They Know Not What They Do!*

IT SEEMS to be a fact of human psychology that when death approaches, the human heart speaks its words of love to those whom it holds closest and dearest. There is no reason to suspect that it is otherwise in the case of the Heart of hearts. If He spoke in a graduated order to those whom He loved most, then we may expect to find in His first three words the order of His love and affection. His first words went out to enemies: "Father, forgive them," His second to sinners: "This day thou shalt be with Me in Paradise," and His third to saints, "Woman, behold thy son." Enemies, sinners, and saints—such is the order of Divine Love and Thoughtfulness.

The congregation anxiously awaited His first word. The executioners expected Him to cry, for every one pinned on the gibbet of the Cross had done it before Him. Seneca tells us that those who were crucified cursed the day of their birth, the executioners, their mothers, and even spat on those who looked upon them. Cicero tells us that at times it was necessary to cut out the tongues of those who were crucified, to stop their terrible blasphemies. Hence the executioners expected a cry but not the kind of cry that they heard. The Scribes and Pharisees expected a cry, too, and they were quite sure that He who had preached "Love your enemies," and "Do good to them that hate you," would now forget that Gospel with the piercing of feet and hands. They felt that the excruciating and agonizing pains would scatter to the winds any resolution He might have taken to keep up appearances. Every one expected a cry, but no one with the exception of the three at the foot of the Cross, expected the cry they did hear. Like some fragrant trees which bathe in perfume the very axe which gnashes them, the great Heart on the Tree of Love poured out from its depths something less a cry than a prayer, the soft, sweet, low prayer of pardon and forgiveness: "Father, forgive them, for they know not what they do."

Forgive whom? Forgive enemies? The soldier in the court-room of Caiaphas who struck Him with a mailed fist; Pilate, the politician, who condemned a God to retain the friendship of Caesar; Herod, who robed Wisdom in the garment of a fool; the soldiers who swung the King of Kings on a tree between heaven and earth—forgive them? Forgive them, why? Because they know what they do? No, because they know not what they do. If they knew what they were doing and still went on doing it; if they knew what a terrible crime they were committing by sentencing Life to death; if they knew what a perversion of justice it was to choose Barabbas to Christ; if they knew what cruelty it was to take the feet that trod everlasting hills and pinion them to the limb of a tree; if they knew what they were doing and still went on doing it, unmindful of the fact that the very blood which they shed was capable of redeeming them, they would never be saved! Why, they would be damned if it were not for the fact that they were ignorant of the terrible thing they did when they crucified Christ! It was only the ignorance of their great sin that brought them within the pale of the hearing of that cry from the Cross. It is not wisdom that saves: it is ignorance!

There is no redemption for the fallen angels. Those great spirits headed by the Bearer of Light, Lucifer, endowed with an intelligence compared with which ours is but that of a child, saw the consequences of each of their decisions just as clearly as we see that two and two make four. Having made a decision, they made it irrevocably; there was no taking it back, and hence there was no future redemption. It is because they knew what they were doing that they were excluded from the hearing of that cry that went forth from the Cross. It is not wisdom that saves: it is ignorance!

In like manner, if we knew what a terrible thing sin was and went on sinning; if we knew how much love there was in the Incarnation and still refused to nourish ourselves with the Bread of Life; if we knew how much sacrificial love there was in the Sacrifice of the Cross and still refused to fill the chalice of our heart with that love; if we knew how much mercy there was in the Sacrament of Penance, and still refused to bend a humble knee to a hand that had the power to loose both in heaven and on earth; if we knew how much life there was in the Eucharist and still refused to take of the Bread which makes life everlasting and still refused to drink of that Wine that produces and enriches virgins; if we knew of all the truth there is in the Church as the mystical body of Christ and still turned our backs to it like other Pilates; if we knew all these things and still stayed away from Christ and His Church, we should be lost! It is not wisdom that saves; it is ignorance! It is only our ignorance of how good God is that excuses us for not being saints!

Prayer

Dear Jesus! I do not want to know the wisdom of the world; I do not want to know on whose anvil snow-flakes are hammered or the hiding-place of darkness or from whose womb came the ice, or why the gold falls to the earth earthly, and fire climbs to the heavens heavenly; I do not want to know literature and science, or the four-dimensional universe in which we live; I do not want to know the length of the universe in terms of light years; I do not want to know the breadth of the earth as it dances about the chariot of the sun; I do not want to know the heights of the stars, chaste candles of the night; I do not want to know the depths of the sea or the secrets of its watery palace. I want to be ignorant of all these things. I want only to know the length, the breadth, the height and the depth of Thy redeeming Love on the Cross, Sweet Saviour of Men. I want to be ignorant of everything in the world—everything but You, dear Jesus. And then, by the strangest of strange paradoxes, I shall be wise!

THE SECOND WORD

*This Day Thou Shalt Be
With Me In Paradise*

THERE IS a legend to the effect that when, to escape the wrath of Herod, Saint Joseph and the Blessed Virgin were fleeing into Egypt with the Divine Child, they stopped at a desert inn. The Blessed Mother asked the lady of the inn for water in which to bathe the Babe. The lady then asked if she might not bathe her own child, who was suffering from leprosy, in the same waters in which the Divine Child had been immersed. Immediately upon touching those waters baptized with the Divine Presence, the child became whole. Her child advanced in age and grew to be a thief. He is Dismas, now hanging on the Cross at the right hand of Christ!

Whether the memory of the story his mother told him now came back to the thief and made him look kindly on Christ, we know not. It might have been that his first meeting with the Saviour was on the day when his heart was filled with compunction on hearing the story of a certain man that went down from Jerusalem to Jericho and fell among robbers. Perhaps, too, his first intimation that he was suffering with the Redeemer came to him as he turned his tortured head and read an inscription which bore His name, "Jesus"; His city, "Nazareth"; His crime, "King of the Jews." At any rate, enough dry fuel of the right kind gathers on the altar of his soul, and now a spark from the central Cross falls upon it, creating in it a glorious illumination of faith. He sees a Cross and adores a Throne; he sees a condemned Man, and invokes a King: "Lord, remember me when Thou shalt come into Thy Kingdom."

Our Blessed Lord was owned at last! Amidst the clamor of the raving crowd and the dismal universal hiss of sin, in all that delirium of man's revolt against God, no voice was lifted in praise and recognition except the voice of a man condemned. It was a cry of faith in Him whom every one else had forsaken, and it was only the testimony of a thief. If the son of the widow of Nain, who had been raised from the dead, had cried out a word of faith in the Kingdom of One who was seemingly losing His Kingdom; if Peter, who on the Mount of Transfiguration had seen His face shine like the sun and His garments whiten like snow, had acknowledged Him; if the blind man of Jericho whose eyes were opened to the light of God's sunshine had been opened anew to proclaim His Divinity, we should not have been surprised. Why, if any of these had cried out, perhaps the timid disciples and friends would have rallied, perhaps the Scribes and Pharisees would have believed ! But at that moment when death was upon Him, when defeat stared Him in the face, the only one outside the small group at the foot of the Cross to acknowledge Him as Lord of a Kingdom, as the Captain of Souls, was a thief at the right hand of Christ.

At the very moment when the testimony of a thief was given, Our Blessed Lord was winning a greater victory than any life can win, and was exerting a greater energy than that which harnesses waterfalls; He was losing His life and saving a soul. And on that day when Herod and his whole court could not make Him speak, nor all the power of Jerusalem make Him step down from the Cross, nor the unjust accusations of a court-room force Him to break silence, nor a mob crying, "He saved others; Himself He cannot save," bring from His burning lips a retort, He turns to a quivering life beside Him, speaks, and saves a thief: "This day thou shalt be with Me in Paradise." No one before was ever the object of such a promise, not even Moses nor John, not even Magdalen nor Mary!

It was the thief's last prayer, perhaps also his first. He knocked once, sought once, asked once, dared everything and found everything. When our spirits stand with John on Patmos, we can see the white-stoled army in Heaven riding after the conquering Christ; when we stand with Luke on Calvary, we see the one who rode first in that procession. Christ, who was poor, died rich. His hands were nailed to a Cross and yet He unlocked the keys of Paradise and won a soul. His escort into Heaven was a thief. May we not say that the thief died a thief, for he stole Paradise?

Oh, what greater assurance is there in all the world of the mercy of God? Lost sheep, prodigal sons, broken Magdalens, penitent Peters, forgiven thieves! Such is the rosary of Divine forgiveness.

God is more anxious to save us than we are to save ourselves. There is a story told to the effect that one day Our Blessed Lord appeared to Saint Jerome, saying to him, "Jerome, what will you give Me?" Jerome answered, "I will give you my writings," to which Our Lord replied that it was not enough. "Then," said Jerome, "what shall I give you? My life of penance and mortification?" But the answer was, "Even that is not enough!" "What have I left to give Thee?" cried Jerome. Our Blessed Lord answered, "Jerome, you can give Me your sins."

Prayer

Dear Jesus! Your kindness to the penitent thief recalls the prophetic words of the Old Testament: "If your sins be as scarlet, they shall be made as white as snow: and if they be as red as crimson, they shall be white as wool." In your words of forgiveness to the penitent thief, I understand now the meaning of your words: "I am not come to call the just, but sinners.... They that are in health need not a physician, but they that are ill." "There shall be joy in Heaven upon one sinner that doth penance more than upon ninety-nine just who need not penance." I see now why Peter was not made Thy first vicar on earth until after he had fallen three times, in order that the Church of which he was the head might forever understand forgiveness and pardon. Jesus, I begin to see that if I had never sinned, I never could call you "Saviour." The thief is not the only sinner. Here am I! But Thou art the only Saviour.

THE THIRD WORD

Woman, Behold Thy Son

AN ANGEL of light went out from the great white Throne of Light and descended over the plains of Esdraelon, past the daughters of the great kingdoms and empires, and came to where a humble virgin of Nazareth knelt in prayer, and said, "Hail, full of grace!" These were not words; they were the Word. "And the Word became flesh." This was the first Annunciation.

Nine months passed and once more an angel from that great white Throne of Light came down to shepherds on Judean hills, teaching them the joy of a "Gloria in excelsis," and bidding them worship Him Whom the world could not contain, a "Babe wrapped in swaddling clothes and laid in a manger." Eternity became time, Divinity incarnate, God a man; Omnipotence was discovered in bonds. In the language of Saint Luke, Mary "brought forth her first-born Son ... and laid Him in a manger." This was the first Nativity.

Then came Nazareth and the carpenter shop where one can imagine the Divine Boy, straitened until baptized with a baptism of blood, fashioning a little cross in anticipation of a great Cross that would one day be His on Calvary. One can also imagine Him in the evening of a day of labor at the bench, stretching out His arms in exhausted relaxation, whilst the setting sun traced on the opposite wall the shadow of a man on a cross. One can, too, imagine His Mother seeing in each nail the prophecy and the tell-tale of a day when men would carpenter to a Cross the One who carpentered the universe.

Nazareth passed into Calvary, and the nails of the shop into the nails of human malignity. From the Cross He completed His last will and testament. He had already committed His blood to the Church, His garments to His enemies, a thief to Paradise, and would soon commend His body to the grave and His soul to His Heavenly Father. To whom, then, could He give the two treasures which He loved above all others, Mary and John? He would bequeath them to one another, giving at once a son to His Mother and a Mother to His friend. "Woman!" It was the second Annunciation! The midnight hour, the silent room, the ecstatic prayer had given way to the mount of Calvary, the darkened sky, and a Son hanging on a Cross. Yet, what consolation! It was only an angel who made the first Annunciation, but it is God's own sweet voice which makes the second.

"Behold thy son!" It was the second Nativity! Mary had brought forth her First-born without labor, in the cave of Bethlehem; she now brings forth her second-born, John, in the labors of the Cross. At this moment Mary is undergoing the pains of childbirth, not only for her second-born, who is John, but also for the millions who will be born to her in Christian ages as "Children of Mary." Now we can understand why Christ was called "her First-born." It was not because she was to have other children by the blood of flesh, but because she was to have other children by the blood of her heart. Truly, indeed, the Divine condemnation against Eve is now renewed against the new Eve, Mary, for she is bringing forth her children in sorrow.

Mary, then, is not only the Mother of Our Lord and Saviour, Jesus Christ, but she is also our Mother, and this not by a title of courtesy, not by legal fiction, not by a mere figure of speech, but by the right of bringing us forth in sorrow at the foot of the Cross. It was by weakness and disobedience at the foot of the tree of Good and Evil that Eve lost the title of the Mother of the Living; it is at the foot of the tree of the Cross that Mary, by sacrifice and obedience, regained for us the title of the Mother of Men. What a destiny to have the Mother of God as my Mother and Jesus as my Brother!

Prayer

O Mary! as Jesus was born to thee in thy first Nativity of the flesh, so we have been born of thee in thy second Nativity of the spirit. Thus thou didst beget us into a new world of spiritual relationship with God as our Father, Jesus as our Brother, and thou as our Mother! If a mother can never forget the child of her womb, then, Mary, thou shalt never forget us. As thou wert Co-Redemptrix in the acquisition of the graces of eternal life, be thou also our Co-Mediatrix in their dispensation. Nothing is impossible for thee, because thou art the Mother of Him who can do all things. If thy Son did not refuse thy request at the banquet of Cana, He will not refuse it at the celestial banquet where thou art crowned as

Queen of Angels and Saints. Intercede therefore to thy Divine Son, that He may change the waters of my weakness into the wine of thy strength. Mary, thou art the Refuge of Sinners! Pray for us, now prostrate at the foot of the Cross. Holy Mary, Mother of God, pray for us sinners, now and at the hour of our death. Amen.

THE FOURTH WORD

*My God! My God!
Why Hast Thou Forsaken Me?*

THE FIRST three words from the pulpit of the Cross were addressed to the three predilections of God: enemies, sinners, and saints. The next two words, the fourth and the fifth, betray the sufferings of the God-man on the Cross. The fourth word symbolizes the sufferings of man abandoned by God; the fifth word the sufferings of God abandoned by man.

When Our Blessed Lord spoke this fourth word from the Cross, darkness covered the earth. It is a common remark that nature is indifferent to our griefs. A nation may be dying of famine, yet the sun starts and plays upon the stricken fields. Brother may rise up against brother in a war which turns poppy fields into Haceldamas of blood; yet a bird, safe from the fire and shell, chants its little song of peace. Hearts may be broken by the loss of a friend; yet a rainbow leaps with joy across the heavens, making a terrible contrast between its smile and the agony it shines upon. But the sun refused to shine on the crucifixion! The light that rules the day, probably for the first and last time in history, was snuffed out like a candle when, according to every human calculation, it should have continued to shine. The reason was that the crowning crime of man, the killing of nature's Lord, could not pass without a protest from nature itself. If the soul of God were in darkness, so should be the sun which He had made.

Truly, all was darkness! He had given up His Mother and His beloved disciple, and now God seemingly abandoned Him. "Eli, Eli, lamma sabacthani?" "My God! My God! Why hast Thou forsaken Me?" It is a cry in the mysterious language of Hebrew to express the tremendous mystery of a God "abandoned" by God. The Son calls His Father, God. What a contrast with a prayer He once taught: "Our Father, Who art in Heaven!" In some strange, mysterious way His human nature seems separated from His Heavenly Father, and yet not separated, for otherwise how could He cry, "My God, My God"? But just as the sun's light and heat can be withdrawn from us by the intervening clouds, though the sun remains in the sky, so there was a kind of withdrawal of His Father's Face in the terrible moment in which He took upon Himself the sins of the world. This pain and desolation He suffered for each of us, that we might know what a terrible thing it is for human nature to be without God, to be deprived of a Divine Remedy and Consolation. It was the supreme act of atonement for three classes of people: those who abandon God, those who doubt the presence of God, and those who are indifferent to God.

He atoned first of all for atheists, for those who on that dark midday half believed in God, as even now at night they half believe in Him. He atoned also for those who know God, but live as if they had never heard His name; for those whose hearts are like waysides on which God's love falls only to be trampled by the world; for those whose hearts are like rocks on which the seed of God's love falls only to be quickly forgotten; for those whose hearts are like thorns on which God's love descends only to be choked by the cares of the world. It was atonement for all who have had faith and lost it; for all who once were saints and now are sinners. It was the Divine Act of Redemption for all abandonment of God, for in that moment in which He was forgotten, He purchased for us the grace of never being forgotten by God.

It was also the atonement for that other class who deny the presence of God; for all those Christians who abandon all effort when they cannot feel God near them; for all who identify being good with feeling good; for all those skeptics beginning with the first who asked, "Why has God commanded you?" It was reparation for all the haunting questions of a doubting world: "Why is there evil?" ... "Why does God not answer my prayers?" ... "Why did God take away my mother?" ... "why" ... "why" ... "why"; and the reparation for all those queries was made when God asked a "why" of God.

Finally, it was atonement for all the indifference of the world which lives as if there had never been a crib at Bethlehem or a Cross at Calvary; it was atonement for all who shake dice while the drama of Redemption is being enacted; for all those who feel themselves as gods beyond all duties of worship and religion, yet bound by none. I suppose that after these twenty centuries the indifference of our modern world is more torturing and crucifying than the pains of Calvary. One can well believe that a crown of thorns, and that steel nails were less terrible to the flesh of our Saviour than our modern indifference which neither scorns nor prays to the Heart of Christ.

Prayer

Jesus! Thou art now atoning for those moments when we are neither hot nor cold, members neither of heaven nor of earth, for now Thou art suffering between the two: rejected by the one, abandoned by the other. Because Thou wouldst not give up sinful humanity, Thy Heavenly Father hid His Face from Thee. Because Thou wouldst not give up Thy Heavenly Father, sinful humanity turned its back to Thee, and thus in holy fellowship Thou didst unite us both. No longer can men say that God does not know what a heart suffers in abandonment, for now Thou art abandoned. No longer can men complain that God does not know the wounds of an inquiring heart which feels not the Divine Presence, for now that sweet Presence is seemingly hid from Thee. Jesus, now I understand pain, abandonment, and suffering, for I see that even the sun has its eclipse. But Jesus, why do I not learn? Teach me that just as Thou didst not make Thy own Cross, neither shall I make my own, but accept the one Thou makest for me. Teach me that everything in the world is Thine, except one thing, and that is my own will; and since that is mine, it is the only real and true gift that I can ever bestow. Teach me to say, "Not my will, but Thine be done, O Lord." Even when I see Thee not, grant me the grace to believe and "although Thou slayest me, yet will I trust Thee." Tell me, how long, how long, O Lord, will I keep Thee writhing on the Cross?

THE FIFTH WORD

I Thirst

THIS IS the shortest of the seven cries. Although it stands in our language as two words, in the original it is one. At the moment when Our Saviour resumes His sermon, it is not a curse upon those who crucify Him, not a word of reproach to the timid disciples at the border of the crowd, not a cry of scorn to the Roman soldiers, not a word of hope to Magdalen, not a word of love to John, not a word of farewell to His own mother. It is not even to God at this moment! Out from the depths of the Sacred Heart there wells through parched lips one awful word: "I thirst!"

He, the God-Man, who threw the stars in their orbits and spheres into space, who "swung the earth a trinket at his wrist," from Whose finger-tips tumbled planets and worlds, who might have said, "The sea is Mine and with it the streams in a thousand valleys and the cataracts in a thousand hills," now asks man—man, a piece of His own handiwork—to help Him. He asks man for a drink! Not a drink of earthly water, that is not what He meant, but a drink of love. "I thirst"—for love!

The last word was a revelation of the sufferings of a man without God; this word was a revelation of the sufferings of a God without man. The Creator cannot live without the creature, the Shepherd without the sheep, the thirst of Christ's love without the soul-water of Christians.

But what has He done to be entitled to my love? How much has God loved me? Oh, if I would know how much God has loved me, then let me sound the depths of meaning of that word "love," a word so often used and so little understood. Love, first of all, means to give and God has given His power to nothingness, His light to darkness, His order to chaos, and this is Creation. Love means to tell secrets to the one loved, and God has told in the Scriptures the secrets of Nature and His high hopes for fallen humanity, and this is Revelation. Love means also to suffer for the one loved, that is why we speak of arrows and darts of love—something that wounds—and God is now suffering for us on the Tree of the Cross, for "greater love than this no man hath, that he lay down his life for his friend." Love means also to become one with the one loved, not only in the unity of flesh but in the unity of spirit, and God has so loved us as to institute the Eucharist, that we may abide in Him and He in us in the ineffable unity of the Bread of Life. Love wishes also to be eternally united with the one loved, and God has so loved us that He has promised us His Father's mansions, where a peace and a joy reign which the world cannot give and time cannot take away, and this is Heaven.

Certainly, love has exhausted itself. There is nothing more that Christ could do for His vineyard than He has done. Having poured forth all the waters of His everlasting Love on our poor parched hearts, it is no wonder that He thirsts for love. If love is reciprocal then certainly He has a right to our love. Why do we not respond? Why do we let the Divine Heart die of the thirst for human hearts? With what justice He might complain:

> *Lo, all things fly thee, for thou fliest Me!*
> *Strange, piteous, futile thing!*
> *Wherefore should any set thee love apart?*
> *Seeing none but I makes much of naught [He said],*
> *And human love needs human meriting:*
> *How hast thou merited—*
> *Of all man's clotted clay the dingiest clot?*
> *Alack, thou knowest not*
> *How little worthy of any love thou art!*
> *Whom wilt thou find to love ignoble thee,*
> *Save Me, save only Me?*[1]

Prayer

Dear Jesus! Thou hast given all for me, and yet I give nothing in return. How often Thou hast come to gather vintage in the vineyard of my soul, and hast found only a few clusters! How often Thou sough test, and found nothing; knocked, and the door of my soul was closed to Thee! How often Thou didst ask for a drink, and I gave Thee only vinegar and gall!

---

[1] Francis Thompson, "The Hound of Heaven."

How often, dear Jesus, I feared lest, having Thee, I must have naught beside. I forget that if I had the flame, I would forget the spark; if I had the sun of Thy love, I could forget the candle of a human heart; if I had the perfect round of Thy happiness, I could forget the broken arc of earth. O Jesus, my story is the sad story of a refusal to return heart for heart, love for love. Give me, above all human gifts, the sweet gift of sympathy for Thee.

> *Am I a stone and not a sheep*
> *That I can stand, O Christ, beneath Thy Cross*
> *To number drop by drop Thy Blood's slow loss,*
> *And yet not weep?*
>
> *Not so those women loved*
> *Who with exceeding grief lamented Thee;*
> *Not so fallen Peter weeping bitterly;*
> *Not so the thief was moved;*
>
> *Not so the sun and moon*
> *Which hid their faces in a starless sky,*
> *A horror of great darkness at broad noon*
> *I, only I.*
>
> *Yet give not o'er,*
> *But seek Thy sheep, true Shepherd of the flock,*
> *Greater than Moses, turn and look once more*
> *And smite a rock.*[2]

---

[2] Christina Rossetti

THE SIXTH WORD

It Is Consummated

FROM ALL eternity God willed to make man to the image of His eternal Son. After having painted the heavens with blue and the earth with green, God then made a garden, beautiful as only God knows how to make a garden beautiful, and in it placed man made to conform to the image of God's Son. In some mysterious way the revolt of Lucifer echoed to earth, and the image of God in man was blurred and ruined.

The Heavenly Father in His divine mercy willed to restore man to his pristine glory. In order that the portrait might once more be true to the Original, God willed to send to earth His Divine Son according to whose image man was made, that the earth might see once more the manner of man God wanted us to be. In the accomplishment of this task, only Divine Omnipotence could use the elements of defeat as the elements of victory. In the Divine economy of Redemption, the same three things which cooperated in our fall shared in our redemption. For the disobedient man Adam, there was the obedient man Christ; for the proud woman Eve, there was the humble virgin Mary; for the tree of the garden, there was the tree of the Cross. The Redemption was now completed. The work which His Father had given Him to do was accomplished. We were bought and paid for. We were won in a battle fought not with five stones like those with which David slew Goliath, but with five wounds, hideous scars on hands and feet and side; in a battle fought not with armor glistening under a noonday sun, but with flesh hanging like purple rags under a darkened sky; in a battle where the cry was not "Crush and kill," but "Father, forgive"; in a battle fought not with spitting steel, but with dripping blood; in a battle in which he who slew the foe lost the day. Now the battle was over. For the last three hours He had been about His Father's business. The artist had put the last touch on his masterpiece and with the joy of the strong He uttered the song of triumph: "It is finished."

His work is finished, but is ours? It belongs to God to use that word, but not to us. The work of acquiring Divine life for man is finished, but not the distribution. He has finished the task of filling the reservoir of Calvary's sacramental life, but the work of letting it flood our souls is not yet finished. He has finished the foundation; we must build upon it. He has finished the ark, opening His side with a spear and clothing Himself in the garment of His precious blood, but we must enter the ark. He stands at the door and knocks, but the latch is on the inside, and only we can open it. He has enacted the consecration, but the communion depends upon us; and whether our work will ever be finished depends entirely on how we relive His life and become other Christs, for His Good Friday and His passion avail us nothing unless we take up His Cross and follow Him. Sin is the great obstacle to the accomplishment of that task, for as long as there is sin in the world, Christ is crucified anew in our hearts.

> *I saw the Son of God go by*
> *Crowned with the crown of thorn.*
> *"Was it not finished, Lord?" I said,*
> *"And all the anguish borne?"*
>
> *He turned on me His awful eyes:*
> *"Hast Thou not understood?*
> *Lo! Every soul is Calvary,*
> *And every sin a rood."*[3]

Prayer

Dear Jesus! redemption is Thy work; atonement is mine, for atonement means at-one-ment with Thy life, Thy truth, and Thy love. Thy work on the cross is finished, but my work is to take you down, for—

> *Whenever there is silence around me*
> *By day or by night—*
> *I am startled by a cry.*
> *It came down from the cross—*
> *The first time I heard it,*
> *I went out and searched—*
> *And found a Man in the throes of crucifixion,*

---

[3] Rachel Annand Taylor.

And I said, "I will take you down,"
And I tried to take the nails out of His feet.
But He said, "Let them be
For I cannot be taken down
Until every man, every woman, and every child
Come together to take Me down."
And I said, "But I cannot bear Your cry.
What can I do?"
And He said, "Go about the world—
Tell everyone that you meet—
There is a Man on the cross." [4]

Thou art on the Cross, but we must take Thee down. Thou hast been hanging there long enough! Through Thy Apostle, Paul, Thou hast told us that those who are Thine crucify their flesh and its concupiscences. My work, then, is not finished until I take Thy place upon the Cross, for unless there is a Good Friday in my life, there will never be an Easter Sunday; unless there is a garment of a fool, there will never be the white robes of wisdom; unless there is the crown of thorns, there will never be the glorified body; unless there is the battle, there will never be the victory; unless there is the thirst, there will never be the Heavenly Refreshment; unless there is the Cross, there will never be the empty tomb. Teach me, Jesus, to finish this task, for it is fitting that the sons of men should suffer and enter into their glory.

---

[4] Elizabeth Cheney.

THE SEVENTH WORD

*Father, Into Thy Hands
I Commend My Spirit*

WHEN ADAM had been driven from the Garden of Paradise, and the penalty of labor imposed upon him, he went out in quest of the bread he was to earn by the sweat of his brow. In the course of that search, he stumbled upon the limp form of his son Abel, picked him up, carried him upon his shoulders, and laid him on the lap of Eve. They spoke to him, but Abel did not answer. He had never been so silent before. They lifted his hand, but it fell back limp; it had never acted that way before. They looked into his eyes, cold, glassy, mysteriously elusive; they had never been so unresponsive before. They wondered, and as they wondered, their wonder grew. Then they remembered: "For in what day soever thou shalt eat of the tree, thou shalt die the death." *It was the first death in the world.*

Centuries whirled around into space, and the new Abel, Christ, is put to death by his jealous brethren of the race of Cain. The life that came out from the boundless deep now prepares to return home. His sixth word was a cry of retrospect: "I have finished the work." His seventh and last one is a word of prospect: "I commend My Spirit." The sixth word was man-ward; the seventh word was God-ward. The sixth word was a farewell to earth; the seventh His entrance into Heaven. Just as those great planets only after a long time complete their orbit and return again to their starting-point, as if to salute Him who sent them on their way, so He who had come from Heaven had finished His work and completed His orbit, now goes back to the Father to salute Him who sent Him out on the great work of the world's redemption: "Father, into Thy hands I commend My Spirit."

The Prodigal Son is returning to His Father's house, for is not Christ the Prodigal? Thirty-three years ago He left His Father's eternal mansion and went off into the foreign country of this world. Then He began spending Himself and being spent; dispensing with an infinite prodigality the divine riches of power and wisdom and bestowing with a heavenly liberality the divine gifts of pardon and mercy. In this last hour His whole substance is wasted among sinners, for He is giving the last drop of His precious blood for the redemption of the world. There is nothing to feed upon except the husks of human sneers and the vinegar and gall of bitter human ingratitude. He now prepares to take the road back to His Father's house, and when yet some distance away He sees the face of His Heavenly Father He breaks out into the last and perfect prayer from the pulpit of the Cross: "Father, into Thy hands I commend My Spirit."

All the while Mary is standing at the foot of the Cross. In a short time the new Abel, slain by His brethren, will be taken down from the gibbet of salvation and laid in the lap of the new Eve. It will be the death of Death! But when the tragic moment comes it may seem to the tear-dimmed eyes of Mary that Bethlehem has come back. The thorn-crowned head which had nowhere to lay itself in death, except on the pillow of the Cross, may, through Mary's clouded vision, seem the head which she drew to her breast at Bethlehem. Those eyes at whose fading even the sun and moon were darkened were to her the eyes that glanced up from a crib of straw. The helpless feet riveted with nails once more seem to her the baby feet at which were cast gold, frankincense, and myrrh. The lips now parched and crimsoned with blood seem the ruddy lips that once at Bethlehem nourished themselves on the Eucharist of her body. The hands that can hold nothing but a wound, seem once more the baby hands that were not quite long enough to touch the huge heads of the cattle. The embrace at the foot of the Cross seems the embrace at the side of the crib. In that sad hour of death which always makes one think of birth, Mary may feel that Bethlehem is returning again.

PRAYER

No, Mary! Bethlehem is not come back. This is not the crib, but the Cross; not birth, but death; not the day of companionship with Shepherds and Kings, but the hour of a common death with thieves; not Bethlehem, but Calvary.

Bethlehem is Jesus, as thou, His sinless mother, gave Him to man; Calvary is Jesus, as sinful man gave Him back to thee. Something intervened between Thy giving at the manger and thy receiving at the Cross, and that which intervened is my sins. Mary, this is not thy hour; it is my hour—my hour of wickedness and sin. If I had not sinned, death would not now hover on its black wings about His crimsoned body; if I had not been proud, the atoning crown of thorns would never have been woven; if I had been less rebellious in treading the broad way which leads to destruction, the feet would never have been pierced with nails; if I had been more responsive to His shepherding calls from the thorns and thistles, His lips would have never been on fire; if I had been more faithful, His cheeks would never have been blistered with the kiss of Judas.

Mary, it is I who stand between His birth and His approaching redemptive death. I warn thee, Mary, think not when thy arms come to clasp Him, that He is white as He came from the Father; He is red as He came from me. In a few short seconds thy Son shall have surrendered His soul to His Heavenly Father, and His body to thy caressing hands. The last few drops of blood are falling from that great chalice of Redemption, staining the wood of the Cross and crimsoning the rocks soon to be rent in horror; and a single drop of it would be sufficient to redeem ten thousand worlds. Mary, my Mother, intercede with thy Divine Son for forgiveness of the sin of changing thy Bethlehem into Calvary. Beg Him, Mary, in these last remaining seconds, to grant us the grace of never crucifying Him again nor piercing thy own heart with seven swords. Mary, plead to thy dying Son that as long as I live ... Mary! Jesus is dead.... Mary!

The Cross and the Beatitudes

[1937]

INTRODUCTION

THIS little book is a correlation of the Seven Beatitudes and the Seven Last Words. The eighth beatitude in the language of St. Thomas Aquinas "is a confirmation and a declaration of all those that precede. Because from the very fact that a man is confirmed in poverty of spirit, meekness and the rest, it follows that no persecution will induce him to renounce them. Hence the eighth beatitude corresponds in a way to all the preceding seven."

There is no strict correspondence between the Seven Beatitudes and the Seven Words, but this work assumes they are not unrelated, for one seems to be related to the other as precept and deed. Both were delivered on a mountain; Our Lord began His Public Life on the Mount of the Beatitudes and closed it on the Mount of Calvary. The story of how He practiced the meekness, the mercy and the poverty of the Beatitudes is here told. If it brings just one soul closer to Our Lord and His Blessed Mother it will have been eminently worth while.

Fulton J. Sheen

THE FIRST WORD

*"Blessed are the meek; for they shall possess
the land."—"Father, forgive them, for
they know not what they do."*

Our Blessed Lord began His Public Life on the Mount of Beatitudes, by preaching: "Blessed are the meek: for they shall possess the land." He finished His Public Life on the Hill of Calvary by practicing that meekness: "Father, forgive them, for they know not what they do."

How different this is from the beatitude of the world! The world blesses not the meek but the vindictive; it praises not the one who turns the other cheek but the one who renders evil for evil; it exalts not the humble but the aggressive. Communism has carried that spirit of violence, class-struggle and the clenched fist to an extreme the like of which the world before has never seen.

To correct such a war-like attitude of the clenched fist, Our Lord both preached and practiced meekness.

He preached it in those memorable words which continue the Beatitudes: "You have heard that it hath been said: An eye for an eye, and a tooth for a tooth. But I say to you not to resist evil: but if one strike thee on thy right cheek, turn to him also the other: and if a man will contend with thee in judgment, and take away thy coat, let go thy cloak also unto him. And whosoever shall force thee one mile, go with him other two.... You have heard that it hath been said: Thou shalt love thy neighbor, and hate thy enemy. But I say to you: Love your enemies: do good to them that hate you: and pray for them that persecute and calumniate you that you may be the children of your Father who is in heaven, who maketh His sun to rise upon the good and bad, and raineth upon the just and the unjust. For if you love them that love you, what reward shall you have? do not even the publicans this? And if you salute your brethren only, what do you more? do not also the heathens this? Be you therefore perfect, as also your heavenly Father is perfect."

But He not only preached meekness; He practiced it. When His own people picked up stones to throw at Him, He threw none back in return; when His fellow townsmen brought Him to the brow of the hill to cast Him over the precipice, He walked through the midst of them unharmed; when the soldier struck Him with a mailed fist, and made the Saviour feel by anticipation the clenched fist of Communism He answered meekly: "If I have spoken evil, give testimony of the evil: but if well, why strikest thou me."

When they swore to kill Him, He did not use His power to strike dead even a single enemy; and now on the Cross, meekness reaches its peak, when to those who dig the Hands which feed the world, and to those who pierce the Feet which shepherd souls, He pleads: "Father, forgive them, for they know not what they do."

Which is right—the violence of Communism or the meekness of Christ? Communism says meekness is weakness. But that is because it does not understand the meaning of Christian meekness. Meekness is not cowardice; meekness is not an easy-going temperament, sluggish and hard to arouse; meekness is not a spineless passivity which allows everyone to walk over us. No! Meekness is self-possession. That is why the reward of meekness is possession.

A weak man can never be meek, because he is never self-possessed; meekness is that virtue which controls the combative, violent and pugnacious powers of our nature, and is therefore the best and noblest road to self-realization.

The meek man is not a man who refuses to fight, nor is he a man who will never become angry. A meek man is a man who will never do one thing: he will never fight when his conceit is attacked, but only when a principle is at stake. And there is the keynote to the difference of the anger of the Communist and the anger of the meek man.

Communism begins at the moment conceit is attacked; fists clench and rise as soon as the ego is challenged; cheeks flush as soon as self-love is wounded, and blood boils and flows at that split second when pride is humbled.

The anger of the Communist is based on selfishness; he hates the rich not because he loves the poor in spirit, but because he wants to be rich himself. Every Communist is really a capitalist without any cash in his pockets. Selfishness is the world's greatest sin; that is why the world hates those who hate it, why it is jealous of those who have more; why it is envious of those who do more; why it dislikes those who refuse to flatter, and why it scorns those who tell us the truth about ourselves; its whole life is inspired by the egotistical, and the personal, and its wrath is born of that self-love.

Now consider the anger of the meek man. For the meek man, not selfishness but righteousness is his guiding principle. He is so possessed, he never allows his fists to go up for an unholy purpose, or in defense of his pride or vanity, or conceit, or because he wants the wealth of another. Only the principles of God's righteousness arouse a meek man. Moses was a meek man, but he broke the tablets of stone when he found his people were disobeying God.

Our Lord is Meekness Itself, and yet He drove the buyers and sellers from the Temple when they prostituted His Father's House; but when He came to the doves, He was so self-possessed He gently released them from the cages. He is so much master of Himself, that He is angry only when holiness is attacked, but never when His Person is attacked. That is why when the Gerasenes besought Our Lord to leave their coasts, without a single retort, "entering into a boat, He passed over the water and came into His own city."

That is why when men laughed Him to scorn. He said nothing but approached the dead daughter of Jairus, and went on His work of mercy oblivious to their insults, and restored her to life. That is why He addressed Judas as "Friend" when he blistered His lips with a kiss. That is why Our Lord from the Cross prays for the forgiveness of His enemies. Their wrath directed against His Body He would not return, though He might have smitten them all dead by the power of His Divinity. Rather He forgave them for "they know not what they do."

If ever innocence had a right to protest against injustice, it was in the case of Our Lord. And yet He extends pardon. Their insults to His Person, He ignores. Had He not preached meekness? Now must He not practice it?

And how could He practice it better than to pray for those who were crucifying Him? And what greater meekness could there be than to excuse them because they knew not what they did. What a lesson for us to remember, that those who do us harm, may, too, be of the same type of misguided consciences as those who crucified Christ?

From that dread day on, there have been two motives for withdrawing from battle: either because we are afraid, or because we are husbanding our energies for a more important battle. The second kind is the meekness of Our Lord.

Be not angry then when your conceit is attacked. It will do no harm. As Our Lord reminded us: "Blessed are they that suffer persecution for justice's sake; for theirs is the kingdom of heaven."

In contrast to this Christian philosophy of forgiveness, there exists for the first time in the history of the world a philosophy and a political and social system based not on love, but on hate, and that is Communism. Communism believes that the only way it can establish itself is by inciting revolution, class-struggle, and violence. Hence its regime is characterized by a hatred of those who believe the family is the basic unit of society. The very Communistic gesture of the clenched fist is a token of its pugnacious and destructive spirit, and a striking contrast indeed to the nailed hand of the Saviour pleading forgiveness for the clenched-fisted generation who sent Him to the Cross.

It is startling indeed to recall that we followers of Our Lord believe in violence just as much as do the Communists. Has not Our Lord said: "the kingdom of heaven suffereth violence, and the violent bear it away." But here is the difference: Communists believe in violence to one's neighbor; we believe in violence to ourselves. Communists struggle against all who refuse to have the same hate; we struggle against ourselves, our lower passions, our concupiscences, our selfishness, our egotism, our sensuality, our meanness—in a word, against all that prevents us from realizing the best and highest things in our nature. Communism crucifies its enemies; we crucify that which makes us think anyone is our enemy. Communism hates the love of Christians; we hate that which makes us hate Communists. If Communists used as much violence on their selfishness as they use on others, they would all be saints!

Their hatred is weakness, for it refuses to see that collective selfishness is just as wrong as individual selfishness; it is the weakness of the man who is not self-possessed, who uses his fist instead of his mind, who resorts to violence for the same reason the ignorant man resorts to blasphemy; namely, because he has not sufficient intellectual strength to express himself otherwise.

What then must be our attitude toward the hatred Communists bear to us? It must be the attitude of the Holy Father who asked us to pray for the Communists. It must be the attitude of those Spanish priests who before being shot by the Communists asked them to kneel down and receive their blessing and their forgiveness. And what is this but a reflection of Our Lord's attitude on the Cross: meekness, love, and forgiveness?

What must be our attitude toward Communism? We must possess a strength, a force, and a daring which exposes its errors and goes down to death on the Cross, rather than accept the least of its principles of hate.

They will not love us for our meekness, and it will be hard for us not to be angry when our conceit and our pride, and possibly our possessions, are attacked; but there is no escaping the Divine injunction: "Blessed are ye when they shall revile you, and persecute you, and speak all that is evil against you, untruly, for my sake: Be glad and rejoice for your reward is very great in heaven." "If the world hate you, know ye that it hath hated me before you. If you had been of the world the world would love its own; but because you are not of the world, but I have chosen you out of the world, therefore the world hateth you." "The hour cometh that whosoever killeth you will think that he doth a service to God."

If then we have enemies, let us forgive them. If we suffer unjustly, then we can practice the virtue of charity. If we suffer justly, and we probably do, for we have sins to atone for, then we can practice the virtue of justice.

What right have we to hate others, since our own selfishness is often the cause of their hatred. The first word from the Cross and the Beatitude of meekness both demand that we tear up self-love by the roots; love our executioners; forgive them, for they know not what they do; do a favor for those who insult us; be kind to the thieves who accuse us of theft; be forgiving to liars who denounce us for lying; be charitable to the adulterers who charge us with impurity.

Be glad and rejoice for their hate. It will only harm our pride, but not our character; it will cauterize our conceit, but not blemish our soul —for the very insult of the world is the consecration of our goodness.

We know it is not the worldly thing to do— to pray for those who nail us to a cross. But that is just the point, Christianity is not worldliness; it is turning the world upside down. We know it is not "common sense" to love our enemies, for to love our enemies means hating ourselves; but that is the meaning of Christianity—hating that which is hateful in us. And in reference to Communism let me say: I hate Communism because it is destructive of civilization as Russia and Spain so well prove, but I love the Communists. I love them because they are potential children of God.

Our enemy is often our saviour; our persecutor is often our redeemer; our executioners are often our allies; our crucifiers are often our benefactors—for they reveal what is selfish, base, conceited, and ignoble in us. But we must not hate them for that. To hate them for hating us is weakness.

If we go on answering hate with hate, how will hate ever end? The violent answer to violence is the propagation of further violence; strife increases the sum of bitterness regardless of who triumphs. Hate is like a seed; if we sow it we reap more hate. If then hatred is to be overcome, the sting must be taken out of it; it must not be nourished, or cultivated, or propagated. But how can this be, except by returning good for evil?

How else can we banish hatred from the earth? Suppose 5,000 men are in line and before them is a Communist propagandist telling them that the only way they can overthrow governments and property is by violence, revolution and the clenched fists. Suppose the first man in line, inspired by that Communist's hatred, strikes the second man in line on the right cheek; the second raises his clenched fist to strike the third; the third wishes to strike the right cheek of the fourth, and on and on clenched fists fly—because their Gospel is hate.

Is there any way at all to stop that hatred and violence? Yes, on one condition, and that is if one man in that line who is struck on his right cheek, instead of striking his neighbor, turns and offers to the one who struck him his left cheek. He would kill hatred, because he refused to sow it.

Hatred would no longer have soil on which it could grow, for hatred can grow on a right cheek but never on a left cheek: "If any man strike thee on the right cheek, turn the other cheek."

That is not weakness; it is strength, the strength that makes man master of himself and the conqueror of hate.

If you doubt it try it some time to see how much strength it takes. It took so much strength that only Divinity's cry of forgiveness could overcome the hatred of those who crucify.

If you have enemies, if they hate you, if they revile you, and persecute you and say all manner of evil things against you, and you wish to stop their hatred, to release the hatred in their clenched fists, drive them off the face of the earth—then there is but one way to do it—Love them!

THE SECOND WORD

"Blessed are the merciful: for they shall obtain mercy."—"This day thou shalt be with me in paradise."

At the beginning of His Public Life, on the Hill of the Beatitudes, Our Lord preached: "Blessed are the merciful: for they shall obtain mercy." At the end of His Public Life, on the Hill of Calvary, He practiced that Beatitude as He addressed the thief: "This day thou shalt be with me in paradise."

The Beatitude of the world is quite different; it runs like this: "Blessed is the man who thinketh first about himself." Life for the world is a struggle for existence in which victory belongs only to the egotists. Liberality, generosity, and graciousness are rare. How often the world insists on "rights," how rarely does it emphasize "duties"; how often it uses the possessive "mine," and how rarely the generous "thine."

How full it is of "courts of justice," but how few are its "courts of mercy."

Our Lord came to correct such an exaggerated justice which knew no mercy. Mercy, he reminded us, was something more than a sentimental, emotional tenderheartedness. The very word mercy is derived in Latin from miserum cor, a sorrowful heart. Mercy is therefore a compassionate understanding of another's unhappiness.

A person is merciful when he feels the sorrow and misery of another as if it were his own. Disliking misery and unhappiness, the merciful man seeks to dispel the misery of his neighbor just as much as he would if the misery were his own. That is why, whenever mercy is confronted not only with pain, but with sin and wrong-doing, it becomes forgiveness which not merely pardons, but even rebuilds into justice, repentance, and love.

Mercy is one of the dominant notes in the preaching of Our Lord. His parables were parables of mercy. Take for example the hundred sheep, the ten pieces of money, and the two sons. Of the hundred sheep, one was lost; of the ten pieces of money, one was lost; of the two sons, one led a life of dissipation.

It is interesting to note that the lost sheep is the one that was sought, and the shepherd finding it, places it upon his shoulders and brings it into the house rejoicing. But there is no record in the Gospels of any such attention being paid to the ninety-nine sheep who were not lost.

When the woman lost a piece of money and found it, she called in her neighbors to rejoice. But there is no record that she ever called in her neighbors to rejoice in the possession of the other nine which were never lost.

One son went into a foreign country and wasted his substance living riotously. And when he came back he was given the fatted calf. But the brother who stayed at home was not so rewarded. All these illustrations Our Lord followed with the simple truth: "There shall be more joy in heaven upon one sinner that doth penance more than upon ninety-nine just who need not penance."

One day Peter went to Him to inquire just what limitation should be placed upon mercy. And so he asked Our Lord a question about mercy and gave what he thought was rather an extravagant limit: "How often shall my brother offend against me, and I forgive him? till seven times?" And Our Lord answered, "Not till seven times, but till seventy times seven times." And that does not mean four hundred and ninety—that means infinity.

Developing the idea of infinite mercy Our Lord said He had come "to heal the contrite of heart"; and that "they that are in health need not a physician, but they that are ill ... For I am not come to call the just, but sinners."

Some were scandalized at Him because He "dined with publicans and sinners," but He never ceased to remind us that we should be merciful because the heavenly Father was merciful. "That you may be the children of your Father who is in heaven, who maketh his sun to rise upon the good and bad, and raineth upon the just and the unjust. For if you love them that love you, what reward shall you have? Do not even the publicans this? ... Be ye therefore perfect as also your heavenly Father is perfect."

Here He is suggesting that we must, like Our Heavenly Father, be merciful to those who according to human estimation least deserve it. That is why He was merciful to Magdalen, to the woman at the well, to

Peter who denied Him, to Zaccheus, and even to Judas whom He addressed as "friend."

There was no mistaking His point of view; He was interested in sinners not because of their merits, but because of their misery. And now at the close of His Life, He fulfills the beatitude of mercy in His second word from the Cross.

There were three crosses on Calvary: the crosses of two thieves and the Cross of the Good Shepherd. Of the three who hung silhouetted against that blackened sky, one only was selfish and thought of himself, and that was the thief on the left. He was interested neither in the Saviour who suffered patiently, nor in the thief who begged for mercy. He had no thought but for himself as he addressed the Man on the central cross: "If thou be Christ, save thyself and us."

The thief on the right, on the contrary, thought not of himself, but about others, namely the thief on the left and Our Blessed Lord. His compassion went out to the thief on the left, because he was not turning to God in this the last hour of his life, and begging for forgiveness: "Neither doest thou fear God, seeing thou art under the same condemnation."

He also thought of the meek Man crucified between the two of them, who had just prayed for His executioners and was innocent and good: "We indeed (suffer) justly, for we receive the due reward of our deeds; but this man hath done no evil."

It is interesting to inquire why the Merciful Saviour not only forgave the penitent thief, but even gave him the Divine Promise: "This day thou shalt be with me in paradise." Why did not Our Lord address the same words to the thief on the left? The answer is to be found in the Beatitude of Mercy: "Blessed are the merciful: for they shall obtain mercy."

Because the thief on the right was merciful and compassionate, he received mercy and compassion. Because he was thoughtless of self, someone thought of him. There is a law about mercy just as rigid as the laws of nature. What we sow that also we reap. If we sow sparingly we reap sparingly. If we sow generously, we reap an abundant harvest. Raised to a spiritual level this means, as Our Lord has said: "For with what judgment you judge, you shall be judged; and with what measure you mete, it shall be measured to you again."

In other words, by thinking of others we get God to think of us. If the seed of the springtime thought only of self, but never of the soil, the rain, and the sun, it would never bloom and blossom into flower and fruit. But once it forgets itself and goes outside itself, and even dies to seed-life for the sake of the soil and sun and air, lo! it finds itself renewed and beautified a thousand times. If the coal in the bowels of the earth thought only of itself, it would never release its imprisoned sunlight as light and heat.

And so it is with us. Mercy is a compassion which seeks to unburden the sorrows of others as if they were our own. But if we have no such compassion, then how can compassion ever come back to us?

Unless we throw something up, nothing will come down; unless there is an action there can never be a reaction; unless we give, it shall not be given to us; unless we love, we shall not be loved; unless we pardon evil, our evil shall not be forgiven; unless we are merciful to others, God cannot be merciful to us.

If our heart is filled with the sand of our ego, how can God fill it with the fire of His Sacred Heart? If there is no "for sale" sign on the selfishness of our souls, how can God take possession of them?

If then we wish to receive mercy, we must, like the good thief, think of others, for it seems that God finds us best when we are lost in others. Blessed are the merciful; for they shall obtain mercy.

In a negative way Our Lord has reminded us of this Law of Mercy in the parable of the unjust steward: "Therefore is the kingdom of heaven likened to a king, who would take an account of his servants. And when he had begun to take the account, one was brought to him that owed him ten thousand talents. And as he had not wherewith to pay it, his lord commanded that he should be sold, and his wife and children, and all that he had, and payment to be made. But that servant falling down, besought him, saying: 'Have patience with me, and I will pay thee all.' And the lord of that servant, being moved with pity, let him go and forgave him the debt.

"But when that servant was gone out, he found one of his fellow-servants that owed him a hundred pence: and laying hold of him, he throttled him, saying: 'Pay what thou owest.' And his fellow-servant falling down, besought him, saying: 'Have patience with me, and I will pay thee all? And he would not, but went and cast him into prison, till he paid the debt.

"Now his fellow-servants seeing what was done, were very much grieved, and they came, and told their lord all that was done. Then his lord called him, and said to him: 'Thou wicked servant, I forgave thee all the debt, because thou besoughtest me. Shouldst not thou then have had compassion also on thy fellow-servant, even as I had compassion on thee?' And his lord being angry, delivered him to the torturers until he paid all the debt. So also shall my heavenly Father do to you, if you forgive not every one his brother from your hearts."

Be merciful then, to others, if you would have God kind to you at the last day. Think of others, rather than of yourself. Our Lord has made mercy the very soul of His Church. I think that is the reason why He chose as the head of His Church, not the innocent, not the pure, not the virgin disciple John, but that impetuous, strong man called Peter—the one who had denied Him, and who, the night of the trial, cursed and swore that he knew not the Man.

His merciful Lord passed him en route to the ignominy of that sorrowful night preceding Good Friday, and Peter seeing Him, went out, and "wept bitterly." And tradition adds that Peter wept so much during his life that even his cheeks became furrowed with tears.

And so he who knew by experience the mercy and forgiveness of Our Lord was chosen the head of the Church, in order that the Church might forever practice mercy and kindness.

There is every reason in the world for mercy. There is some good in the worst of us, and there is some bad in the best of us. The good are those who try to find some good in others, and they generally do find it. The evil are those who look for the faults of others, and as a result never see their own.

It was these Our Lord rebuked: "And why seest thou the mote that is in thy brother's eye; and seest not the beam that is in thy own eye? Or how sayest thou to thy brother: Let me cast the mote out of thy eye; and behold a beam is in thy own eye! Thou hypocrite, cast out first the beam out of thy own eye, and then shalt thou see to cast out the mote out of thy brother's eye."

If then on the last day we would receive a merciful judgment, we must begin here below to be merciful to others. Just as the clouds release only the moisture which they gathered from the earth, so too can Heaven release only the mercy we have sent heavenward.

By constantly thinking of ourselves, we render ourselves incapable of receiving the kindness of others. Only to the extent that we have emptied ourselves of ourselves can God fill us with Himself. And likewise, the best way to have our prayers answered is to pray for the intentions of others: for God begins to think of us when we cease to think of ourselves.

Therein probably must be sought the reason why more of our prayers are not answered. How can God answer the prayers we address to Him unless we answer the prayers others address to us? Do we answer the prayers of the poor? the maimed? the lame? the sinner? the missionary? If not, then by what right can we expect God to answer our requests?

How can God give us His gifts, if we never give others our gifts? How can God fill our coffers with His treasures, unless we empty them to others?

The law is as simple as that: sow and you reap; do not keep your seed in your barns; give it away—scatter it over the fields; do the foolish thing; dissipate it, so that even the birds may eat of your bounty. And lo! in a short time you will find your seed increased five, ten, one hundred-fold. But keep it in your barn, and the birds starve and you have no increase.

Give and you shall receive; be merciful and you shall receive mercy. When therefore you are on a cross of pain or sorrow always think of that cross as the cross of the thief on the right.

As such, let your prayers go out to those on the left cross that they may be mindful of the expiatory value of their suffering; let your love also go out to the Good Shepherd on the Central Cross who suffers so innocently for all men, and because you never once thought of yourself but of others, or in other words, because you were merciful, you will hear the reward of Mercy from the Central Cross: "This day thou shalt be with me in paradise." In that way you become another Good Thief, for a Good Thief is one who steals Paradise!

THE THIRD WORD

"Blessed are the clean of heart: for they shall see God."—"(Son) behold thy mother, Woman, behold thy son."

ON the Hill of the Beatitudes, at the beginning of His Public Life, Our Lord preached: "Blessed are the clean of heart, for they shall see God." Now at the end of His life, on the Hill of Calvary, He speaks to the clean of heart: "(Son) behold thy mother, Woman, behold thy son."

This of course, is not the beatitude of the world. The world is living today in what might be described as an era of carnality, which glorifies sex, hates restraint, identifies purity with coldness, innocence with ignorance, and turns men and women into Buddhas with their eyes closed, hands folded across their breasts, intently looking inward, thinking only of self.

It is just precisely against such a glorification of sex, and such egocentrism which is so characteristic of the flesh, that Our Lord reacted in His third Beatitude: "Blessed are the clean of heart."

The third Beatitude and the Third Word are related as theory to practice and as doctrine to example, for it was the purity of Our Lord that made the gift of His Mother possible. This is the one supreme lesson to be drawn from this word, namely, that Mary became Our Mother because her Divine Son was Purity itself. On no other condition could He have given her to us so completely and whole-heartedly.

In order to understand how Mary became Our Mother through purity, dwell for a moment on the nature of flesh. Flesh is essentially selfish even in its legitimate satisfaction. All its pleasures look to itself and not to another. Even the law of self-preservation implies, as the word itself states, a kind of selfishness. In its illegitimate pursuits flesh is even more selfish still, for to satisfy itself it must tyrannize over others, and consume them to enkindle its own fires.

But God in His wisdom has instituted two escapes from the selfishness of the flesh: the Sacrament of Matrimony and the vow of chastity. Each not only breaks the circle of selfishness but makes possible a greater and wider field of service. Or to turn the truth around: the greater the purity of heart, the less the selfishness.

The first escape from the selfishness of the flesh which God has instituted, is the Sacrament of Matrimony. Matrimony crushes selfishness, first of all, because it merges individuals into a corporate life in which neither lives for self but for the other; it crushes selfishness also because the very permanence of marriage is destructive of those fleeting infatuations, which are born with the moment and die with it; it destroys selfishness, furthermore, because the mutual love of husband and wife takes them out of themselves into the incarnation of their mutual love, their other selves, their children; and finally it narrows selfishness because the rearing of children demands sacrifice, without which, like unwatered flowers, they wilt and die.

But these are only negative aspects of Matrimony in relation to the flesh. What is more important to note is that matrimony cures selfishness by calling the flesh to the service of others. New horizons and vistas of devotion and sacrifice are opened to the eyes of flesh; others become more important than self; the ego becomes less circumscribed and more expansive. It reaches out to others at times even forgetting self.

And so true is this that there is generally less selfishness in large families than in small. A husband and wife may live only for one another, but a father and mother must die to themselves in order to live for their offspring. All unregulated and egotistic attachments which destroy the integrity of a common life are left behind them. Where their heart is, there is their treasure also. They lay their flesh on the altar of sacrifice that others may live, and this is the beginning of love.

But God has provided still another escape from the selfishness of flesh, one more complete than the Sacrament of Matrimony, and that is the vow of chastity. The man or woman who takes this vow does so, not to escape the sacrifices which marriage demands, but to detach himself from all the ties of the flesh, in order that he may be free for greater service.

As St. Paul puts it: "He that is with a wife is solicitous for the things of the world, how he may please his wife; and he is divided. He that is without a wife is solicitous for the things that belong to the Lord, how he may please God."

The vow is a higher form of sacrifice than matrimony, simply because it purchases greater release from the claims of the flesh. The greater the purity the less the selfishness. He or she who takes it may be free to serve and love not just another man or woman and a few children, but all men and all women and all children in the bonds of charity in Christ Jesus Our Lord.

Marriage releases the flesh from its individual selfishness for the service of the family; the vow of chastity releases the flesh not only from the narrow and circumscribed family where there can still be selfishness, but also for the service of that family which embraces all humanity. That is why the Church asks those who consecrate themselves to the redemption of the world to take a vow and to surrender all selfishness, that they may belong to no one family and yet belong to all.

That is why in that larger family of the Kingdom of God, the priest is called "Father"—because he has begotten children not in the flesh, but in the spirit. That is why the superior of a religious community of women is called "Mother"—she has her little flock in Christ. That too is why certain teaching orders of men are called "Brothers," and why women bound in religious life by the vow of chastity are called "Sisters."

They are all one family in which new relations have been established, not by their birth in the flesh but by their birth in Christ—all selflessly seeking the glory of God and the salvation of sinners, under the one whom they love most on earth: their Holy Father, the successor of Peter, the Vicar of Jesus Christ.

Now if matrimony and the vow provide releases from the selfishness of the flesh, and if increasing purity prepares for a wider service of others, then what should we expect when we meet perfect purity?

If a person becomes less and less egocentric as he becomes more pure, then what should we look for in perfect sinlessness and perfect purity? If greater purity means greater selflessness then what should we expect of innocence? The answer is: perfect sacrifice.

Given a character in whom there is no selfishness, either for his own comfort or even for his own life, and you have the sacrifice of the cross. "For greater love than this no man hath, that a man lay down his life for his friends." Given a purity which arises above all family ties and bonds of blood, and then, as Our Lord told us: "He that doth the will of the Father in heaven is a father, a mother, a brother, and a sister."

Given a purity which is the Purity of Our Lord on the Cross, and you have someone so detached from the ego, so strange to selfishness, so thoughtless of the flesh that He looks upon His Mother, not uniquely as His own, but as the Mother of us all. Perfect Purity is perfect selflessness. That is why Christ gives His Mother to us, as represented in the person of John: "Behold thy mother."

He would not be selfish about her; He would not keep just for Himself the loveliest and most beautiful of all mothers; He would share His own mother with us: and so at the foot of the Cross He gave her who is the Mother of God to us as the mother of men. No human person could do that because the ties of flesh and the selfishness of the flesh are too close. The flesh is too close to us to enable us to share our mother with others. But absolute purity can.

That is why the Beatitude of Purity is one with the Third Word, where selflessness, reaching its perfection in Purity, gave His life that we might be saved, and gave us His Mother that we might not be orphans.

Purity then is not something negative; it is not just an unopened bud; it is not something cold; it is not ignorance of life. Is justice merely the absence of dishonesty? Is mercy merely the absence of cruelty? Is faith merely the absence of doubt? Purity is not merely the absence of sensuality; it is selflessness born of love and the highest love of all.

Everyone with a vow is in love, but not in love with that which dies, but with that love which is eternal—the love of God. There is a passion about chastity—what Thompson calls a "passionless passion and wild tranquillity."

Chastity is not an impossible virtue. Even those who have it not, may yet possess it. St. Augustine calls Mary Magdalen, "the arch-virgin." Think of it! the "arch-virgin." He puts her next to the Blessed Mother in virginity; Magdalen, this common prostitute of the streets! She recovered purity, we might almost say, by receiving in anticipation of the Eucharist, the night she bathed the Feet of Our Lord with tears.

That day she came in contact with purity, and she so lived out its implications that within a short time we find her at the foot of the cross on Good Friday. But who stands beside her? It is no other than the Blessed Mother.

What a remarkable companionship! a woman whose name a few months ago was synonymous with sin, and the Blessed Virgin! If Mary loved Magdalen, then why cannot she love us? If there was hope for Magdalen, then there can be hope for us. If she recovered purity, then it can be recovered by us. But how, except through Mary, for why is she called Mother Most Pure except to make us pure?

Everyone can go to Mary, not only converted sinners like Magdalen, but holy virgins and good mothers, for she is both Virgin and Mother. Virginity alone seems to lack something. There is a natural incompleteness about it—a faculty unused. Motherhood alone seems to have lost something. There is something surrendered in motherhood. But in Mary there is "neither lack nor loss."1 There is Virginity and Motherhood—"springtime of eternal May."

Purity then is not selfishness; it is surrender, it is thoughtfulness of others, it is sacrifice. It can even reach a peak where the Mother of

Jesus can become our mother. Away then with that false maxim of the world which tells us that love is blind. It cannot be blind. Our Lord says it is not blind. "Blessed are the clean of heart, for they shall see"—see even God. Mary, open our eyes!

Sheila Kay Smith.

THE FOURTH WORD

*"Blessed are the poor in spirit, for theirs is
the kingdom of heaven."—"My God, My
God, why hast thou forsaken me?"*

AT the beginning of His Public Life on the Hill of the Beatitudes Our Lord preached: "Blessed are the poor in spirit, for theirs is the Kingdom of Heaven." At the end of His life on the Hill of Calvary He now practices that poverty of spirit by His Fourth Word from the cross: "My God, My God, why hast thou forsaken me?"

Both the Beatitude and the Word are foreign to the spirit of the world. Modern society is what might be characterized as acquisitive, for its primary concern is to acquire, to own, to possess; its aristocracy is not one of blood or virtue, but of money; it judges worth not by righteousness but in terms of possessions.

Our Blessed Lord came into the world to destroy this acquisitiveness and this subservience of moral to economic ends by preaching the blessedness of the poor in spirit. It is worth noting immediately that "the poor in spirit" does not necessarily mean the indigent or those in straitened circumstances of life; "Poor in spirit" means interior detachment, and as such includes even some who are rich in the world's goods, for detachment can be practiced by the rich just as avarice can be practiced by the poor.

The poor in spirit are those who are so detached from wealth, from social position, and from earthly knowledge that, at the moment the Kingdom of God demands a sacrifice, they are prepared to surrender all.

The Beatitude means then: Blessed are those who are not possessed by their possessions; blessed are they who whether or not they are poor in fact are poor in their inmost spirit.

Our Lord not only preached Poverty of Spirit; He also lived it, and He lived it in such a way as to conquer the three kinds of pride: — the pride of what one has, which is economic pride; the pride of what one is, which is social pride; and the pride of what one knows, which is intellectual pride.

First of all, to counteract the wild exaltation of the economic, the pursuit of wealth as the noblest end of man, and the glorying in what one has, Christ became economically poor. He chose His Mother from the poorer classes who could afford to offer only doves in the Temple, and His foster father from the village tradesmen; and He Who owned the earth and the fullness thereof, chose for His birthplace a deserted shepherd's cave.

He was poor in His mission as He explained at Nazareth: "The Spirit of the Lord is upon me, wherefore he hath anointed me to preach the gospel to the poor." He was poor in His public life: "The foxes have holes, and the birds of the air nests; but the Son of man hath not where to lay his head."

He was poor in the eyes of government, for when asked to pay the tax, He had no money. He was poor in His death, for He was stripped of His garments—the last remnant of earthly possessions—; He was executed on a cross erected at public expense, and buried in a stranger's grave.

Thus did He atone for those who are proud of what they have, by having nothing, and becoming the Universal Poor Man of the World. He who was rich became poor for our sakes that we might be rich, and He is therefore the only one in all history of whom both the rich and poor can say: "He came from our ranks. He is one of our own."

Reparation had to be made not only for the pride of wealth, but also for the snobbery and pride of social position. The world is full of those who either through the accident of birth or circumstance count themselves better than their fellowmen and who glory in what they are.

These too He atoned for not only by veiling the glory of His Godhead under human form, but also by the most poignant social abandonment. The very beginning of His life bears the record: "He came unto his own, and his own received him not." Cities abandoned Him: Bethlehem refused Him an inn; Nazareth drove Him from its gates, and Jerusalem stoned Him.

Truly indeed He could say: "A prophet is not without honour, but in his own country, and in his own house, and among his own kindred." Men abandoned Him. Some of His disciples hearing Him say He would give Himself humbly under the form of Bread said: "This saying is hard, and who can hear it?" ... and they walked with Him no more.

Teachers of the Law abandoned Him calling Him "a glutton, a wine-drinker, a friend of publicans and sinners." The needy abandoned Him and drew from Him the sweet complaint: "You will not come to me that you may have life."

One of His Apostles abandoned Him for thirty pieces of silver, one for shame at the word of a maid-servant, and three for sleep. Even those whom He helped abandoned Him: "Were not ten made clean? and where are the other nine? There is no one found to return and give glory to God, but this stranger."

And now at the end of His Life, the Roman Governor could say: "Thy own nation ... has delivered Thee up to me." Thus did He Who is King of Kings become socially poor and an outcast from the snobs of the earth, in order that through that abandonment we might become—let us pause at the very thought of it—children of God!

Finally, He atoned for the intellectually proud, for all those who think they know, and who rely on the sufficiency of human knowledge without faith, by becoming spiritually poor.

During His Public Life He rejoiced that the sublime truths of the Kingdom of Heaven were given only to the humble: "I confess to Thee, O Father, Lord of heaven and earth, because Thou hast hid these things from the wise and prudent, and hast revealed them to little ones."

The night of His agony in the garden when that atonement for pride began in all horror, He described His soul as "sorrowful unto death"; and now on the cross He lives the Beatitude of the Poor in Spirit by proclaiming the last and greatest poverty of all—the spiritual poverty of seeming abandonment by God: "My God, Why hast thou forsaken me?"

Even the sun at mid-day hid its light as a symbol of the spiritual desolation of His soul. The Father had not really abandoned Him, but Our Lord restrained His Divinity from mitigating even with one drop of consolation the bitterness of His chalice.

The cry was of abandonment and not one of despair. A soul that despairs never cries to God. Just as the keenest pangs of hunger are felt not by the dying man who is completely exhausted, but by the man battling for his life with the last ounce of strength, so abandonment is felt not by the ungodly and unholy, but by the most holy of men, Our Lord on the Cross.

This was the hardest reparation of all. It was not difficult to be economically poor; it was not so difficult to be socially poor and stripped of His friends; but it was hard to surrender Divine consolation in a moment of agony to atone for self-wise, the intelligentsia and the conceited who refuse to bow their heads to the wisdom of God, for the atheists who live without God and for the Communists who blot His name from the land of the living.

This word from the Cross was a revelation of how much mental agony there must be in the world in those minds and souls and hearts who are without God.

He knew at that one moment what it was to be without God! He knew something of the loneliness of godlessness and something of the misery of Communism, for it was the one moment in which He suffered the desolation of both, that we might have the consolation of never being without Him. By feeling without God, he redeemed those who live without Him.

Behold the Poor Man. Economically poor because stripped of garments; socially poor because deserted by friends; spiritually poor because abandoned by God. From that day to this, then: Blessed are the poor in Spirit. Blessed are the economically poor in spirit for by desiring nothing, they possess all, even the mansions of the Father's House.

Some years ago when the Cloister of a Carmelite convent was broken by a Cardinal and opened to the public, a good Carmelite nun was showing a visiting priest through the convent. From the roof of it one could look over a valley, and on to an opposite hill where there stood a large and beautiful home that seemed to stand as a symbol for all that was sweet and beautiful and lovely in life.

Recalling the economic poverty of this poor nun, the visitor said to her, "Sister, just suppose that before you entered Carmel, you could have lived in that home. Suppose that you could have had all the wealth, refinement, and opportunities for worldly enjoyment that such a home would give you. Would you have left that house to have become a poor Carmelite?" And she answered, "Father, that is my house!"

Blessed also are the poor in spirit socially. Blessed are they who know of only one aristocracy—the blue-bloods born at the Baptismal font and the royalty of the King of Kings.

There is going to be a tremendous transformation of social position at the last day, for God is no respecter of persons. Our social position in the Kingdom of God will depend not upon our human popularity of propaganda, but only upon those things we carry with us in the shipwreck of the world—a clear conscience and the love of God.

The world has little use for either, that is why Our Lord warned us that a full-hearted love of Him would draw down the world's hatred: "Yea, the hour cometh, that whosoever killeth you, will think that he doth a service to God. And these things will they do to you, because they have not known the Father, nor me. But these things I have told you, that when the hour shall come, you may remember that I told you of them."

How completely His point of view reverses that of the world's estimate of position is evidenced in those equally striking words: "Blessed shall you be when men shall hate you, and when they shall separate you, and shall reproach you, and cast out your name as evil, for the Son of man's sake. Be glad in that day and rejoice; for behold, your reward is great in heaven."

Blessed finally are the poor in spirit intellectually. Blessed are the humble, and the teachable who like the Shepherds know they know nothing, or like the Wise Men who know they do not know everything. Faith in God, faith in prayer, hope in Christ, devotion to Our Blessed Mother, belief in the Eucharist and in infallibility—all this may seem foolish to the self-wise, but "the foolishness of God is wiser than men."

Personally, we feel that if our eternal salvation were conditioned upon saving either one hundred corrupt men and women of the streets like Magdalen and Zaccheus, or converting one proud university professor who felt his tiny mind had solved all the riddles of the universe, we should choose to go out and convert the hundred.

And there is a divine warrant for the choice, for Our Lord said to those who thought themselves wise: "Amen, I say to you, that the publicans and the harlots shall go into the Kingdom of God before you."

Why then are we proud? Why do we set all the energies of life on becoming rich: "What doth it profit a man, if he gain the whole world, and suffer the loss of his own soul?" Why do we seek social prestige and seek out the first places at tables—the Divine injunction is just the contrary: "When thou art invited, go, sit down in the lowest place; that when he who invited thee cometh, he may say to thee: Friend, go up higher.... Because every one that exalteth himself shall be humbled; and he that humbleth himself shall be exalted."

Why are we proud? Whom in all the world could we find to love us in poverty, in friendless abandonment, and in ignorance, other than Our Lord. In the beautiful words of Francis Thompson:

> "Strange, piteous, futile thing!
> Wherefore should any set thee love apart?
> Seeing none but I make much of naught"
> (He said),
> "And human love needs human meriting:
> How hast thou merited—
> Of all man's clotted clay, the dingiest clot?
> Alack, thou knowest not
> How little worthy of any love thou art!

> Whom wilt thou find to love ignoble thee,
> Save Me, save only Me?
> All which I took from thee I did but take,
> Not for thy harms,
> But just that thou might'st seek it in My arms.
> All which thy child's mistake
> Fancies as lost, I have stored for thee at home:
> Rise, clasp My hand, and come."

If then we are called to be poor economically, poor socially, and poor intellectually, let us rejoice in the hope that for us is reserved the Kingdom of heaven, and for the present see in our fleeting poverty "the shade of His hand, outstretched caressingly."

THE FIFTH WORD

*"Blessed are they that hunger and thirst after justice:
for they shall have their fill."—"I thirst."*

At the beginning of His Public Life on the Hill of the Beatitudes Our Lord preached the necessity of zeal: "Blessed are they that hunger and thirst after justice: for they shall have their fill." At the end of His Public Life on the Hill of Calvary He practiced that beatitude as there fell from His lips the cry of apostleship: "I thirst."

The world cannot understand either this Beatitude or this Word, for the world by its nature is seated in indifference. It is very fond of talking about religion, but dislikes doing anything about it. It dismisses zeal and intense love of God with the sneer of "mysticism," and regards religion as something incidental to human life, like poetry.

It is not uncommon therefore to find Catholics who say: "I knew I should not eat meat on Friday out of respect for the day on which Our Lord sacrificed His life for me, but I did not want to embarrass my host," or "I was staying with some unbelieving friends over the week-end and I did not want to embarrass them, so I did not go to Mass on Sunday," or "when they made fun of devotion to the Blessed Mother and ridiculed veneration of saints, and the crucifix, I said nothing, because I did not want to start an argument about religion."

Such is the indifference of the world—a fear of being identified whole-heartedly with the God for whom we were made. If the world does hunger and thirst it is always for something less than the justice of this Beatitude.

Communists, for example, hunger and thirst, but not for the Justice of God; they hunger and thirst for a system built, not upon love, but upon class-struggle and revolution. They seek to fill a want, but only the wants of the stomach.

It is just against such filling of the animal in us, and the starving of the spiritual, that Our Lord said: "Woe to you that are filled: for you shall hunger." "Your Father know-eth that you have need of all these things. Seek ye therefore first the kingdom of God, and his justice, and all these things shall be added unto you."

And against that compromising indifference which fears to assert God's justice He warned: "Everyone therefore that shall confess me before men, I will also confess him before my Father who is in heaven. But he that shall deny me before men, I will also deny him before my Father who is in heaven"; and against justice which limits itself to economic rights and excludes the duties of man to his Maker, He said: "For I tell you, that unless your justice abound more than that of the Scribes and Pharisees, you shall not enter into the kingdom of heaven."

Not only negatively but positively did He preach the necessity of zeal for the Justice of the Kingdom of God. His circumcision was a kind of impatience to run His course of Justice which led to the Garden and the Cross; His teaching the Doctors in the Temple at twelve years of age was an impatience to teach men the sweetness of His Father's ways.

At the beginning of His Public Life we find Him driving merchants out of the Temple, in fulfillment of the prophecy of apostleship: "The zeal of thy house hath eaten me up." Later on, He made use of a dinner invitation to save the soul of Magdalen, and on a hot day, made use of a common love of cold water to bring the Samaritan woman to a knowledge of everlasting fountains.

He came, He said, "not to destroy souls, but to save"; and, "seeing the multitude, he had compassion on them; because they were distressed, and lying as sheep having no shepherd. Then he said to His disciples: "The harvest indeed is great, but the laborers are few. Pray ye therefore the Lord of the harvest, that he send forth laborers into his harvest." His whole mission in life was one of zeal, a hunger and thirst for the Justice of God, which He perhaps best expressed in words of fire: "I am come to cast fire on the earth: and what will I, but that it be kindled? And I have a baptism where with I am to be baptized: and how am I straitened until it be accomplished!" "And other sheep I have, that are not of this fold: them also I must bring, and they shall hear my voice, and there shall be one fold and one shepherd."

And now at the end of His life, He yearns still more for justice as He who called himself the Fountain of Living Waters and He who was figuratively the Rock that gave forth water as Moses struck it in the desert, now lets well from out His Sacred Heart the shepherd's call to all the souls of the world: "I thirst."

It was not a thirst for earthly waters, for the earth and its oceans were His. And when they offered Him vinegar and gall as a sedative for His sufferings He refused it. It was therefore not a physical, but a spiritual thirst that troubled Him—the thirst for the Beatitude of Justice—an insatiable thirst for the souls of men.

The world that dislikes zeal for God's justice, first hated it in Him. It was His zeal which brought Him to the cross. The world loves the indifferent, the mediocre, the ordinary, but it hates two classes of people: those who are too good, and those who are too bad.

Hence on Calvary, we find Our Lord crucified with thieves. Both Innocence and Injustice fell foul of the law. Some go to the cross because they are too good for the majority or for the system; and others go to the cross because they are too bad for it.

The world hates the zealous, such as Our Lord, because they are a reproach to its mediocrity; it hates also the wicked, such as the thieves, because they are an annoyance to its self-complacency.

The race of quantity has always persecuted the race of quality. The good go down to death, because they are good; the wicked go to death because they are wicked—the mediocre survive. As Our Lord put it: "The world cannot hate you; but me it hateth: because I give testimony of it, that the works thereof are evil." And if this was true of Our Lord, it must be true of us. The servant is not above the master.

If our passionate quest of God's cause makes us disliked by men, we cannot say we were not warned by Him who was hated first. "If the world hate you, know ye that it hath hated me before you. If you had been of the world, the world would love its own: but because you are not of the world, but I have chosen you out of the world, therefore the world hateth you.... If they have persecuted me, they will also persecute you.... That the word may be fulfilled which was written in their law: They hated me without cause." Apostles of Christ then will never be popular. Their end is crucifixion.

And yet we must thirst for Justice and be on fire for the Kingdom of God. And why? Because everything that is good diffuses itself. The sun is good, and it diffuses itself in light and heat; the flower is good, and it diffuses itself in perfume; the animal is good and it diffuses itself in the generation of its kind; man is good and he diffuses himself in the communication of thought; a Christian is good, he must therefore diffuse his Christianity, throw sparks from the flame of His love, enkindle fires in the inflammable hearts of men, and speak of his Lover because He is Love, for "out of the abundance of the heart the mouth speaketh."

Strong love makes strong actions, and the measure of our zeal in bringing souls to the feet of Christ is the measure of our love of Him.

Converting souls to Christ then is not based on the pride of propaganda, but on a desire for perfection. An apostle desires to bring men and women to Our Lord not for the same reason a business man wishes to increase his trade.

The business man advertises to increase his profits; the Christian propagandizes to increase the happiness of others. He wants to bring souls to Our Lord for the same reason he wants to see the sun shine, the flowers bloom, and lambs grow into sheep—because it is their perfection and therefore their happiness.

If a pencil is made for writing, we do not want to see it used for digging; if a bird is made for flying, we do not want to see it change places with the mole; if a soul is made for the fullness of Life, then we do not want to see it clip its wings and wallow in hatred, half-truths, and marred loveliness. We want to see it united with its perfection which is the Life and Truth and Love and Beauty of God.

That is why a Christian soul is apostolic—it loves perfection, wholeness, completeness, happiness: God. And therefore it wants everyone to be God-like and God-ward.

And no cost is too great to achieve that end for in the language of Paul: "Who then shall separate us from the love of Christ? Shall tribulation? or distress? or famine? or nakedness? or danger? or persecution? or the sword? (As it is written: For Thy sake we are put to death all the day long. We are accounted as sheep for the slaughter.) But in all these things we overcome, because of Him that hath loved us. For I am sure that neither death, nor life, nor angels, nor principalities, nor powers, nor things present, nor things to come, nor might, nor height, nor depth, nor any other creature shall be able to separate us from the love of God, which is in Christ Jesus Our Lord."

If there be hate, enmity, jealousy, and war on the face of the earth today is it not due in the last analysis to our want of zeal for the cause of God?

Just suppose that outside of the necessary structure of the Church, there was only one in all the world who believed in it, who received Communion, acknowledged the Primacy of Peter, and assisted at Holy Mass. Just suppose that that one zealous believer the first year converted one un-believer to Christ and His Church. Suppose that the next year these two each made a convert; then there would be four the second year.

And suppose the next year, these four made one apiece next year, then there would be eight converts at the end of the third year. Now how many would there be, from that one zealous believer, at the end of only thirty years? There would be at the communion rails of the Church at the end of the 30th year, one billion, seventy-three million, seven hundred and forty-one thousand, eight hundred and twenty-four souls breaking their fast with the Bread of Life.

It is a tremendous thought, and a reminder of how much we have failed to do our duty and to spread the love and knowledge of Christ in the souls of men. Are we unmindful that thirst for justice will save our own souls? Have we forgotten the words of St. James: "He who causeth a sinner to be converted from the error of his way, shall save his soul from death, and shall cover a multitude of sins."

Have we forgotten that the cold must burn; that the tepid must flame like torches of the night, that the Kingdom of heaven suffereth violence and only the violent shall bear it away? If we have, then we know why Our Lord cried: "I thirst." It is because we have reached Him the vinegar and gall of indifference.

Away with mediocrity! Lift up your hearts! The world is looking for light. Will you hide yours under bushels? The earth is looking for savor, will you let the salt lose its savor? Think of the Communists who are hungering for justice without knowing it! Think of the atheists who are starving for peace without knowing it! Think of the great mass of men and women in this country who set for themselves no higher life than that of animals, namely, to eat and drink, sleep and search for prey.

Think of those who hate the good, really because they hate their own wickedness! They have a passion for God hid beneath the ashes of their lives, but they presently live in fear "lest having Him they must have naught else beside."

We plead particularly for the Communists, who hate religion, who hate classes, and who hate God. But that does not mean we must hate them.

They are yearning for something which their own Communism cannot give them. They are hungering and thirsting for the justice of God, whether they know it or not. Therefore we must not hate them just because they hate us. Rather we must feel sorry for them because they miss so much, and because their zeal is bent on destruction rather than construction.

In fact our sympathy for them should be so deep that we will strive to save them from the very ruins which, Samson-like, they pull down on their heads. This is our Christian duty, for we do not save our souls alone, but only in companionship with others.

On Judgment Day we shall be asked: Where are your children? If we can point to those whom we have saved, or can point to one Communist whom we have made a Communionist, then we who hungered and thirsted shall be filled—filled even from the fountains of God.

THE SIXTH WORD

*"Blessed are the peace-makers: for they shall
be called the children of God."—"It is
consummated."*

AT the beginning of His Public Life on the Hill of Beatitudes, Our Lord preached: "Blessed are the peace-makers: for they shall be called the children of God." At the end of His life on the Hill of Calvary He practiced that Beatitude as, concluding peace between man and God, He uttered the triumphant cry: "It is consummated."

Like all the other Beatitudes this was at utter variance with the spirit of the world, where right is might, and where pugnacity and aggressiveness are virtues. This is putting it mildly, for in our generation there has arisen a philosophy of life whose first principle is class struggle.

Never before in the history of the world did any political system profess, and much less act, on the motive of hate. We have it now in Communism, which has almost drowned out the voice of the Prince of Peace.

But what is the peace spoken of in this Beatitude? The most perfect definition of peace ever given was that of St. Augustine: "Peace is the tranquillity of order." It is not tranquillity alone, for some nations such as Russia are tranquil through fear.

Rather it is the tranquillity of order in which there is no oppression from without, but rather a subordination of all things to the sovereign good which is God. Therefore the subjection of senses to reason, reason to faith, and the whole man to God as his eternal end and final perfection—that is the basis of peace.

It was just such a tranquillity of order which Our Lord brought to earth as the angels sang at His birth: "Glory to God in the highest, and on earth peace to men of good will." He bade His disciples to have peace with one another. Into whatsoever house they entered, they were first to say: "Peace be to this house."

The very Beatitude we are considering is a blessing on such peace-makers, and His words over Jerusalem a reminder of His sorrow at those who loved not peace: "If thou also hadst known, and that in this thy day, the things that are to thy peace; but now they are hidden from thy eyes."

The night of His arrest in the garden, when Peter drew his sword and cut off the right ear of the servant of the high priest, Our Lord rebuked him saying: "Put up again the sword into its place: for all that take the sword shall perish with the sword." Touching the ear of the wounded servant He made it whole.

The next afternoon, He who came to preach peace, was put to death in the first world war of man against his Redeemer; but before He died He pronounced the last and final words of peace: "It is finished."

What is finished? War is finished! The war against sin! The war against evil! The war against God! The work of atonement, which is at-one-ment with God was completed. He has finished His Father's decade of the sorrowful mysteries, and the glorious ones were now about to begin.

The last farthing was paid. The Treaty of Peace was signed: "Blessed are the peacemakers." And now that He has made peace He could cry in triumph: "It is finished." It was not just an armistice; it was victory; it was a consummation—something done that could not be undone—Peace with God.

Thus far we have spoken of peace which Our Lord brought to earth. Now we must consider a difficulty against it. If Christ is the Prince of Peace, and if they who take the sword perish with it, and if a kingdom divided against itself will be brought to desolation, and if the Resurrection greeting is pax, then how reconcile these other seemingly contradictory words of Our Lord: "Do not think that I came to send peace upon earth: I came not to send peace, but the sword." "Think ye, that I am come to give peace on earth? I tell you, no; but separation. For there shall be from henceforth five in one house divided three against two, and two against three. The father shall be divided against the son, and the son against the father, the mother against the daughter, and the daughter against the mother, the mother-in-law against her daughter-in-law and the daughter-in-law against her mother-in-law." "He that hath not, let him sell his coat and buy a sword."

The explanation of these apparent contradictions is to be found in the words He addressed to His apostles the night of the last supper in which He made an important distinction between two kinds of peace:

"My peace I give unto you; not as the world giveth, do I give unto you." "These things I have spoken to you, that in me you may have peace. In the world you shall have distress: but have confidence: I have overcome the world." There is a difference then between His Peace and the peace of the world.

It is evident from these words that Our Lord offers a peace and a consolation which He alone can confer, a peace which comes from the right ordering of conscience, from justice, charity, love of God and love of neighbor. And blessed are those peace-makers who continue to spread that message of peace for they shall be called the children of God; that is, they shall be recognized as possessing a divine characteristic which shall stamp them as God-like.

But these very lovers of peace, who follow in His footsteps, who take up their crosses daily, who love Him more than all the world, who surrender all to be completely His, who trust in the Providence which feeds the birds, who have the faith of little children, and who love Christ and therefore seek that interior peace of conscience which only Christ can give —they will by that very fact be hated by the world.

The poor in spirit will be hated by those who pursue self-interest; the meek will be opposed by the self-assertive; those who hunger and thirst after justice will be scorned by the indifferent; the merciful will be ridiculed by the unforgiving; the pure of heart will be the laughingstock of the Freudians. The world whose false peace is based on self-love will make war against those whose peace is based on conscience.

In that sense Our Lord brought the sword— we might say, He even made war, war against war, war against selfishness, war against sin, war against godlessness. And if His war against evil brought Him to the cross, then His followers who preach His peace must also expect to be crucified.

The son who enters the priesthood rather than business may be hated by his father; the daughter who enters the convent rather than the social whirl may be hated by her mother; and the mother-in-law who pleads for the sanctity of the marriage bond may be hated by the daughter-in-law; and the daughter-in-law who is received into the Church to enjoy the security of its truth and the life of its Eucharist may be hated by her mother-in-law. This is the meaning of Our Lord's words about a house being divided against itself.

A young man goes to college. He could there join an Oriental sun cult, or become a Buddhist, or a Confucianist, or start a new religion of his own, and his parents would probably only remonstrate; but let him join the Church and there would be war!

Truly indeed: "I came not to bring peace but the sword"—but Our Lord encouragingly reminds that young man that the war against him is only temporary. "In the world you shall have distress; but have confidence: I have overcome the world."

The Prince of Peace then brings war—war against a false peace, war against tranquillity without order. If there is anything in life of which we must beware it is the danger of a false peace. Our Lord could have made a false peace with the world.

Did not the very ones who put Him to death ask Him to make terms with them? Did they not shout up to the throne: "Come down from the cross and we will believe"; in other words, "Come down and make a false peace. You are too insistent in the rights of your heavenly Father. You are too uncompromising about sin. You are too intolerant about your divinity. Can you not see that your claim to be the Son of God and Redeemer of the world is upsetting the world? Did you not hear one of the judges say to you last night 'One man must die for the nation to keep peace'? Come down and we will have peace."

Yes, if He had come down, there would have been peace; but a false peace! Our Lord stayed on the cross until it was finished. He would not compromise His divinity. He would not compromise obedience to His Father's Will. He would not minimize the horror of sin.

And so He stayed on the cross making war against evil until the battle was over, like a dying soldier who feebly fights with ebbing strength until his cause is victorious. That is why He could cry at the end: "It is consummated."

So too we must beware of a false peace. The Communists for example ask us to join them in a League for Peace, but we cannot, simply because it is a false peace. Communists want peace among non-Communist nations only because it offers them a better opportunity for their propaganda, which ends in the destruction of peace.

Furthermore, to a Communist there is no real peace until all nations are subject to the Communist regime and the leadership of Stalin. Communism thus becomes identified with the overthrow of the family, of religion, of justice, and of God. Such is peace as the world gives it.

Because we refuse to accept that false peace, because we refuse to come down from our cross and join in their false peace based on injustice, we bring down upon our heads their violence and their hate. But we cannot expect the world to treat us differently than it treated Our Lord.

Peace for us means a right conscience, not a dictatorship over the proletariat; it means the tranquillity of order, not the overthrow of society; it means loving our enemies, not despising them; it means something in the inside of a man's soul, not something outside like a sickle and a hammer.

We must beware, then, of concluding a false peace, of selling the Saviour for thirty pieces of silver because He does not make us rich; of denying Him before men because of the ridicule of maid servants; of sleeping in hours of great need; and above all else, of stepping down from the cross, even after two hours and fifty-nine minutes of the world's crucifixion.

We must be prepared to suffer scorn, if for no other reason than because we are peacemakers; we must ever be ready to be hated by the world, for Our Lord told us we would be hated because of Him. We must stay until "it is finished," even though that staying makes our fellow-men hate us.

This life is not a victory; this life is a war, and God hates peace in those who are destined for war!

THE SEVENTH WORD

*"Blessed are they that mourn; for they shall
he comforted."—"Father, into thy hands
I commend my spirit."*

AT the beginning of His Public Life on the Hill of the Beatitudes Our Lord preached: "Blessed are they that mourn; for they shall be comforted." At the end of His Public Life on the Hill of Calvary, He found that blessed comfort: "Father, into thy hands I commend my spirit."

Like all the other beatitudes, this beatitude of mourning is quite different from the beatitude of the world: "Eat, drink, and be merry, for tomorrow we die." The world never regards mourning as a blessing, but always as a curse. Laughter is the gold it is seeking, and sorrow is the enemy it flees.

It can no more understand the beatitude of mourning, than it can understand the cross. In fact, the modern man steels himself even against the suffering of another by wearing the mask of indifference, quite unmindful that such a thickening of his spiritual skin, though it may sometimes protect him from sorrow, nevertheless shuts in his own morbidity until it festers and corrupts.

But it must not be thought that the beatitude of Our Lord is either a condemnation of laughter and joy or a glorification of sorrow and tears. Our Lord did not believe in a philosophy of tragedy any more than we do. As a matter of fact, He upbraided the Pharisees because they wore long faces and looked sad when they fasted, and His Apostles summed up His Life and Resurrection in the one word "Rejoice."

The difference between the beatitude of the world, "Laugh and the world laughs with you," and the beatitude of Our Lord, "Blessed are they that mourn," is not that the world brings laughter and Our Lord brings tears. It is not even a choice of having or not having sadness; it is rather a choice of where we shall put it: at the beginning or at the end. In other words, which comes first, laughter or tears?

Shall we place our joys in time or in eternity, for we cannot have them in both. Shall we laugh on earth, or laugh in heaven, for we cannot laugh in both. Shall we mourn before we die or after we die, for we cannot mourn in both. We cannot have our reward both in heaven and on earth.

That is why we believe one of the most tragic words in the life of Our Lord is the word He will say to the worldly at the end of time: "You have already had your reward."

Which of the two roads then shall we take: the royal road of the Cross which leads to the Resurrection and Eternal Life, or the road of selfishness which leads to Eternal Death? The first road is filled with thorns, but if we traverse it far enough, we find it ends in a bed of roses; the other road is filled with roses, but if we traverse it far enough, it ends in a bed of thorns.

But we cannot take both roads or make the best of both worlds, because we cannot love both God and Mammon, any more than we can be both alive and dead at the same time. No man can serve two masters: "either he will hate the one, and love the other; or he will sustain the one, and despise the other."

If we save our life in this world we lose it in the next; if we lose our life in this world we save it in the next. If we sow in sin, we reap corruption; if we sow in truth, we reap life everlasting. But we cannot do both.

With which then shall we begin—the fast or the feast? This is the problem of the beatitudes. Our Lord begins with the fast and ends with the feast; the world begins with the feast and ends with want.

The contrast between these two philosophies is recorded on every page of the Gospel. Dives was rich on this earth, but he had not even a drop of cold water after his death; Lazarus was a beggar on earth, but he became a rich man in the bosom of Abraham. Therefore, in the words of Our Lord: "Woe to you that now laugh: for you shall mourn and weep"; "Blessed are ye that weep now, for you shall laugh."

It is not surprising then to find that Our Lord who came into such utter conflict with the evil of the world should be described as the "Man of Sorrows," and one "Who in the days of His flesh with a strong cry and tears, offering up prayers and supplications to Him that was able to save Him from death, was heard for his reverence."

There is no record in the Gospels that He ever laughed; though there are many records of His tears. He openly wept at the grave of His friend Lazarus. He wept over the city that was to kill Him, and amidst tears glistening on that heavenly face bemoaned: "Jerusalem, Jerusalem, thou that killest the prophets, and stonest them that are sent unto thee, how often would I have gathered together thy children, as the hen doth gather her chickens under her wings, and thou wouldest not!"

And not a long time afterwards He wept tears of crimson in the garden, as the "desperate tides of the great world's anguish forced through the channels of a single heart." And finally on the Cross after three hours of blood weeping He comes to the end of His mourning.

Tears and crucifixions are not final; they are only the momentary death that even the seed endures before it bursts into the bloom and blossom of life.

Had He not said: "Blessed are ye that weep now, for you shall laugh." He had had His fast, now He would have the feast; He had worn the thorns, now He would have the diadem of gold; He had mourned, now He would rejoice.

And in fulfillment of the beatitude of mourning, He lets ring out over Golgotha's hills in a commanding voice the last word He ever uttered on this earth as a suffering man, and it was a word of joy and triumph: "Father, into Thy hands I commend My spirit." It was the word of one who is strong and vigorous. No one was taking His life away. He was laying it down of Himself and nowhere does Sacred Scripture say that He died.

Death was not coming to Him; it was He who was going to it. Death did not open its portals to Him; He unlocked them of Himself, for He knew whither He was going.

His last hour was not like the pushing out of a boat into a trackless sea bound for unknown lands and under starless skies. His goal was fixed. He knew where He was going. The exiled King was going back home; the Prodigal Son was returning to the Father's House; the Heavenly Planet that thirty-three years before started out on its orbit to illumine a world, now returns to salute Him who sent Him on His way; the Great Captain now goes back to His native land bearing the glorious scars of victory.

The sorrowful mysteries are over; now begin the glorious ones. Truly indeed, "Blessed are they that mourn, for they shall be comforted."

The sorrow of Our Lord is over. He who mourned is comforted. But how about us? Which beatitude are we going to follow? Are we going to take all our laughter here below, or save some of it for eternity? Are we going to flee the cross now, or are we going to embrace it? Are we going to plan our life so that at the end we can say: "Father, into Thy hands I commend my spirit." If we are, then we must mourn. But why must we mourn?

We must mourn, first of all, because the world will make us mourn if we follow the Redeemer's beatitudes. If we practice meekness, the world will try to provoke us to anger; if we are merciful, the world will accuse us of not being just; if we are clean of heart, the world will shout "Prudes"; if we hunger and thirst after justice, we shall not succeed; if we are peace-makers, the world will say we are cowards; if we are poor in spirit, the world will look down upon us.

In a word, suffering naturally follows the Christian's conflict with the evil of the world. Because we have been taken out of the world, the world will hate us. The servant is not above the master; if it made Him weep crimson tears, it will make us weep too.

That is the first reason then why we must mourn: Because we have chosen the Man of Sorrows. But "blessed are ye when they shall revile you and persecute you, and speak all that is evil against you, untruly for my sake: Be glad and rejoice, for your reward is very great in heaven."

There is another reason why we should mourn, and that is because of the sorrow we caused Our Lord's Blessed Mother. We can never grieve enough for grieving her who is Our Mother too. And we did make her suffer, for there is never a wicked deed done in the world but that there is an innocent victim.

The repercussion of sin is enormous. We throw a stone into the sea, and it causes a ripple that disturbs even the most distant shore. Calvary had its innocent victim too—one who had no share in bringing Our Lord to the cross, in fact the only one who could ever say: "Iam innocent of the blood of this man,"—that innocent victim was Mary.

What had she done to deserve the Seven Swords? What crimes had she committed to rob her of her Son? She had done nothing; but we have. We have sinned against Her Divine Son, we have sentenced Him to the Cross; and in sinning against Him we wounded her.

In fact, we thrust into her hands the greatest of all griefs, for she was not losing a brother, or a sister, or a father, or a mother, or even just a son—she was losing God: And what greater sorrow is there than this!

And finally, we should mourn for the greatest of all reasons, namely, because of what our sins have done to Him. If we had been less proud, His crown of thorns would have been less piercing; if we had been less avaricious, the nails in the Hands would have been less burning; if we had travelled less in the devious ways of sin, His feet would not have been so deeply dug with steel; if our speech had been less biting, His lips would have been less parched; if we had been less sinful, His agony would have been shorter; if we had loved more, He would have been hated less.

There is a personal equation between that Cross and us. Life with its rebellions, its injustices, its sins, all played a role in the Crucifixion.

We can no more wash our hands of our guilt than Pilate could wash his as he held them up under a noon-day sun and declared himself innocent.

It was not so much the Crucifixion that hurt and wounded, it was not Annas, it was not Caiphas, it was not the executioner, for "they knew not what they did"; it was not His enemies who caused His greatest sorrow: "If my enemies had done this, I could have borne it."

It was we who grieved Him most, for we know what we do; we have tasted His sweetmeats; we have broken Bread with Him; we are His familiars. That is our sorrow—that He who came to heal the broken hearts had His own Heart broken by us.

But mourning is not despair. If we have crucified Christ, there is pardon: "Father, forgive them"; if we have pierced Mary's heart, there is pardon still: "Son, behold thy mother"; if there are tears in our eyes, they shall be wiped away: "Blessed are they that mourn, for they shall be comforted."

Think not then that the beatitude of mourning means the enthronement of sorrow, for it ends in the triumphant flight into the Father's embrace. All of you, therefore, who for months and years have lain crucified on beds of pain, remember that an hour will come when you will be taken down from your cross, and the Saviour shall look upon your hands and feet and sides to find there the imprint of His wounds which will be your passport to eternal joy; for being made like Him in His death, you shall be made like Him in His glory.

All you husbands, wives, brothers, and sisters, who have been bereaved of loved ones, remember that the Good Shepherd has taken His sheep to the green pastures that you, like other sheep, might follow your beloved even to the arms of Love.

To you whose life is as a fountain of tears for sins, remember that just as baptismal water washed away your original sin, so your tears will wash away your actual sins, and a day will come when God Himself will wipe them all away.

To you who have lost faith, who have fear of confession, who dread casting yourself at the feet of Our Lord for absolution, remember that even your fear and your sin is a mourning, for you are most miserable on the inside.

You have broken your own heart, but be not disturbed. Take it to the anvil of Calvary and under the fires of Love, it shall be mended into that wholeness where it will never sorrow again, because when God mends a heart, it loses its capacity to sorrow and can only rejoice.

To all you who mourn, He has said: "Blessed are you, for you shall be comforted." You have had your fast with Christ, now you shall have

His feast. He has saved much for you; He kept something back when He was on earth. He has reserved it for those who have wept.

And that thing which he has kept for eternity, which will make your life's crucifixion seem as naught, which will make your eternity a blissful ecstatic passionless passion of love, which will be the ending of all beatitudes and the crown of all living, that thing which He has guardedly treasured for eternity, and which will make heaven heaven, will be—His Smile!

Victory Over Vice

[1939]

DEDICATED

TO

THE MOTHER OF SORROWS

IN HUMBLE PETITION

FOR

VICTORY OVER VICE

INTRODUCTION

THIS book is the fourth in a series on the Seven Last Words in which the Crucifixion of Our Divine Lord is used as the basis of spiritual meditation.

In the first book, "Calvary and the Mass," a correlation was made between the Sacrifice of the Cross and the Sacrifice of the Mass; in the second book, "The Cross and the Beatitudes," each word from the cross was used as a background for the Sermon on the Mount; in the third book, "The Rainbow of Sorrows," the Seven Words, like the seven colors from the rainbow, illumined the problem of suffering. In this book, "Victory over Vice," each of the Seven Words is considered from the point of view of one of the seven capital sins, which might be rightly considered the seven pallbearers of the soul.

There is no claim made that the reparation for the capital sins was made in these Seven Words, but only that they do offer a convenient meditation-point for the soul and its advancement in the love of Christ Jesus, Our Lord.

THE FIRST WORD: ANGER

*"Father, forgive them for
they know not what they do."*

THE one passion in man which has deeper roots in his rational nature than any other, is the passion of anger. Anger and reason are capable of great compatibility, because anger is based upon reason which weighs the injury done and the satisfaction to be demanded. We are never angry unless someone has injured us in some way—or we think he has.

But not all anger is sinful, for there is such a thing as just anger. The most perfect expression of just anger we find in Our Blessed Lord cleansing the temple. Passing through its shadowed doorways at the festival of the Pasch, He found greedy traders, victimizing at every turn the worshippers who needed lambs and doves for the temple sacrifices.

Making a scourge of little cords He moved through their midst with a calm dignity and beautiful self-control even more compelling than the whip. The oxen and sheep He drove out with His scourge; with His Hands He upset the tables of the money changers who scrambled on the floor after their rolling coins; with His finger He pointed to the vendors of doves and bade them leave the outer court; to all He said: "Take these things hence, and make not the house of my Father a house of traffic."

Here was fulfilled the injunction of the Scriptures, "Be angry, and sin not," for anger is no sin under three conditions: 1—If the cause of anger be just, for example, defense of God's honor; 2—if it be no greater than the cause demands, that is, if it be kept under control; and 3—if it be quickly subdued: "Let not the sun go down upon your anger."

Here we are not concerned with just anger, but with unjust anger, namely, that which has no rightful cause—anger which is excessive, revengeful and enduring; the kind of anger and hatred against God which has destroyed religion on one sixth of the earth's surface, and which recently in Spain burned 25,000 churches and chapels and murdered 12,000 servants of God; the kind of hatred which is not only directed against God, but also against fellowman, and is fanned by the disciples of class conflict who talk peace but glory in war; the red anger which rushes the blood to the surface, and the white anger which pushes it to the depths and bleaches the face; the anger which seeks to "get even," to repay in kind, bump for bump, punch for punch, eye for eye, lie for lie; the anger of the clenched fist prepared to strike not in defense of that which is loved but in offense against that which is hated; in a word, the kind of anger which will destroy our civilization unless we smother it by love.

Our Blessed Lord came to make reparation for the sin of anger, first by teaching us a prayer: "Forgive us our trespasses as we forgive those who trespass against us"; and then by giving us a precept: "Love your enemies, do good to them that hate you." More concretely still, He added: "Whosoever will force thee one mile, go with him another two ... if a man ... take away thy coat, let go thy cloak also unto him."

Revenge and retaliation were forbidden: "You have heard that it has been said: an eye for an eye, and a tooth for a tooth. But I say unto you, Love your enemies." These precepts were made all the more striking because He practised them.

When the Gerasenes became angry at Him because He put a higher value on an afflicted man than on a herd of swine, Scripture records no retort: "And entering into the boat, he passed over the water." To the soldier who struck Him with a mailed fist, He meekly responded: "If I have spoken evil, give testimony of the evil, but if well, why strikest thou me?"

The perfect reparation for anger was made on Calvary. We might also say that anger and hate led Him up that hill. His own people hated Him for they asked for His crucifixion; the law hated Him, for it forsook justice to condemn Justice; the Gentiles hated Him for they consented to His death; the forests hated Him for one of its trees bore the burden of His weight; the flowers hated Him as they wove thorns for His brow; the bowels of the earth hated Him as it gave its steel as hammer and nails.

Then as if to personalize all that hatred, the first generation of clenched fists in the history of the world stood beneath the Cross and shook them in the face of God. That day they tore His body to shreds as in this day they smash His tabernacle to bits. Their sons and daughters have shattered crucifixes in Spain and Russia as they once smote the Crucified on Calvary.

Let no one think the clenched fist is a phenomenon of the twentieth century; they whose hearts freeze into fists today are but the lineal descendants of those who stood beneath the Cross with hands lifted like clubs against Love as they hoarsely sang the first International of hate.

As one contemplates those clenched fists, one cannot help but feel that if ever anger would have been justified, if ever Justice might have fittingly judged, if ever Power might have rightfully struck, if ever Innocence might have lawfully protested, if ever God might have justly revenged Himself against man—it was at that moment.

And yet just at that second when a sickle and a hammer combined to cut down the grass on Calvary's hill to erect a cross, and drive nails through Hands to render impotent the blessings of Love Incarnate, He, like a tree which bathes in perfume the axe which kills it, lets fall from His lips for the earth's first hearing the perfect reparation for anger and hate—a prayer for the army of clenched fists, the first Word from the Cross: "Father, forgive them for they know not what they do."

The greatest sinner may now be saved; the blackest sin may now be blotted out; the clenched fist may now be opened; the unforgivable may now be forgiven. While they were most certain that they knew what they were doing, He seizes upon the only possible palliation of their crime and urges it upon His Heavenly Father with all the ardor of a merciful Heart: ignorance—"they know not what they do." If they did know what they were doing as they fastened Love to a tree, and still went on doing it, they would never be saved. They would be damned.

It was only because fists are clenched in ignorance that they may yet be opened into folded hands; it is only because tongues blaspheme in ignorance that they may yet speak in prayer. It is not their conscious wisdom that saves them; it is their unconscious ignorance.

This Word from the Cross teaches us two lessons: 1—The reason for forgiving is ignorance; and 2—There are no limits to forgiveness.

The reason for forgiving is ignorance. Divine Innocence found such a reason for pardon; certainly guilt can do no less. St. Peter's first Pentecostal sermon used this very excuse of ignorance for the Crucifixion so fresh in his mind: "The author of life you killed ... and now, brethren, I know that you did it through ignorance, as did also your rulers."

If there were full consciousness of the evil, perfect deliberation, perfect understanding of the consequences of acts, there would be no room for forgiveness. That is why there is no redemption for the fallen angels. They knew what they were doing. We do not. We are very ignorant—ignorant of ourselves and ignorant of others.

Ignorant of others! How little we know of their motives, their good faith, the circumstances surrounding their actions. When others visit violence upon us we too often forget how little we know about their hearts and say: "I cannot see that they have the slightest excuse; they knew very well what they were doing." And yet in exactly the same circumstances, Jesus found an excuse: "They know not what they do."

We know nothing about the inside of our neighbor's heart and hence we refuse to forgive; He knew the heart inside out and because He did know, He forgave. Take any scene of action, let five people look upon it, and you get five different stories of what happened. No one of them sees all sides. Our Lord does and that is why He forgives.

Why is it that we can find excuses for our anger against our neighbor, and yet we refuse to admit the same excuses when our neighbor is angry with us? We say others would forgive us if they understood us perfectly, and that the only reason they are angry with us is because "they do not understand."

Why is not that ignorance reversible? Can we not be as ignorant of their motives, as we say they are ignorant of ours? Does not our refusal to find an excuse for their hatred tacitly mean that under similar circumstances we ourselves will be unfit to be forgiven?

Ignorance of ourselves is another reason for forgiving others. Unfortunately it is ourselves we know least; our neighbor's sins, weaknesses and failures we know a thousand times better than our own. Criticism of others may be bad, but it is want of self criticism which is worse.

It would be less wrong to criticize others, if we first criticized ourselves, for if we first turned the searchlight into our own souls, we would never feel we had a right to turn it on the soul of anyone else. It is only because we are ignorant of our true condition that we fail to realize how badly we stand in need of pardon.

Have we ever offended God? Has He any right to be angry with us? Then why should we, who need pardon so badly, strive not to purchase it by pardoning others? The answer is because we never examine our own consciences.

We are so ignorant of our true condition that we know little more of ourselves than our name and address and how much we have; of our selfishness, our envy, our detraction, our sin, we know absolutely nothing. In fact, in order that we may never know ourselves we hate silence and solitariness. Lest our conscience should carry on with us an unbearable repartee we drown out its voice in amusements, distractions and noise. If we met ourselves in others we would hate them.

If we knew ourselves better, we would be more forgiving of others. The harder we are on ourselves, the easier we will be on others; the man who has never learned to obey knows not how to command;

and the man who has never disciplined himself knows not how to be merciful.

It is always the selfish who are unkind to others, and those who are hardest on themselves are the kindest to others, as the teacher who knows the least is always the most intolerant to his pupils.

Only a Lord Who thought so little of Himself as to become man and die like a criminal could ever forgive the weakness of those who crucified Him.

It is not hatred that is wrong; it is hating the wrong thing that is wrong. It is not anger that is wrong, it is being angry at the wrong thing that is wrong. Tell me your enemy and I will tell you what you are. Tell me your hatred and I will tell you your character.

Do you hate religion? Then your conscience bothers you. Do you hate capitalists? Then you are avaricious and you want to be a capitalist. Do you hate the laborer? Then you are selfish and a snob. Do you hate sin? Then you love God. Do you hate your hate, your selfishness, your quick temper, your wickedness? Then you are a good soul, for "If any man come to me ... and hate not his own life he cannot be my disciple."

The second lesson to be derived from this First Word from the Cross is that there is no limit to pardon. Our Lord forgave when He was innocent and not because He Himself had been forgiven. Hence we must forgive not only when we have been forgiven, but even when we are innocent.

The problem of the limits of pardon once troubled Peter and He asked Our Lord: "How often shall my brother offend against me, and I forgive him till seven times?" Peter thought he was stretching forgiveness by saying seven times, for it was four more than the Jewish Masters enjoined.

Peter proposed a limit beyond which there was to be no forgiveness. Peter assumed the right to be forgiven is automatically renounced after seven offenses. It is equivalent to saying: "I renounce my right to collect debts from you if you never owe me more than seven dollars, but if you exceed that sum, then my duty of further cancellation ceases. I can throttle you for eight dollars."

Our Lord in answering Peter says forgiveness has no limits; forgiveness is the surrender of all rights and the denial of limits. "I say not to thee till seven times but till seventy times seven." That does not mean 490 literally, but infinitely. The Saviour then proceeded to tell the parable of the unjust steward who immediately after being forgiven by his lord a debt of 10,000 talents, choked a fellow servant who owed him a hundred pence. The unmerciful steward by refusing to be merciful to his debtor had his own mercy revoked. His guilt was not that, needing mercy he refused to show it, but having received mercy, he was unmerciful still. "So also shall my heavenly Father do to you if you forgive not every one his brother."

Forgive then and we will be forgiven; remit our anger against others and God will remit His anger against us. Judgment is a harvest where we sow what we reap. If we sowed anger against our brethren during life, we will reap the just anger of God. Judge not and we shall not be judged.

If during life we forgive others from our hearts, on Judgment Day the All Wise God will permit something very unusual to Himself: He will forget how to add and will know only how to subtract. He Who has a Memory from all eternity will no longer remember our sins. Thus we will be saved once again through Divine "Ignorance."

By forgiving others on the ground that they know not what they do, Our Lord will forgive us on the ground that He no longer remembers what we did. It may well be that if He looks on a hand that, now after hearing the first Word on the Cross gives a kindly blessing to an enemy, He will even forget that it was once a clenched fist red with the blood of Christendom.

> *"And dars't thou venture still to live in sin,*
> *And crucify thy dying Lord again?*
> *Were not His pangs sufficient? Must he bleed*
> *Yet more? O, must our sinful pleasures feed*
> *Upon his torments, and augment the story*
> *Of the sad passion of the Lord of glory!*
> *Is there no pity? Is there no remorse*
> *In human breasts? Is there a firm divorce*
> *Betwixt all mercy and the hearts of men?*
> *Parted for ever—ne'er to meet again?*
> *No mercy bides with us: 'tis thou alone,*
> *Hast it, sweet Jesu, for us, that have none*
> *For thee: thou hast forestall'd our markets so*
> *That all's above, and we have none below:*
> *Nay, blessed Lord, we have not wherewithal*
> *To serve our shiftless selves: unless we call*
> *To thee, thou art our Saviour, and hast power*
> *To give, and whom we crucify each hour:*
> *We are cruel, Lord, to thee, and ourselves too;*
> *Jesu forgive us; we know not what we do."*

Francis Quarles

THE SECOND WORD: ENVY

*"This day thou shalt
be with Me in Paradise."*

Envy is sadness at another's good, and joy at another's evil. What rust is to iron, what moths are to wool, what termites are to wood, that envy is to the soul: the assassination of brotherly love.

We are not here concerned with just envy or zeal which inspires us to emulate good example and to progress with those who are our betters, for the Scriptures enjoin us to "be zealous for spiritual gifts"; rather we here touch on that sinful envy which is a wilful grieving at another's good, either spiritual or temporal, for the reason that it seems to diminish our own good. The honor paid to another is regarded by the envious man as a reflected disgrace on himself and he is sad in consequence. Envy manifests itself in discord, hatred, malicious joy, back-biting, detraction, imputing of evil motives, jealousy, and calumny.

A sample of this kind of envy we find in one of the two women who asked Solomon to adjudicate their dispute. The first woman said: "I and this woman dwelt in one house ... And this woman's child died in the night: for in her sleep she overlaid him. And rising in the dead time of the night she took my child from my side, while I thy handmaid was asleep ... and laid her dead child in my bosom." To which the other woman answered: "It is not so as thou sayest, but thy child is dead, and mine is alive."

Since there were no witnesses, Solomon ordered a sword to be brought to him, for he rightly judged that the motherly heart of the real mother would rather give up her child than see it killed. Brandishing the glittering sword he said: "Divide the living child in two, and give half to the one, and half to the other." Hearing this the woman whose child was alive cried out in terror and pity: "I beseech thee, my lord, give her the child alive, and do not kill it." But the other said: "Let it be neither mine or thine, but divide it."

Then the king commanded the child be given to her who would rather give it up to another than have it killed, knowing that she must be the mother. The point of the story is that envy which is so jealous of the good of another may reach a point where it scruples not to take a life.

In our times, envy has taken on an economic form. The avarice of the rich is being matched by the envy of the poor. Some poor hate the rich not because they have unjustly stolen their possessions, but because they want their possessions. Certain have-nots are scandalized at the wealth of the haves, only because they are tempted by lust for their possessions.

The Communists hate the Capitalists only because they want to be Capitalists themselves; they envy the rich not because of their need, but because of their greed.

Combined with this is social envy or snobbery which sneers at the higher position of others, because the snobs want to sit in their chairs and enjoy their applause. They assume that in not arriving at such popular favor themselves they were deprived of their due. That is why we hate those who do not pay sufficient attention to us and why we love those who flatter us.

If envy is on the increase today, as it undoubtedly is, it is because of the surrender of the belief of a future life and righteous Divine Justice. If this life is all, they think they should have all. From that point on, envy of others becomes their rule of life.

Our Lord was unceasing in His preaching against envy. To those who were envious of the mercy extended to lost sheep He pictured the angels of Heaven rejoicing more at the one sinner doing penance than at the ninety-nine just who needed not penance. To those who were envious of wealth He warned: "Lay not up to yourselves treasures on earth: where the rust and moth consume, and where thieves break through, and steal. But lay up to yourselves treasures in heaven: where neither the rust nor moth consume, and where thieves do not break through, nor steal."

To those who were envious of power, such as the Apostles quarreling about first place, He placed a child in the midst of them and "putting His arms around him" reminded them that heaven was open only to those who were as simple children, for Christ is not in the great but in the little: "Whosoever shall receive one such child as this in my name, receiveth me. And whosoever shall receive me, receiveth not me, but him that sent me."

But His preaching against envy did not save Him from the envious. Pilate was envious of His power; Annas was envious of His innocence;

Caiphas was envious of His popularity; Herod was envious of His moral superiority; the Scribes and Pharisees were envious of His wisdom. Each of these had built his judgment seat of mock moral superiority from which to sentence Morality to the Cross. And in order that He might no longer be a person to be envied, they reputed Him with the wicked.

Born between an ox and an ass, they now crucify Him between two criminals. That was the last insult they could give Him. To the public eye they created the impression that three thieves and not two were silhouetted against the sky. In a certain sense it was true: two stole gold out of avarice, one stole hearts out of love. Salvandus, Salvator, and Salvatus: The thief who could have been saved; the thief who was saved; and the Saviour who saved them. The crosses spelled out the words Envy, Mercy, and Pity.

The thief on the left envied the Power which Our Blessed Lord claimed. As the chief priests, scribes, and ancients ridiculed the Saviour, sneering: "He saved others—himself he cannot save," the thief on the left added to their revilings: "If thou be Christ, save thyself and us." In other words: 'If I had that power of yours, that power which you claim as the Messias, I would use it differently than to hang helpless on a tree. I would step down from the Cross, smite my enemies, and prove what power really is.'

Thus did Envy reveal that if it had the gifts which it envies in others it would misuse them, as the thief on the left would have surrendered redemption from sin for release from a nail. In like manner many in the world today who are envious of wealth would probably lose their souls if they had that wealth. Envy never thinks of responsibilities. Looking only to self it misuses every gift that comes its way.

Pity has quite a different effect on the soul. The thief on the right had no envy of the Master's Power but only pity for the Master's sufferings. Rebuking his companion on the left, the good thief said: "Neither dost thou fear God, seeing thou art under the same condemnation? And we indeed, justly, for we receive the due reward of our deeds; but this man hath done no evil."

There was not a spark of envy in him. He wanted nothing in all the world, not even to be removed from tragic companioning with his cross. He was not envious of God's Power, for God knows best what to do with His Power. He was not envious of his fellowmen, for they had nothing worth giving.

So he threw himself upon Divine Providence and asked only for forgiveness: "Lord, remember me when thou shalt come into thy kingdom." A dying man asked a dying Man for life; a man without possessions asked a Poor Man for a Kingdom; a thief at the door of death asked to die a thief and steal Paradise. And because He envied nothing, He received all: "Amen I say to thee, this day thou shalt be with me in paradise."

One would have thought a saint would have been the first soul purchased over the counter of Calvary by the red coins of redemption, but in the Divine plan it is a thief who steals that privilege and marches as the escort of the King of Kings into Paradise.

Two lessons are taught us by this Second Word from the Cross. The first is that envy is the source of our wrong judgments about others. The chances are that if we are envious of others, nine times out of ten we will misjudge their characters.

Because the thief on the left was envious of the Power of Our Lord, he misjudged Him and missed both the Divinity of the Saviour and his own salvation. He falsely argued that Power should always be used the way he would have used it, namely to turn nails into rosebuds, a cross into a throne, blood into royal purple, and the blades of grass on the hillside into bayonets of offensive steel.

No one in the history of the world ever came closer to Redemption, and yet no one ever missed it so far. His envy made him ask for the wrong thing: he asked to be taken down when he should have asked to be taken up. It makes one think of how much the envy of Herod resulted in an equally false judgment: He massacred the Innocents because He thought the Infant King came to destroy an earthy kingdom, whereas He came only to announce a heavenly one.

So it is with us. Backbiting, calumny, false judgments, are all born of our envy. We say: "Oh, he is jealous," or "she is jealous"; but how do we know that he or she is jealous unless we ourselves have felt that way? How do we know others are acting proudly unless we know how pride asserts itself? Every envious word is based on a false judgment of our own moral superiority. To sit in judgment makes us feel that we are above those who are judged and more righteous and more innocent than they.

To accuse others is to say: "I am not like that." To be envious of others, is to say: "You have stolen that which is mine." Envy of others' wealth has resulted in the gross misjudgment that the best way to do away with its abuse in the hands of the rich is to dispossess them violently, so that the dispossesses may in their turn enjoy its abuse.

Envy of others' political power has given rise to the erroneous philosophy that even governments may be overthrown if organized violence is strong enough to do so.

Envy thus becomes the denial of all justice and love. In individuals it develops a cynicism which destroys all moral values, for by bankrupting others do we ourselves become bankrupt. In groups it produces a deceit which extends the glad hand of welcome to those who differ, only until they are strong enough to cut it off.

Since envy is so rampant in the world today, it is extremely good counsel to disbelieve 99/100 per cent of the wicked statements we hear about others. Think of how much the thief on the right had to discount in order to arrive at the truth. He had to disbelieve the judgment of four envious judges, the raillery of envious scribes and ancients, the blasphemous utterances of curious onlookers who love murders, and the envious taunts of the thief on the left who was willing to lose his soul if only he could keep his fingers nimble for more thefts.

But if he had been envious of the Lord's power, he would never have been saved. He found peace by disbelieving the envious scandal mongers. Our peace is found in the same incredulity.

The chances are that there is a bit of jealousy, a bit of envy, behind every cutting remark and barbed whispering we hear about our neighbor. It is always well to remember that there are always more sticks under the tree that has the most apples. There should be some consolation for those who are so unjustly attacked to remember that it is a physical impossibility for any man to get ahead of us who stays behind to kick us.

A second lesson to be learned from this Word is that the only way to overcome envy is, like the thief on the right, to show pity. As Christians in good faith we are all members of the Mystical Body of Christ, and should therefore love one another as Christ has loved us.

If our arm suffers an injury our whole body feels the pain. In like manner, if the Church in any part of the world suffers martyrdom we should feel pity toward it as part of our body, and that pity should express itself in prayer and good works. Pity should be extended not only to those outside the Church who are living as if the earth never bore a Cross, but even to the enemies of the Church who would destroy even the shadow of the cross. God is their Judge; not we.

And as potential brothers of Christ, sons of a Heavenly Father and children of Mary, they must be worth our pity since they were worth the Saviour's blood. Unfortunately, there are some who blame the Church for receiving great sinners into the Church on their deathbeds.

A few years ago one who was generally believed to be a racketeer and murderer met death at the hands of his fellow criminals. A few minutes before his death, he asked to be received into the Church, was baptized, received First Communion, was anointed and given the last blessing. Some who should have known better protested against the Church. Imagine! Envy at the salvation of a soul!

Why not rather rejoice in God's Mercy, for after all did he not belong to the same profession as the thief on the right—and why should not Our Lord be just as anxious to save twentieth century thieves as first century thieves? They both have souls. It would seem that sinful envy of the salvation of a thief is a greater sin than thievery.

One thief was saved: therefore let no one despair. One thief was lost: therefore let no one presume. Have pity then on the miserable and Divine Mercy will be the reward for your pity. When the Pharisees accused Our Lord of eating with publicans and sinners He retorted by reiterating the necessity of mercy: "The healthy have no need of a physician, but the sick have. Now go and learn what this means; "I will have mercy and not sacrifice. For I am not come to call the just, but sinners."

One day a woman went to the saintly Father John Vianny, the Cure of Ars, in France, and said: "My husband has not been to the sacraments or to Mass for years. He has been unfaithful, wicked, and unjust. He has just fallen from a bridge and was drowned —a double death of body and soul." The Cure answered: "Madam, there is a short distance between the bridge and the water, and it is that distance which forbids you to judge."

There was just that distance between the two crosses which saved the penitent thief. If the thief on the right had been self-righteous, he would have looked down on Jesus and lost his soul. But because he was conscious of his own sin, he left room for Divine Pardon.

And the answer of the Redeemer to his request proves that to the merciful, love is blind—for if we love God and our neighbor, who may even be our enemy, Divine Love will go blind as it did for the thief on the right. Christ will no longer be able to see our faults, and that blindness will be for us the dawn of the vision of Love.

THE PENITENT THIEF

"Say, bold but blessed thief,
That in a trice
Slipped into paradise,
And in plain day
Stol'st heaven away,
What trick couldst thou invent
To compass thy intent?
What arms?
What charms?"

"Love and belief."
"Say, bold but blessed thief,
How couldst thou read
A crown upon that head?
What text, what gloss—
A kingdom and a cross?
How couldst thou come to spy
God in a man to die?
What light?
What sight?"
"The sight of grief—"
"I sight to God his pain;
And by that sight
I saw the light,
Thus did my grief
Beget relief.
And take this rule from me,
Pity thou him he'll pity thee.
Use this,
Ne'er miss,
Heaven may be stolen again."

(Anonymous)

THE THIRD WORD: LUST

*"Woman, behold thy son ...
behold thy mother."*

Lust is an inordinate love of the pleasures of the flesh. The important word here is inordinate for it was Almighty God Himself who associated pleasure with the flesh. He attached pleasure to eating in order that we might not be remiss in nourishing and preserving our individual lives; He associated pleasure with the marital act in order that husband and wife might not be remiss in their social obligations to propagate mankind and raise children for the Kingdom of God.

The pleasure becomes sinful at that point where, instead of using it as means, we begin to use it as an end. To eat for the sake of eating is a sin, because eating is a means to an end, which is health. Lust, in like manner, is selfishness or perverted love.

It looks not so much to the good of the other, as to the pleasure of self. It breaks the glass that holds the wine; it breaks the lute to snare the music. It subordinates the other to self for the sake of pleasure. Denying the quality of "otherness" it seeks to make the other person care for us, but not to make us care for the other person.

We are living today in what might properly be called an era of carnality. As the appeal to the spiritual relaxes, the demands of the flesh increase. Living less for God, human nature begins to live only for self, for "no man can serve two masters: For either he will hate the one, and love the other: or he will sustain the one, and despise the other."

Peculiar to this era of carnality is the tendency to equate the perpetuity of marriage with the fleshly pleasure, so that when the pleasure ends the bond is presumed to be automatically dissolved. In America, for example, there is one divorce for every four marriages—an indication of how much we have ceased to be a Christian nation and how much we have forgotten the words of Our Lord: "What therefore God hath joined together, let no man put asunder."

The regrettable aspect of it all is that with this increased sin there is a decreased sense of sin. Souls sin more, but think less about it. Like sick who are so moribund they have no desire to be better, sinners become so caloused they have no yearning for redemption. Having lost their eyes, they no longer want to see; the only pleasure left them in the end is to mock and sneer at those who do.

It is never the pure who say chastity is impossible, but only the impure. We judge others by ourselves, and attribute to others the vices from which we ourselves refuse to abstain.

Some reparation had to be made for the sin of lust which in Old Testament times became so hideous to God that He would have withheld the destruction of the cities of Sodom and Gomorrah could but ten just men have been found within their gates.

Our Lord began making reparation for it at the first moment of the Incarnation for He chose to be born of a virgin. Why did He choose to transcend the laws of nature? The answer is very simple. Original sin has been propagated to every human being from Adam to this very hour, with the exception of Our Lady. The prolongation of this taint in human nature takes place through the carnal act, of which man is the active principle, for man was the head of the human race. Every time there is generation of one human being by another, through the union of man and woman, there is the propagation of original sin.

The problem confronting the Second Person of the Blessed Trinity in becoming man was: how become man without at the same time becoming sinful man, that is, man-infected by the sin to which all flesh is heir? How become man without inheriting original sin? He had to be a true man in order to suffer for man, but He could not be a sinful man if He were to redeem man from sin. How could He be both man and yet sinless?

He could be man by being born of a woman; He could be sinless man, without original sin, by dispensing with man as the active principle of generation—in other words, by being born of a virgin. Thus it was that when the Angel Gabriel appeared to Mary and told her that she was to conceive the Messias whose name would be called Jesus, she answered: "How can this be done, because I know not man?" She had the vow of virginity and she intended to keep it.

The Angel answered that the conception of the Son of man would take place without man, through the power of the Holy Ghost who would overshadow her. Being assured of her continued virginity, she accepted the motherhood of God Incarnate. "Be it done unto me, according to thy Word."

So it was that the reparation for sins of the flesh began the first moment of the Incarnation through the Virgin Birth. That same love He manifested for virginity in the beginning, He re-echoed in the first sermon of His public life: "Blessed are the clean of heart: for they shall see God."

Later on, to the Scribes and Pharisees who sought to malign His good name, He challenged them to find anything impure in His life. "Which of you shall convince me of sin?"

The final atonement and reparation is made on Calvary where, in reparation for all the impure desires and thoughts of men, Our Lord is crowned with thorns; where, in reparation for all the sins of shame, He is stripped of His garments; where, in reparation for all the lusts of the flesh, He is almost dispossessed of His flesh, for according to Sacred Scripture the very bones of His Body could be numbered.

We are so used to looking upon artistic crucifixes of ivory and the beautiful images in our prayer books, that we think of Our Blessed Lord as being whole on the Cross. The fact is that He made such reparation for sins of the flesh that His Body was torn, His blood poured forth, and Scripture refers to Him on the Cross as a leper, as one struck by God and afflicted, so that "there is no beauty in him, nor comeliness: ... that we should be desirous of him."

Our Lord chose to go even further in reparation for the sins of lust by dispossessing Himself of the two most legitimate claims of the flesh. If there was ever a pure and legitimate claim in the realm of the flesh, it is the claim to the love of one's own Mother. If there is any honest title to affection in the universe of the flesh, it is the bonds of love which attach one to a fellow man. But the flesh was so misused by man and so perverted that Our Divine Saviour renounced even these legitimate bonds of the flesh in order to atone for the illegitimate.

He became totally un-fleshed, in order to atone for the abuse of the flesh, by giving away His Mother and His best friend. So to His own Mother He looks and bids farewell: "Woman, behold thy son"; and to His best friend He looks and bids farewell again: "Behold, thy mother."

How different from the world! A mother will deprive her son of an advanced education in a foreign land, saying: "I cannot give up my son"; or a wife will deprive her husband of good material advancement through a short absence, saying: "I cannot give up my husband." These are not the cries of noble love but of attachment. Our Lord did not say: "I cannot give up My Mother." He gave her up. He loved her enough to give her away for her life's plan and destiny, namely, to be our Mother.

Here was a love that was strong enough to forget itself, in order that others might never want for love. He made the sacrifice of His Mother that we might have her; He wounded Himself like the pelican, that we might be nourished by her motherhood. Mary accepted the poor exchange to carry out her Son's redemptive work. And at that moment when Jesus surrendered even the legitimate claims of the flesh and gave us His Mother, Mary, and His best friend, John—selfishness died its death.

Two lessons are to be learned from this Third Word from the Cross: 1—The only real escape from the demands of the flesh is to find something more than the flesh to love; and 2—Mary is the refuge of sinners.

If we could ever find anything we loved more than the flesh, the demands of the flesh would be less imperative. This is the "escape" a mother offers her boy when she says: "Don't do anything of which your mother would ever be ashamed." If there is that higher love of his mother, the boy will always have a consecrated sense of affection, something for which he will be willing to make sacrifices.

When a mother makes such an appeal to her son she is merely re-echoing the lesson of the Saviour, who, in giving His Mother to us as our Mother, equivalently said: "My children, never do anything of which your Mother would be ashamed." Let a soul but love that Mother and He will love her Divine Son Jesus, Who, in order to make satisfaction for the unlawful pleasure of the flesh, surrendered to us His last and lawful attachment—His Mother.

The psychology of this enthusiasm for a higher love of Jesus and Mary as an escape from the unlawful attachments of the flesh is this: by it we avoid undue concentration on lower loves and their explosions. Think about your mouth for five minutes and you will have an undue concentration of saliva. Think about your heart for five minutes and you will believe you have heart trouble, though the chances are nine out of ten that you have not. Stand on a stage and think about your hands and they will begin to feel as big as hams.

The balance and equilibrium of the whole system is disturbed when an organ is isolated from its function in the whole organism, or divorced from its higher purpose. These people who are always talking, reading, and thinking about sex are like singers who think more about their larynx than about singing. They make that which is subordinate to a higher purpose so all important that the harmony of life is upset.

But suppose that instead of concentrating on an organ, one fitted that organ into a pattern of living—then all the uneasiness would end. The skilled orator never feels his hands are awkward because, being enthused about his speech, he makes the hands subordinate to their higher purpose.

Our Lord practically said the same thing: "Be not solicitous ... what you shall eat." So it is with the flesh. Cultivate a higher love, a purpose of living, a goal of existence, a desire to correspond to all that God wants us to be, and the lower passion will be absorbed by it.

The Church applies this psychology to the vow of chastity. The Church asks her priests and nuns to surrender even the lawful pleasures of the flesh, not because she does not want them to love, but because she wants them to love better. She knows that their love for souls will be greater as their love for the flesh is less, just as Our Lord died on the Cross for men because He loved His Own life less.

Nor must it be thought that the vow of chastity is a burden. Thompson has called it a "passionless passion, a wild tranquillity." And so it is. A new passion is born with the vow of chastity, the passion for the love of God. It is the consolation of that higher love which makes the surrender of the lower love so easy. And only when that higher love is lost does the vow begin to be a burden, just as honesty becomes a burden only to those who have lost the sense of others' rights.

The reason why there is a degeneration in the moral order and a decay of decency is because men and women have lost the higher love. Ignoring Christ their Saviour, who loved them unto the death on Calvary, and Mary who loved them unto becoming Queen of Martyrs beneath that Cross, they have nothing for which to make the sacrifice.

The only way love can be shown in this world is by sacrifice, namely, the surrender of one thing for another. Love is essentially bound up with choice, and choice is a negation and negation is a sacrifice. When a young man sets his heart upon a maid and asks her to marry him, he is not only saying "I choose you," he is also saying "I do not choose, I reject all others. I give them all up for you." Apply this to the problem of lust.

Take away all love above the flesh, take away God, the Crucifix, the Sorrowful Mother, salvation, eternal happiness—and what possibility is there for choice, what is to be gained by denying the imperious and revolutionary demands of the flesh? But grant the Divine, and the flesh's greatest joy is to throw itself on the altar of the one loved where it counts its sorrow a cheap price for the blissful joy of giving.

Then its greatest despair is not to be needed; it could almost find it in its heart to inflict a wound that it might bind and heal. Such is the attitude of the pure: they have integrated their flesh with the Divine, they have sublimated its cravings with the Cross; having a higher love, they now make the surrender of the lower, that their Mother may never be put to shame.

Mary is the refuge of sinners. She who is Virgin Most Pure is also the Refuge of Sinners. She knows what sin is, not by the experience of its falls, not by tasting its bitter regrets, but by seeing what it did to her Divine Son.

She looked upon His torn and bleeding flesh hanging from Him like rays of a purple sunset —and she came to know how much flesh sinned by seeing what His flesh suffered. What better way in all the world was there to measure the heinousness of sin than by seeing when left alone with Him for three hours what it could do to Innocence and Purity.

She is the Refuge of Sinners not only because she knows sin through Calvary, but also because she chose, during the most terrifying hours of her life, a converted sinner as her companion. The measure of our appreciation of friends is our desire to have them about us in the moment of our greatest need.

Mary heard Jesus say: "The harlots and publicans will enter the Kingdom of Heaven before the Scribes and Pharisees." So she chose the absolved harlot, Magdalen, as her companion at the Cross. What the scandalmongers of that day must have said when they saw Our Blessed Mother in the company of a woman, who everyone knew was the kind who sold her body without giving away her soul.

Magdalen knew that day why Mary is the Refuge of Sinners, and certainly our day too can learn that if she had Magdalen as a companion then, she is willing to have us as companions now.

Mary's purity is not a holier-than-thou purity, a stand-offish holiness which gathers up its robes lest they be stained by the sinful; nor is it a despising purity which looks down upon the impure. Rather it is a radiating purity which is no more spoiled by solicitude for the fallen than a ray of sunshine is sullied by a dirty window pane through which it pours.

There is no reason for the fallen being discouraged. Hope is the message of Golgotha. Find a higher love than the flesh, a love pure, understanding, redeeming, and the struggle will be easy. That higher love is on the Cross and beneath it.

We almost seem to forget that there is a Cross at all. He begins to look more like a red rose and she begins to look like the stem. That stem reaches down from Calvary into all our wounded hearts of earth, sucking up our prayers and petitions and conveying them to Him. That is why roses have thorns in this life—to keep away every disturbing influence that might destroy our union with Jesus and Mary.

Acknowledgment

If Christ should come on earth some summer day
And walk unknown upon our busy street
I wonder how 'twould be if we should meet,
And being God—if He would act that way.

Perhaps the kindest thing that He would do
Would be just to forget I failed to pray
And clasp my hand, forgivingly, and say,
"My child, I've heard My Mother speak of you."

                                        Mrs. Frederick V. Murphy

The Fourth Word: Pride

*"My God, My God,
why hast thou forsaken me."*

PRIDE is an inordinate love of one's own excellence, either of body or mind or the unlawful pleasure we derive from thinking we have no superiors. Pride being swollen egoism, it erects the human soul into a separate center of originativeness apart from God, exaggerates its own importance, and becomes a world in and for itself. All other sins are evil deeds, but pride insinuates itself even unto good works to destroy and slay them. For that reason Sacred Scriptures says: "Pride goeth before destruction."

Pride manifests itself in many forms: atheism, which is a denial of our dependence on God, our Creator and our final end; intellectual vanity, which makes minds unteachable because they think they know all there is to know; superficiality, which judges others by their clothes, their accent, and their bank account; snobbery, which sneers at inferiors as the earmark of its own superiority, "they are not of our set"; vain-glory, which prompts some Catholic parents to refuse to send their boys and girls to Catholic colleges, because they would there associate only with the children of carpenters; presumptuousness, which inclines a man to seek honors and positions quite beyond his capacity; and exaggerated sensitiveness which makes one incapable of moral improvements because so unwilling to hear one's own faults.

Pride it was that made Satan fall from heaven and man fall from grace. By its very nature such undue self-exaltation could be cured only by self-humiliation. That is why He who might have been born in a palace by the Tiber as befitting His Majesty as the Son of God, chose to appear before men in a stable as a child wrapped in swaddling bands.

Added to this humility of His Birth was the humility of His profession—a carpenter in an obscure village of Nazareth whose name was a reproach among the great. Just as today there are those who sneer at the humble walks of life, so too there were then those who sneered: "Is not this the carpenter's son?" There was also the humility of His actions, for never once did He work a miracle in His own behalf not even to supply Himself with a place to lay His head.

Humility of example there was too, when on Holy Thursday night He who is the Lord of heaven and earth, girds Himself with a towel, gets down on His knees, and with basin and water washes the twenty-four calloused feet of His Apostles saying: "The servant is not greater than his lord ... If then I being your Lord and Master have washed your feet; you also ought to wash one another's feet." Finally, there was humility of precept: "Unless you be converted, and become as little children, you shall not enter into the kingdom of heaven."

But the supreme humiliation of all was the manner of death He chose, for "He humbled himself ... even to the death of the cross." To atone for false pride of ancestry, He thrusts aside the consolation of Divinity; for pride of popularity, He is laughed to scorn as He hangs cursed upon a tree; for pride of snobbery, He is put in the company of thieves; for pride of wealth, He is denied even the ownership of His own deathbed; for pride of flesh, He was scourged until "there was no beauty in Him"; for pride in influential friends, He is forgotten even by those whom He cured; for pride of power, He is weak and abandoned; for pride of those who surrender God and their faith, He wills to feel without God.

For all the egotism, false independence, and atheism, He now offers satisfaction by surrendering the joys and consolations of His Divine Nature. Because proud men forgot God, He permits Himself to feel God-lessness and it broke His heart in the saddest of all cries: "My God, my God, why hast thou forsaken me?" There was union even in the separation; but they were words of desolation uttered that we might never be without consolation.

Two lessons emerge from this Word: 1— Glory not in ourselves for God resists the proud; and 2—Glory in humility for humility is truth and the path to true greatness.

Why should we be proud? As St. Paul reminds us "Or what hast thou that thou hast not received? And if thou hast received, why dost thou glory, as if thou hadst not received it?" Is it our voice, our wealth, our beauty, our talents of which we are proud? But what are these but gifts of God, anyone of which He might revoke this second?

From a material point of view, we are worth so little. The content of a human body is equivalent to as much iron as there is in a nail, as much sugar as there is in two lumps, as much oil as there is in seven bars of soap, as much phosphorus as there is in 2200 matches, and as much magnesium as it takes to develop one photograph. In all, the human body, chemically, is worth a little less than two dollars—"O why should the spirit of mortal be proud?"

But spiritually we are worth more than the universe: "For what shall it profit a man, if he gains the whole world, and suffer the loss of his soul?" Or what shall a man give in exchange for his soul?"

God resists the proud. The Pharisee who praised his own good deeds in the forefront of the temple is condemned; the poor publican in the rear of the temple, who calls himself a sinner and strikes his breast in a plea for pardon, goes to his house justified. The harlots and the publicans who are conscious of their sin enter the kingdom of Heaven before the Scribes and the Pharisees, who are conscious of their righteousness.

The Heavenly Father is thanked for concealing His Wisdom from the self-wise and the conscious intellectuals and for revealing it to the simple: "I confess to thee, O Father, Lord of heaven and earth, because thou hast hidden these things from the wise and prudent and hast revealed them to little ones."

Surely anyone who has had experience with the proud will bear witness to the truth of this statement: If my own eternal salvation were conditioned upon saving the soul of one self-wise man who prided himself on his learning, or one hundred of the most morally corrupt men and women of the streets, I should choose the easier task of converting the hundred. Nothing is more difficult to conquer in all the world than intellectual pride. If battleships could be lined with it instead of with armor, no shell could ever pierce it.

This is easy to understand, for if a man thinks he knows it all, then there is nothing left for him to know, not even what God might tell him. If the soul is filled to the brim with the ego, there is no place left for God. If a vessel is filled with water it cannot also be filled with oil. So it is with the soul.

God can give His Truth and Life only to those who have emptied themselves. We must create a vacuum in our own souls in order to make room for grace. We live under the impression that we do more than we actually do. Take, for example, the simple fact of drinking liquid through a straw. We erroneously believe that we draw up the liquid through the straw. We do not, for strictly speaking there is no such thing as suction. All that we do is create a vacuum; the atmosphere presses down on the liquid with a weight equal to that of an ocean covering the earth to a depth of thirty-four feet. It is this pressure that pushes the liquid up through the straw when we create the vacuum.

So too in our spiritual lives. The good we accomplish is not through the action of ourselves, as much as it is through the spiritual pressure of God's grace. All that we have to do is create a vacuum, to count ourselves as nothing—and immediately God fills the soul with His Power and Truth.

The paradox of apostolate is, then: the less we think we are, the more good we do. It was only when Peter had labored all the night and taken nothing, that Our Lord filled his boat with the miraculous draught of fishes. The higher the building the deeper the foundation; the greater the virtue the more the humility.

God's instruments for good in the world are for that reason only the humble; reducing themselves to zero they leave room for infinity, whereas those who think themselves infinite, God leaves with their little zero.

Even in the world we find a natural basis for humility. As long as we are small, everything else seems big. A boy mounts a broomstick which is no more than four feet long and yet to him it is a Pegasus travelling through space; he can hear the hoofs beating the clouds as he clings to the "whistling mane of every wind." His world is peopled with giants because he is so little; tin soldiers to him are real soldiers fighting real battles and the red of the carpet is the blood of the battle field.

When he grows to be a big man, the giants shrink in size; the horses become broom-sticks and the soldiers are painted tin no more than three inches high. In the spiritual order, it is the same; as long as there is a God who is wiser than we, greater than we, more powerful than we, then the world is a house of wonders.

Truth is then something so vast that not even an eternity can sound its depths. Love then is so abiding that not even heaven can dull its ecstasies. Goodness becomes so profound that thanks must ever be on one's lips.

But just forget God, make yourself a god, and then your little learning is your title to omniscience. Then the saints become for you stupid fools; the martyrs, "fanatics"; the religious, "dumb"; confession, a "priestly invention"; the Eucharist, a "vestige of paganism"; heaven, a "childish fancy"; and truth, a "delusion." It must be wonderful to know so much, but it must be terrible to find out in the end that one really knows so little.

The second lesson to be derived from this Fourth Word from the Cross is that humility is truth. Humility is not an underestimation of our talents or gifts or powers, nor is it their exaggeration. A man who is six feet tall is not humble if he says he is only five feet four inches tall, just as he is not humble if he says he is seven feet tall. Humility is truth or the recognition of gifts as gifts, faults as faults. Humility is dependence on God as pride is independence of Him.

It was that sense of independence or being without God which wrung out of the heart of Our Lord on the Cross this pitiable cry of abandonment: "My God, my God, why hast thou forsaken me?" The humble soul, conscious of his dependence on God, is always the thankful soul.

How many singers, orators, musicians, actors, doctors, professors ever think of thanking God for the special talents which made them outstanding in their profession? Out of the ten lepers who were made clean only one returned to give thanks. "Were not ten made clean? and where are the nine?" probably represents the proportion of the ungrateful who thank not because they are not humble.

The humble soul will always avoid praising his own good works and thus making void the virtues of his deeds. Self-praise devours merit; and those who have done good things to be seen by men, and who trumpet their philanthropies in the market places, will one day hear the saddest words of tongue or pen: "Thou hast already had thy reward."

The humble man, even though he be great in the eyes of the world, will esteem himself less than others, for he will always suspect that their internal greatness may far overreach his insignificant external greatness. He will therefore not flaunt his accidental superiority before his fellowman, for to do so is to prove one is not truly great. The really big men are the humble men; they are always approachable, kind, and understanding.

It is the little men who must put on airs. The really rich boy need not wear good clothes to impress his friends with his wealth, but the poor boy must do so to create the false impression of wealth. So it is with those who have nothing in their heads; they must be eternally creating the impression of how much they know, the books they have read, and the university from which they were graduated.

The learned man never has to "seem" learned, as the saint never has to appear pious —but the hypocrite does. The fact that so many men take honors seriously, change their voices, and cultivate poses, proves they never should have had the honors—the honors were too big for them. They could not assimilate the honors; rather the honors assimilated them. Instead of wearing the purple, the purple wears them.

A sponge can absorb so much water and no more; a character can absorb so much praise and no more; the point of saturation is reached when the honor ceases to be a part of him and begins to stick out like a sore thumb. The truly great are like St. Phillip Neri who one day, seeing a criminal being led off to prison, said: "There goes Phillip Neri, except for the grace of God."

Suppose we began to be humble and esteemed others at least no less than ourselves. Suppose to those who wounded us with their slanderous darts, we answered: "Father, forgive!" Suppose to those who classified us with thieves, we made the best of it and converted them saying: "This day, Paradise." Suppose out of those who shamed us before relatives, as Jesus was shamed before His Mother, we made a new friend for our heavenly Mother: "Behold thy son!" Suppose to those beneath us in worldly dignity we humbled ourselves and asked them for a drink: "I thirst!"

Suppose we began to be truthful, and estimated ourselves at our real worth. If we did these things for but one hour, we would completely revolutionize the world. We are not wanting an example for we have before our eyes Him who humbled Himself to the death on the Cross, who surrendered Divine consolation as Power put on the rags of weakness and Strength girded itself in abandonment, and, being God, appeared to be without God.

And why did He do this? Because we have been trying to lead our lives without God— to be independent. By choosing the humiliation of the Cross in reparation for pride He takes us back again to the story of David and Goliath.

Goliath was a great giant clothed in an armor of steel and carrying in his hand a mighty sword. David was the shepherd boy without defensive steel and carrying no other weapon than a staff, and five little stones from a nearby brook. Goliath scorned him, saying: "Am I a dog, that thou comest to me with a staff"? David answered; humbly, not trusting in his own power: "I come to thee in the name of the Lord..." The outcome we know. The boy with a stone killed the giant with the armor and sword.

The victory of David symbolized the reality of Good Friday. Pride is Goliath. Our Lord is the humble David who comes to slay pride with the staff of His Cross and five little stones—five wounds, in hands, feet, and side. With no other weapon than these Five Wounds and the staff of the Cross do we gain victories over the Goliath of pride on the battlefield of our soul.

To the worldly they seem ill-fitted for battle, and impotent to conquer, but not if we understand God's plan from the beginning that: "...the foolish things of the world hath God chosen, that he may confound the wise; and the weak things of the world hath God chosen that he may confound the strong." It was with a cross and a crowned brow that God won the day. As Oscar Wilde puts it:

O smitten mouth! O forehead crowned with thorn!
O chalice of all common miseries!
Thou for our sakes that loved thee not has borne
An agony of endless centuries,
And we were vain and ignorant nor knew
That when we stabbed thy heart it was our
own real hearts we slew.
Being ourselves the sowers and the seeds,
The night that covers and the lights that fade,
The spear that pierces and the side that bleeds,
The lips betraying and the life betrayed;
The deep hath calm: the moon hath rest: but we
Lords of the natural world are yet our own dread enemy.
Nay, nay, we are but crucified, and though
The bloody sweat falls from our brows like rain,
Loosen the nails—we shall come down I know,
Stanch the red wounds—we shall be whole again,
No need have we of hyssop-laden rod,
That which is purely human, that is Godlike, that is God.

Oscar Wilde.

THE FIFTH WORD: GLUTTONY

"I thirst."

GLUTTONY is an inordinate indulgence in food or drink, and may manifest itself either in taking more than is necessary, or in taking it at the wrong time, or in taking it too luxuriously. It is sinful because reason demands that food and drink be taken for the necessities and conveniences of nature but not for pleasure alone.

The Gospel describes Dives as being guilty of this sin. There is no mention in the story given to us by Our Blessed Lord that Dives was a wicked man. We have no record of him ever underpaying his servants or of being guilty of any moral turpitude. Our Lord tells us only that he was "clothed in purple and fine linen; and feasted sumptuously every day."

"And there was a certain beggar, named Lazarus, who lay at his gate, full of sores, desiring to be filled with the crumbs that fell from the rich man's table, and no one did give him; moreover the dogs came, and licked his sores. And it came to pass, that the beggar died, and was carried by the angels into Abraham's bosom. And the rich man also died: and he was buried in hell. And lifting up his eyes when he was in torments, he saw Abraham afar off, and Lazarus in his bosom. And he cried, and said: "Father Abraham, have mercy on me, and send Lazarus, that he may dip the tip of his finger in water, to cool my tongue; for I am tormented in this flame."

And Abraham said to him: "Son, remember that thou didst receive good things in thy lifetime, and likewise Lazarus evil things, but now he is comforted; and thou art tormented. And besides all this, between us and you, there is fixed a great chaos: so that they who would pass from hence to you, cannot, nor from thence come hither."

And he said: "Then, father, I beseech thee, that thou wouldst send him to my father's house, for I have five brethren, that he may testify unto them, lest they also come into this place of torments." And Abraham said to him: "They have Moses and the prophets; let them hear them." But he said: "No, father Abraham: but if one went to them from the dead, they will do penance." And he said to him: "If they hear not Moses and the prophets, neither will they believe, if one rise again from the dead."

If there is any indication of the present degeneration of society better than another, it is the excess of luxury in the modem world. When men begin to forget their souls, they begin to take great care of their bodies. There are more athletic clubs in the modern world than there are spiritual retreat houses; and who shall count the millions spent in beauty shops to glorify faces that will one day be the prey of worms.

It is not particularly difficult to find thousands who will spend two or three hours a day in exercising, but if you ask them to bend their knees to God in five minutes of prayer they protest that it is too long. Added to this is the shocking amount that is yearly spent, not in the normal pleasure of drinking, but in its excess.

The scandal increases when one considers the necessary wants of the poor which could have been supplied by the amount spent for such dehumanization. The Divine judgment upon Dives is bound to be repeated upon many of our generation, who will find that the beggars for whose service they refused to interrupt their luxuries, will be seated at the Banquet of the King of Kings, while they, like Dives, will be the beggars for but a drop of water.

Some reparation had to be made for gluttony, drunkenness, and excessive luxury. That reparation began at the birth of Our Lord when He who might have pulled down the heavens for His house-top and the stars for His chandeliers, chose to be rejected by men and driven as an outcast to a cave in the hillsides of the least of the cities of Israel.

The very first sermon He preached was a plea for detachment: "Blessed are the poor in spirit: for theirs is the kingdom of heaven." He began His public life by fasting forty days and bade men "Be not solicitous for your life, what you shall eat, nor for your body, what you shall put on."

Travelling about as an itinerant prophet, He admitted He was as homeless as at His birth and that the beasts and birds had a better habitation than He: "The foxes have holes, and the birds of the air nests; but the Son of man hath not where to lay his head." There was no luxury in the way He dined, for we know of but one meal which He himself prepared and it consisted only of bread and fish.

Finally, at the Cross He is stripped of His garments and denied a death-bed, in order to go out of His own world as He came into it— Lord of it and yet possessing nothing. The waters of the sea were His and all the fountains of the earth had sprung up at His word; He it was who drew the bolt of Nature's waterfalls and shut up the seas with doors; He it was who said: "Whosoever drinketh of this water, shall thirst again; but he that shall drink of the water that I will give him, shall not thirst for ever. If any man thirst, let him come to me, and drink."

But now He lets fall from His lips the shortest of the seven cries from the Cross and the one which expresses the keenest of all human sufferings in reparation for those who have had their fill: "I thirst."

A soldier immediately put a sponge full of vinegar on a stick and pressed it to His mouth. Thus was fulfilled the prophecy uttered by the Psalmist a thousand years before: "In my thirst they gave me vinegar to drink."

He who fed the birds of the air is left unfed; He who changed water into wine, now thirsts; the everlasting fountains are dry; the God-man is poverty stricken. The Divine Lazarus stands at the door of the world and begs for a crumb and a drop, but the door of generosity is closed in His face.

Thus was reparation made for the luxury of eating and drinking. When Mirabeau was dying he called for opium, saying: "You promised to spare me needless suffering.... Support this head, the greatest head in France." When Christ is dying, He refuses the drug to alleviate His suffering. He deliberately wills to feel the most poignant of human wants, that He might balance in the scales of justice those who had more than they needed.

He even made Himself the least of all men by asking them for a drink—not a drink of earthly water. That is not what He wanted, but a drink for His thirsty heart—a drink of love: I thirst for love.

This word from the Cross reveals that there is a double hunger and a double thirst: one of the body, the other of the soul. On many previous occasions Our Lord had distinguished between them: "Woe to you that are filled: for you shall hunger. Woe to you that now laugh: for you shall mourn and weep." "Blessed are ye that hunger now, for you shall be filled. Blessed are ye that weep now, for you shall laugh."

Then to the multitude who followed Him across the sea in search of bread, He said: "Labour not for the meat which perisheth, but for that which endureth unto life everlasting, which the Son of man will give you."

To the Samaritan woman who came to draw water at Jacob's well He foretold: "Whosoever drinketh of this water, shall thirst again; but he that shall drink of the water that I will give him, shall not thirst forever: But the water that I will give him, shall become in him a fountain of water, springing up into life everlasting." But above all other references to the food and drink of the inner man as contrasted with that of the outer man, He promised the supreme nourishment of Himself: "For my flesh is meat indeed: and my blood is drink indeed."

It is in the light of this double hunger and thirst of body and soul that the distinction between dieting and fasting becomes clear. The Church fasts; the world diets. Materially there is no difference, for a person can lose twenty pounds one way as well as the other. But the difference is in the intention.

The Christian fasts not for the sake of the body, but for the sake of the soul; the pagan fasts not for the sake of the soul, but for the sake of the body. The Christian does not fast because he believes the body is wicked, but in order to make it pliable in the hands of the soul, like a tool in the hands of a skilled workman.

That brings us down to the basic problem of life. Is the soul the tool of the body, or the body the tool of the soul? Should the soul do what the body wants, or should the body do what the soul wants? Each has its appetites and each is imperious in the satisfaction of its wants. If we please one, we displease the other, and vice versa. Both of them cannot sit down together at the banquet of life.

The development of character depends upon which hunger and thirst we cultivate. To diet or to fast—that is the problem. To lose a double chin in order to be more beautiful in the eyes of creatures or to lose it in order to keep the body tamed and ever obedient to the spiritual demands of the soul—that is the question. Human worth can be judged by human desires.

Tell me your hungers and your thirsts and I will tell you what you are. Do you hunger for money more than mercy, for riches more than virtue, and for power more than service? Then you are selfish, pampered, and proud. Do you thirst for the Wine of Everlasting Life more than for pleasure, and for the poor more than the favor of the rich, and for souls more than for the first places at table? Then you are a humble Christian.

The great pity is that so many have been so concerned with the body that they neglect the soul, and in neglecting the soul they lose the appetite for the spiritual. Just as it is possible in the physiological order for a man to lose all appetite for food, so it is possible in the spiritual order to lose all desire for the supernatural. Gluttonous about the perishable, they become indifferent to the everlasting.

Like deaf ears which are dead to the environment of harmony and blind eyes which are dead to the environment of beauty, so warped souls become dead to the environment of the Divine.

Darwin tells us in his autobiography that in his love for the biological he lost all the taste which he once had for poetry and music, and he regretted the loss all the days of his life. Nothing so much dulls the capacity for the spiritual as excessive dedication to the material.

Excessive love of money destroys a sense of value; excessive love of the flesh kills the values of the spirit. Then comes a moment when everything seems to rebel against the higher law of our being. As the poet has put it: "All things betrayest thee, who betrayest Me." Nature is so loyal to its Maker that it is always in the end disloyal to those who abuse it. "Traitorous trueness and loyal deceit" is its best poetic description, for in faithfulness to Him it will always be fickle with us.

The Fifth Word from the Cross is God's plea to the human heart to satisfy itself at the only satisfying fountains. God cannot compel men to thirst for the holy in place of the base, or for the divine rather than the secular; that is why His plea is merely an affirmation. "I thirst," meaning I thirst to be thirsted for. And His thirst is our salvation.

A twofold recommendation is hidden in this short sermon from the Cross; first, to mortify bodily hunger and thirst, and second, to cultivate a spiritual hunger and thirst.

We are to mortify bodily hunger and thirst not because the flesh is wicked, but because the soul must ever exercise mastery over it, lest it become a tyrant. Quite apart from avoiding all excesses, the Cross commits us even to the minimizing of expenditures for luxuries, for the sake of the poor. How many ever think of foregoing an elaborate dinner and theater party, or a debut, out of genuine sympathy and affection for Christ's poor? Dives did not, and he lost his soul because of that forgetfulness. How many in less ample circumstances even mortify themselves one movie a month in order to drop its equivalent in the poor box, that He who sees in secret may reward in secret?

The Divine counsel concerning such restraint of bodily appetites is unmistakable. On one occasion when Our Lord was invited to the home of the Prince of the Pharisees, He addressed the host himself saying: "When thou makest a dinner or a supper, call not thy friends, nor thy brethren, nor thy kinsmen, nor thy neighbours who are rich; lest perhaps they also invite thee again, and a recompense be made to thee. But when thou makest a feast, call the poor, the maimed, the lame, and the blind; And thou shalt be blessed, because they have not wherewith to make thee recompense: for recompense shall be made thee at the resurrection of the just."

The money we spend in the excesses of bodily hunger and thirst will do us no good on the last day; but the poor whom we have assisted by our restraint and mortification will stand up as so many advocates before the bar of Divine Justice, and will plead for mercy on our souls, even though they once were heavily laden with sin.

The Heavenly Judge cannot be bought with money, but He can be swayed by the poor. On that last day, the only one which really counts, will be fulfilled the beautifully prophetic words of the Mother of Our Lord: "He hath filled the hungry with good things; and the rich he hath sent empty away."

When such surrenders of the superfluous food and drink are made for the soul's sake, let it all be done in a spirit of joy. "And when you fast, be not as the hypocrites, sad. For they disfigure their faces, that they may appear unto men to fast. Amen I say to you, they have received their reward. But thou, when thou fastest anoint thy head, and wash thy face; That thou appear not to men to fast, but to thy Father who is in secret; and thy Father who seeth in secret, will repay thee."

We are, in addition, to cultivate a spiritual hunger and thirst. Mortification of the bodily appetites is only a means, not an end. The end is union with God, the soul's desire. "Taste and see that the Lord is sweet." The great tragedy of life is not so much what men have suffered, but what they have missed. It comes but within the compass of a few to satisfy their earthly desires with wealth, but there is no man living, who, if he willed it, could not enjoy the spiritual food and drink which God serves to all who ask.

And yet how few there are who ever think of nourishing their souls. How few there must have been in Jerusalem to have drawn from Our Lord the sweet complaint: "How often would I have gathered together thy children, as the hen doth gather her chickens under her wings, and thou wouldst not?"

Well indeed might the Saviour say to us as we listen to the cry: "I thirst" the words he addressed to the woman at the well. "If thou didst know the gift of God, and who he is that saith to thee, Give me to drink; thou perhaps wouldst have asked of him, and he would have given thee living water."

But how many ask? Consider the greatest gift of God to men: the Bread of Life and the Wine that germinates virgins. How few avail themselves of the Divine presence to break their fast each morning on the Heavenly food of the soul!

How many are sufficiently conscious that Our Lord is present in the tabernacle to pay a daily visit to Him in His Prison of Love? And if we do not, what does it witness to but the deadening of our spiritual sense. Our body would miss a dessert more than our soul would miss a Communion.

No wonder Our Crucified Redeemer thirsted for us on the Cross—thirsted for our unresponsive hearts and dulled souls. Nor let us think that His thirst is a proof of His need, but of our own. He does not need us for His perfection any more than we need the flower that blooms outside our window for our perfection. In dry seasons we desire rain for the flower, not because we need the rain, but because the flower needs it.

In like manner, God thirsts for us not because He needs us for His happiness, but because we need Him for our happiness. Without Him it is impossible for us to develop. Just as certain diseases, such as rickets and anemia, arise in the body from a deficiency of necessary vitamins, so too our characters fail because of a deficiency of the Spirit.

The vast majority of men and women in the world today are so under-developed spiritually that if a like deficiency showed in their bodies they would be physical monstrosities.

How many millions of minds there are today that are devoid of one single satisfying truth which they can carry through life to sustain them in their sorrows and console their death? How many millions of wills there are that have not yet found the goal of life and which, because they are presently without it, flit like butterflies from one colored emotion to another, unable to find repose?

Let them cultivate a taste for something more than bread and circuses; let them sound the depths of their beings to discover there the arid wastes crying for the refreshment of everlasting fountains. Of course these emaciated hungry souls are not altogether to blame. They have heard preachers without end preaching Go to Christ! But what does that mean? Go back 1900 years? If so, then have they not a right to doubt the Divinity of Him who could not project Himself through time?

Look up to heaven? If so, then what has become of His blessing, His forgiveness of sinners, His Truth that He said would endure unto the end of time? Where is His authority? His Power? His Life now? If it is not some place on earth, then why did He come to earth? To leave only the echo of His words, the record of His deeds, and then to slip away leaving us only a history and its teachers?

Somewhere on earth today is His Truth: "He that heareth you, heareth me." Somewhere on earth is His Power: "Behold, I have given you power ..." Somewhere on earth is His Life: "The bread that I will give, is my flesh, for the life of the world." Where find it?

There is an institution on the face of the earth which claims to be that, and to those who have knocked at its portals and have asked for a drink has come the elixir of Divine Life and with it the peace which comes to those who drink and never thirst again, and eat and never hunger again.

To each and everyone of us, inside and outside the Church, Our Lord asks: "Will you accept the cup of My Love?" He took our cup of hate and bitterness in Gethsemane and its dregs were so bitter they made Him cry out: "My Father, if it be possible, let this chalice pass from me."

But He drank every drop of it. If He drank our cup of hates why do we not drink His Chalice of pardon? Why then, when He cries, "I thirst," do we reach Him vinegar and gall?

> *I cannot tell the half of it, yet hear*
> *What rush of feeling still comes back to me,*
> *From that proud torture hanging on His Cross,*
> *From that gold rapture of His Heart in mine.*
> *I knew in blissful anguish what it means*
> *To be a part of Christ, and feel as mine*
> *The dark distresses of my brother limbs,*
> *To feel it bodily and simply true,*
> *To feel as mine the starving of His poor,*
> *To feel as mine the shadow of curse on all,*
> *Hard words, hard looks, and savage misery,*
> *And struggling deaths, unpitied and unwept.*
> *To feel rich brothers' sad satieties,*
> *The weary manner of their lives and deaths,*
> *That want in love, and lacking love lack all.*
> *To feel the heavy sorrow of the world*
> *Thicken and thicken on to future hell,*
> *To mighty cities with their miles of streets,*
> *Where men seek work for days, and walk and starve,*
> *Freezing on river-banks on winter nights,*
> *And come at last to cord or stream or steel.*
> *The honor of the things our brothers bear!*
> *It was but naught to that which after came,*
> *The woe of things we make our brothers bear,*
> *Our brothers and our sisters! In my heart*
> *Christ's Heart seemed beating, and the world's whole sin, —*
> *Its crimson malice and grey negligence, —*
> *Rose up and blackening hid the Face of God.*

Arthur Shearly Cripps

The Sixth Word: Sloth

"It is finished."

Sloth is a malady of the will which causes us to neglect our duties. Sloth may be either physical or spiritual. It is physical when it manifests itself in laziness, procrastination, idleness, softness, indifference, and nonchalance. It is spiritual when it shows itself in an indifference to character betterment, a distaste for the spiritual, a hurried crowding of devotions, a lukewarmness and failure to cultivate new virtue.

The classic description of the effects of sloth are to be found in the Book of Proverbs: "I passed by the field of the slothful man, and by the vineyard of the foolish man: And behold it was all filled with nettles, and thorns had covered the face thereof, and the stone wall was broken down. Which when I had seen, I laid it up in my heart, and by the example I received instruction. Thou wilt sleep a little, said I, thou wilt slumber a little, thou wilt fold thy hands a little to rest: And poverty shall come to thee as a runner, and beggary as an armed man."

Of such indifference to duty Our Lord spoke in the Apocalypse: "But because thou art lukewarm, and neither cold, nor hot, I will begin to vomit thee out of my mouth."

The Life and teaching of Our Lord lend no support to the slothful man. When yet only twelve years of age He speaks of being about His "Father's business" which was nothing less than redeeming the world. Then for eighteen years He worked as a manual laborer transforming dead and useless things into the child's crib, the friend's table, Nazarene roofs, and the farmers' wagons, as symbols of His later work by which He would transform hard money changers and prostitutes into useful citizens of the Kingdom of Heaven.

Beginning a public life with calloused hands He preached the Gospel of work: "I must work the works of him that sent me, whilst it is day; the night cometh, when no man can work." His whole life, in His own words, was spent not in receiving but in giving: "the Son of man is not come to be ministered unto, but to minister, and to give his life as a redemption for many."

He earned the right to teach the necessity of work, and lest we live under any illusions that any other work is more important than the saving of souls, even the burial of our fathers, He said to the disciple who asked for such permission: "Follow me, and let the dead bury their dead."

To the young man who wished to be His disciple but first wanted to bid farewell to his friends at home, Our Lord said: "No man putting his hand to the plough, and looking back, is fit for the kingdom of God." Laboring for bread alone is no fulfillment of His commandment, for to those who wanted more bread He pleaded: "Labour not for the meat which perisheth, but for that which endureth unto life everlasting, which the Son of man will give you."

The business of salvation is no easy task. There are two roads through this world and two gates into the future life. "Enter ye in at the narrow gate; for wide is the gate, and broad is the way that leadeth to destruction, and many there are who go in thereat. How narrow is the gate, and strait is the way that leadeth to life: and few there are that find it!"

Curiously enough, His invitation goes out only to those who labor for the eternal prize: "Come to me, all you who labour, and are burdened, and I will refresh you. Take up my yoke upon you, and learn of me, for I am meek, and humble of heart: And you shall find rest to your souls. For my yoke is sweet, and my burden light."

So completely had He fulfilled the smallest detail of His Father's business that the very night of His Agony, in the Upper Room in the presence of His Apostles, He could raise His eyes to heaven and pray: "Father ... I have glorified thee on earth; I have finished the work which thou gavest me to do." Then the following afternoon, as the Carpenter is put to death by His own profession, He cries out from the Cross in a loud voice the final reparation for sloth and the song of triumph: "It is consummated."

He did not say: "I die," because death did not come to take Him. He walked to it to conquer it. The last drop in the chalice of Redemption was drained; the last nail had been driven in the mansion of the Father's House; the last brush touched to the canvas of salvation! His work was done!

But ours is not. It is important to realize this for there are the slothful who justify themselves by saying they need only faith in Christ to save their souls. Surely He who worked so hard for the world's redemption came not to dispense His followers from work. The servant is not above the master. Faith in Him alone does not save, for "faith without good works is dead." It is not enough for the student to have faith in his teacher's knowledge; he must also study. It is not enough for the sick to have faith in their doctor; their organism must cooperate with him and his medicine. It is not enough to believe that Washington was the "father of our country," we must also assume and fulfill our duties as American citizens.

In like manner it is not enough to believe in Christ; we must live Christ and to some extent die Christ-like. His words permit of no equivocation: "And he that taketh not up his cross, and followeth me, is not worthy of me. He that findeth his life, shall lose it: and he that shall lose his life for me, shall find it."

St. Paul understood the labor involved in being a Christian and wrote the same message to the Romans: "For if we have been planted together in the likeness of his death, we shall be also in the likeness of his resurrection." What He hath done with His human nature, we must do with ours—plant it in the soil of the Cross and await the Resurrection of the Eternal Easter.

Later on, to the Corinthians, Paul repeated it: "As you are partakers of the sufferings, so shall you be also of the consolation." And St. Peter who knew so well the scandal of the Cross pleaded for joy in reliving the Cross: "But if you partake of the sufferings of Christ, rejoice that when his glory shall be revealed, you may also be glad with exceeding joy."

There is no hope for the spiritually slothful in these injunctions. Our Lord is the die; we must be stamped by it. He is the pattern; we must be remodelled to it. The Cross is the condition; we must be nailed to it. Our Lord loved His Cross so much that He keeps its scars even in His glory. He who had won victory over death, kept the record of its wounds.

If so precious to Him, they cannot be meaningless for us. In their preservation is the reminder that we too must be signed with those signs and sealed with those seals.

On Judgment Day He will say to each of us: "Show Me your hands and feet. Where are your scars of victory? Have you fought no battles for truth? Have you won no wars for goodness? Have you made no enemy of evil?"

If we can prove we have been His warriors and show the scars on our apostolic hands, then we shall enjoy the peace of victory. But woe unto us who come down from the Calvary of this earthly pilgrimage with hands unscarred and white!

Two lessons emerge from this Sixth Word from the Cross witnessing to His finished work and our own unfinished tasks: First, we must beware of spiritual sloth for its penalties are tremendous; and second, we must work for a complete life.

The Gospel records three instances of sloth. There were the foolish virgins, chaste but lazy. The wise virgins fill their lamps with oil and wait to hear the step of the approaching bridegroom. The foolish virgins do not think of oil, and tired of waiting, they fall asleep. When the bridegroom comes, the wise virgins light their lamps and welcome the bridegroom. The foolish virgins go out to buy oil, but everybody is asleep, the shops are closed. They go back to the wedding feast, but the door is closed. They cry: "Lord, Lord open to us." But His answer is: "Amen I say to you, I know you not . . ." Our Lord concludes the parable with these words: "Watch ye therefore, because you know not the day nor the hour."

The second instance of sloth was the parable of the barren fig tree: "And the next day when they came out from Bethania, he was hungry. And when he had seen afar off a fig-tree having leaves, he came if perhaps he might find anything on it. And when he was come to it, he found nothing but leaves. For it was not the time for figs. And answering, he said to it: May no man hereafter eat fruit of thee any more forever."

The third was the parable of the buried talent. He who received five talents earned another five; he who had received two earned another two; but he who received one hid it in the ground. Of him the lord of the servants said: "Wicked and slothful servant! . . . Take ye away therefore the talent from him, and give it him that hath ten talents. For to every one that hath shall be given, and he shall abound: but from him that hath not, that also which he seemeth to have shall be taken away. And the unprofitable servant cast ye out into the exterior darkness. There shall be weeping and gnashing of teeth."

Common to these three parables is the danger of sloth and the necessity of work. Purity without good works will not save any more than it saved the foolish virgins. Those who do nothing run the risk of losing the little that they have. In other words, it is possible to lose our souls by doing nothing. "How shall we escape if we neglect . . . ?" We lose our souls not only by the evil we do, but also by the good we leave undone.

Neglect the body and the muscles stiffen; neglect the mind and imbecility comes; neglect the soul and ruin follows. Just as physical life is the sum of the forces which resist death, so the spiritual life is to some extent the sum of the forces which resist evil. Neglect to take an antidote for a poison in the body, and we die by our neglect. Neglect to take precaution against sin, and we die the death merely because of neglect.

Heaven is a city on a hill, hence we cannot coast into it; we have to climb. Those who are too lazy to mount can miss its capture, as well as the evil who refuse to seek it. Let no one think he can be totally indifferent to God in this life and suddenly develop a capacity for Him at the moment of death.

Where will the capacity for Heaven come from if we have neglected it on earth? A man cannot suddenly walk into a lecture room on higher mathematics and be thrilled by its equations if all during life he neglected to develop a taste for mathematics. A heaven of poets would be a hell to those who never learned to love poetry. And a heaven of Divine Truth, Righteousness, and Justice would be a hell to those who never studiously cultivated those virtues here below. Heaven is only for those who work for heaven.

If we crush every inspiration of the Divine; if we drown every Godward inspiration of the soul; if we choke every inlet to Christ—where will be our relish for God on the last day? The very things we neglected will then be the very cause of our ruin. The very things that should have ministered to our growth will then turn against us and minister to our decay.

The sun which warms the plant can under other conditions also wither it. The rain which nourishes the flower can under other conditions rot it. The same sun shines upon mud that shines upon wax. It hardens the mud but softens the wax. The difference is not in the sun, but in that upon which it shines.

So it is with God. The Divine Life which shines upon a soul that loves Him, softens it into everlasting life; that same Divine Life which shines upon the slothful soul, neglectful of God, hardens it into everlasting death.

Heaven and hell are in like manner both effects of Divine Goodness. Their difference comes from our reaction to that goodness, and to that extent are also our creations. Both God and man are in different senses creators of heaven and hell.

A little heed then to this word from the Cross: "It is consummated." We finish our vocation as He finished His—on a cross and nowhere else. Only to the doors of the truth, and not to its preachers or its hearers, comes the reward of the crown. Doing implies the spending not of what we have, but of what we are.

We need have no undue fear for our health if we work hard for the Kingdom of God; God will take care of our health if we take care of His cause. In any case, it is better to burn out than to rust out.

Burning the candle at both ends for God's sake may be foolishness to the world, but it is a profitable Christian exercise—for so much better the light. Only one thing in life matters: Being found worthy of the Light of the World in the hour of His visitation.

"Take ye heed," He said. "Take ye heed, watch and pray. For ye know not when the time is. Even as a man who going into a far country, left his house; and gave authority to his servants over every work, and commanded the porter to watch. Watch ye therefore (for you know not when the lord of the house cometh: at even, or at midnight, or at the cock crowing, or in the morning), Lest coming on a sudden, he find you sleeping. And what I say to you, I say to all: Watch."

Not only must we beware of spiritual sloth; we must work for a completed life. The important word in the struggle against sloth is "finished." The world judges us by results; Our Lord judges us by the way we fulfill and finish our appointed tasks. A good life is not necessarily a successful life.

The sowers are not always the reapers. Those whom God destines only to sow receive their reward for just that, even though they never garnered a single sheaf into everlasting barns. In the parable of the talents, the reward is according to the development of potentialities and the completion of appointed duties.

One day Our Lord "sitting over against the treasury, beheld how the people cast money into the treasury, and many that were rich cast in much. And there came a certain poor widow, and she cast in two mites, which make about half a cent. And calling his disciples together, he saith to them: Amen I say to you, this poor widow hath cast in more than all they who have cast into the treasury. For all they did cast in of their abundance; but she of her want cast in all she had, even her whole living."

The result was trivial for the treasury, but it was infinite for her soul. She had not half done her duty, she had finished it. This is what is meant by completed living.

In the Christian order it is not the important who are essential, nor those who do great things who are really great. A king is no nobler in the sight of God than a peasant. The head of government with millions of troops at his command is no more precious in the sight of God than a paralyzed child. The former has greater opportunities for evil, but like the widow in the Temple, if the child fulfills its task of resignation to the will of God more than the dictator fulfills his task of procuring social justice for the glory of God, then the child is greater. "God is no respecter of persons."

Men and women are only actors on the stage of life. Why should he who plays the part of the rich man glory in his gold and rich table and consider himself better than him who plays the role of the beggar begging a crumb from his table. When the curtain goes down they are both men. So when God pulls down the curtain on the drama of the world's redemption, He will not ask what part we played, but only how well we played the role assigned to us. The Little Flower has said that one could save one's soul by picking up pins out of love of God.

If we could create worlds and drop them into space from our finger tips, we would please God no more than by dropping a coin into a tin cup. It is not what is done, but why it is done that matters. A bootblack shining a pair of shoes inspired by a Divine motive is doing more good for this world than all the Godless conventions Moscow could ever convene.

It is the intention which makes the work. Duties in life are like marble, canvas, and stone. Marble becomes valuable because of the image given to it by the sculptor; canvas is ennobled by the picture of the artist; and stone is glorified by the pattern of the architect.

So it is with our works. The intention gives them value as the image gives the marble value. God is not interested in what we do with our hands, or our money, or our minds, or our mouths, but with our wills. It is not the work but the worker that counts.

Let those souls who think their work has no value recognize that by fulfilling their insignificant tasks out of a love of God, those tasks assume a supernatural worth. The aged who bear the taunts of the young, the sick crucified to their beds, the ignorant immigrant in the steel mill, the street cleaner and the garbage collector, the wardrobe mistress in the theater and the chorus girl who never had a line, the unemployed carpenter and the ash collector-all these will be enthroned above dictators, presidents, kings, and cardinals if a greater love of God inspires their humbler tasks than inspires those who play nobler roles with less love.

No work is finished until we do it for the honor and glory of God. "Whether you eat or drink, or whatever else you do, do all to the glory of God." When our lease on life runs out there are two questions which will be asked. The world will ask: "How much did he leave?" The angels will ask: "How much did he bring with him?"

The soul can carry much, but in its journey to the judgment seat of God it will be freighted down only with that kind of goods which a man can carry away from a shipwreck—his good works done for the glory of God. All that we leave behind is "unfinished." All that we take with us is "finished."

May we never die too soon! This does not mean not dying young; it means not dying with our appointed tasks undone. It is indeed a curious fact that no one ever thinks of Our Lord as dying too young! That is because He finished His Father's business. But no matter how old we are when we die, we always feel there is something more to be done.

Why do we feel that way, if it is not because we did not do well the tasks assigned to us. Our task may not be great; it may be only to add one stone to the Temple of God. But whatever it is, do each tiny little act in union with your Saviour who died on the Cross and you will finish your life. Then you will never die too young!

> But if, impatient, thou let slip thy cross,
> Thou wilt not find it in this world again,
> Nor in another; here, and here alone
> Is given thee to suffer for God's sake.
> In other words we shall more perfectly
> Serve Him and love Him, praise Him, work for Him,
> Grow near and nearer Him with all delight;
> But then we shall not any more be called
> To suffer, which is our appointment here,
> Canst thou not suffer then one hour,—or two?
> If He should call thee from thy cross to-day,
> Saying, It is finished!—that hard cross of thine
> From which thou prayest for deliverance,
> Thinkest thou not some passion of regret
> Would overcome thee? Thou wouldst say, 'So soon?
> Let me go back and suffer yet awhile
> More patiently;—I have not yet praised God.'
> And He might answer to thee,—'Never more.
> All pain is done with.' Whensoe'er it comes,
> That summons that we look for, it will seem
> Soon, yea too soon. Let us take heed in time
> That God may now be glorified in us;
> And while we suffer, let us set our souls
> To suffer perfectly: since this alone,
> The suffering, which is this world's special grace
> May here be perfected and left behind....
> Endure, Endure,—be faithful to the end!

Harriet Eleanor Hamilton-King

THE SEVENTH WORD: COVETOUSNESS

*"Father, into Thy Hands,
I commend my spirit."*

COVETOUSNESS is an inordinate love of the things of this world. It becomes inordinate if one is not guided by a reasonable end, such as a suitable provision for one's family, or the future, or if one is too solicitous in amassing wealth, or too parsimonious in dispensing it.

The sin of covetousness includes therefore both the intention one has in acquiring the goods of this world and the manner of acquiring them. It is not the love of an excessive sum which makes it wrong, but an inordinate love of any sum.

Simply because a man has a great fortune, it does not follow that he is a covetous man. A child with a few pennies might possibly be more covetous. Material things are lawful and necessary in order to enable us to live according to our station in life, to mitigate suffering, to advance the Kingdom of God and to save our souls.

It is the pursuit of wealth as an end instead of a means to the above ends, which makes a man covetous.

In this class of the covetous are to be placed the young woman who marries a divorced man for his money; the public official who accepts a bribe; the lawyer, the educator or clergyman who sponsors radical movements for Red gold; the capitalist who puts profits above human rights and needs, and the laborer who puts party power above the laborer's rights.

Covetousness is much more general in the world today than we suspect. It once was monopolized by the avaricious rich; now it is shared by the envious poor. Because a man has no money in his pockets is no proof that he is not covetous; he may be involuntarily poor with a passion for wealth far in excess of those who possess.

History bears witness to the fact that almost every radical economic revolutionist in the history of the world has been interested in only one thing:—booty. The only poor who ever attacked the rich and sought nothing for themselves were Our Lord and His followers, like St. Francis of Assisi.

There are very few disinterested lovers of the poor today; most of their so-called champions do not love the poor as much as they hate the rich. They hate all the rich, but they love only those poor who will help them attain their wicked ends.

Such covetousness is ruinous for man, principally because it hardens the heart. Man becomes like unto that which he loves, and if he loves gold, he becomes like it—cold, hard and yellow. The more he acquires, the more he suffers at surrendering even the least of it, just as it hurts to have a single hair pulled out even though your head is full of them.

The more the sinfully rich man gets, the more he believes he is needy. He is always poor in his own eyes. The sense of the spiritual thus becomes so deadened that its most precious treasures are bartered away for the trivial increases, as Judas sold his Master for thirty pieces of silver.

As St. Paul tells us: "The desire for money is the root of all evils, which some coveting have erred from the faith." (I Tim. 6, 10). The Providence of God becomes less and less a reality, and if it still retains value, it is reduced to a secondary role; God is trusted as long as we have a good bank account.

When things go well we are quite willing to dispense with God, like the young man in the Gospel who came to Our Lord only be cause he was being deprived of some of his father's estate. "Master, speak to my brother that he divide the inheritance with me." It was only when economic confusion arose that the young man had recourse to the Divine.

There are many in the world today who feel that the only reason for the existence of the Church is to improve the economic order and if they do not have their fill, they assail the Church for failing. Well indeed might the Church answer in the words of Our Lord: "O man, who hath appointed me judge and divider over you."

To turn man's heart away from perishable things to the eternal values of the soul, was one of the reasons for the Lord's visit to the earth. His teaching from the beginning was not only a warning against covetousness, but a plea for a greater trust in Providence.

"Do not lay up for yourselves treasures upon the earth, where moth and rust consume, and where thieves break through and steal; but lay up for yourselves treasures in heaven, where neither moth nor rust consumes, and where thieves do not break through nor steal. For where thy treasure is, there will thy heart be also." (Matt. 6, 19-21).

"I say to you therefore, do not be anxious about your life, what you shall eat or what you shall drink; nor about your body, what you shall wear. Is not the life of more consequence than the food, and the body than the clothing? Look at the birds of the sky, how they neither sow nor reap nor gather into barns yet your heavenly Father feeds them! Are you not of much more value than they? Yet who among you by anxious thought is able to add a single span to his life?

"And why should you worry about clothing? Observe the field-lilies, how they grow; they neither toil nor spin; yet I tell you that even Solomon in all his magnificence was not arrayed like one of them. But if God so clothes the grass of the field, which exists today and is thrown in the oven tomorrow, will He not much rather clothe you, O you of little faith?

"Do not therefore worry saying, 'What shall we eat?' What shall we drink,' or What shall we wear?' for the heathen seek after all these things; and your heavenly Father knows that you need them all. But seek first the Kingdom of God and His holiness, and all these things shall be given you besides. Do not then be anxious about tomorrow, for tomorrow will take care of itself. Quite enough for the day is its own trouble." (Matt. 6, 25-34).

The man who unduly loves riches is a fallen man, because of a bad exchange; he might have had heaven through his generosity, and he has only the earth. He could have kept his soul, but he sold it for material things. Camels will pass through eyes of needles more easily than the covetous will pass through the gates of heaven. It was easy of course to condemn the rich; our world is too full of those who are doing it now. But our economic revolutionists do it because they envy wealth, not because they love poverty.

It was not so with Our Divine Saviour. He Who condemned Dives and the man who ordered bigger barns the very day he died, and who thundered that no man could serve God and Mammon, lived His Gospel. Not in a hospital, nor a home, or a city, but in a stable in the fields did He bow entrance into the world He made. Not with money did He make money in the markets of exchange, but as a poor carpenter.

He earned His living with the two most primitive instruments used: wood and hammer. During His three years of preaching not even a roof could He claim as His own: "The foxes have burrows, and the birds of the sky have nests; but the Son of Man has not a place where He may lay His head." (Matt. 8, 9, 20).

Then at His death He had no wealth to leave; His Mother he gave to John; His body to the tomb; His blood to the earth; His garments to His executioners. Absolutely dispossessed, He is still hated, to give the lie to those who say religion is hated because of its possessions.

Religion is hated because it is religion, and possessions are only the excuse and pretext for driving God from the earth. There was no quarreling about His will; there was no dispute about how His property would be divided; there was no lawsuit over the Lord of the Universe.

He had given up everything in reparation for covetousness, keeping only one thing for Himself that was not a thing—His Spirit. With a loud cry, so powerful that it freed His soul from His flesh and bore witness to the fact that He was giving up His life and not having it taken away, He said in farewell: "Father, into Thy Hands I commend My Spirit."

It rang out over the darkness and lost itself in the furthermost ends of the earth. The world has made all kinds of noise since to drown it out.

Men have busied themselves with nothing to shut out hearing it; but through the fog and darkness of cities, and the silence of the night that awful cry rings within the hearing of every heart who does not force himself to forget, and as we listen to it we learn two lessons:

1. The more ties we have to earth the harder will it be for us to die.
2. We were never meant to be perfectly satisfied here below.

In every friendship hearts grow and entwine themselves together, so that the two hearts seem to make only one heart with only a common thought. That is why separation is so painful;—it is not so much two hearts separating, but one heart being torn asunder.

When a man loves wealth inordinately, he and it grow together like a tree pushing itself in growth through the crevices of a rock. Death to such a man is a painful wrench, because of his close identification with the material. He has everything to live for, nothing to die for. He becomes at death the most destitute and despoiled beggar in the universe, for he has nothing he can take with him. He discovers too late that he did not belong to himself, but to things, for wealth is a pitiless master.

It would not allow him during life to think of anything else except increasing itself. Now he discovers too late that by consecrating himself to filling his barns, he was never free to save the only thing he could carry with him to eternity:—his soul. In order to acquire a part, he lost the whole; he won a fraction of the earth, now he will need only six feet of it.

Like a giant tied down by ten thousand ropes to ten thousand stakes, he is no longer free to think about anything else than what he must leave. That is why death is so hard for the covetous rich.

On the contrary, as the ties to earth become lessened, the easier is the separation. Where our treasure is, there is our heart also. If we have lived for God, then death is a liberation. Earth and its possessions are the cage which confines us and death is the opening of its door, enabling our soul to wing its way to its Beloved for which it had only lived, and for which it only waited to die.

Our powers of dispossession are greater than our powers of possession; our hands could never contain all the gold in the world, but we can wash our hands of its desire. We cannot own the world, but we can disown it. That is why the soul with the vow of poverty is more satisfied than the richest covetous man in the world, for the latter has not yet all he wants, while the religious wants nothing; in a certain sense the religious has all and is perfectly happy.

It was such poverty of spirit raised to its sublimest peaks, which made the death of Our Lord so easy. He had no ties to earth. His treasure was with the Father and His Soul followed the spiritual law of gravitation.

Gold, like dirt, falls; charity, like fire, rises: "Father, into Thy Hands I commend My Spirit."

The death of Our Lord on the Cross reveals that we are meant to be perpetually dissatisfied here below. If earth were meant to be a Paradise, then He Who made it would never have taken leave of it on Good Friday. The commending of the Spirit to the Father was at the same time the refusal to commend it to earth. The completion or fulfillment of life is in heaven, not on earth.

Our Lord in His last Word is saying that nowhere else can we be satisfied except in God. It is absolutely impossible for us to be perfectly happy here below. Nothing proves this more than disappointment. One might almost say the essence of life is disappointment. We look forward to a position, to marriage, to ownership, to power, to popularity, to wealth, and when we attain them, we have to admit, if we are honest, that they never come up to our expectations.

As children we looked forward to Christmas; when it did come and we had our fill of sweets and tested every toy or rocked every doll, and then crept into our beds, we said in our own little heart of hearts: "Somehow or other, it did not quite come up to expectations." That experience is repeated a thousand times in life.

But why is there disappointment? Because when we look forward to a future ideal, we endow it with something of the infinity of the soul. I can imagine a house with ten thousand rooms studded with diamonds and emeralds, but I shall never see one. I can imagine a mountain of gold, but I shall never see one.

So with our earthly ideals. We color them with the qualities of our spiritual soul. But when they become realized, they are concrete, cabined, cribbed, confined. A tremendous disproportion thus arises between the ideal we conceived and the reality before us.

That disproportion between the infinite and the finite is the cause of disappointment. There is no escaping this fact. We have eternity in our heart, but time on our hands. The soul demands a heaven, and we get only an earth. Our eyes look up to the mountains, but they rest only on the plains. It is easier to strangle our ideals than it is to satisfy them. He who attains his earthly ideal, smashes it.

To touch an ideal in this world is to destroy the ideal. "No man is a hero to his valet." We are no longer thirsty at the border of a well. The satisfaction of earthly ideals turns against us, like a cruel retort from one we paid an underhand compliment.

But there is no reason for being pessimists or cynics. Disappointment is no proof there is no ideal, but only that it is not here. Just as we would have no eyes were there no beauties to see, and as we would have no ears were there no harmonies to hear, so we would have no appetite for the infinite were there no God to love.

In Him alone is the reconciliation of the chase and the capture. Here on this earth we are buffeted between the two. The chase has its thrill for it is the pursuit of an ideal, the quest for satisfaction, and the march to victory. The capture too has its thrill for it is possession, enjoyment and peace.

But while we live in time we can never enjoy both together. The capture ends the excitement of the chase; and the chase without a capture is maddening, like having a refreshing spring withdrawn from our parched lips as we drew near to it.

How combine the chase without the ennui of capture, and the capture without losing the joy of the chase? It is impossible here below, but not in heaven, for when we attain unto God, we capture the Infinite, and because He is Infinite it will take an eternity of chase to discover the undiscoverable joys of Life, Truth, Love and Beauty.

Such is the meaning behind the last and farewell word from the Cross. Centuries ago the sun shone upon plants and trees and imprisoned within them its light and heat. Today we dig up that light and heat in coal, and as its flames mount upward we pay back our debt to the sun.

So now the Divine Light, that for thirty-three years has been imprisoning itself in human hearts, goes back again to the Father, to ever remind us that only by completing a similar circuit and commending our souls to the Father, do we find the answer to the riddle of life, and the end of disappointment and the beginning of eternal peace for our eternal hearts.

Everything is disappointing except the Redemptive Love of Our Lord. You can go on acquiring things but you will be poor until your soul is filled with the love of Him Who died on the Cross for you. As the eye was made for seeing and the ear for hearing, so your spirit was made to be re-commended back again to God.

If it had any other destiny the dying words of the Saviour would have betrayed that destiny. The spirit has a capacity for the infinite; the knowledge of one flower, the life of a single hour, the love of a minute do not exhaust its potencies; it wants the fulness of these things, in a word—it wants God.

The tragedy of our modern life is that so many put their pleasures in desires rather than in discovery. Having lost the one purpose of human living, namely God, they seek substitutes in the petty things of earth.

After repeated disappointments, they begin to put their happiness not in a pleasure, but in the hunt for it, in butterfly existences that never rest long enough at any one moment to know their inner desires; running races hoping they will never end; turning pages but never discovering the plot; knocking at doors of truth and then dashing away lest its portals be opened and they be invited in. Existence becomes a flight from peace, rather than an advance; a momentary escape from frustration instead of its sublimation in victory.

Every now and then there comes to some a light through the clouds of Calvary and the echo of the word commending a spirit to God, but instead of making a supreme effort to satisfy the goal of life, they crucify it.

"But the husbandmen said one to another, this is the heir; come, let us kill him and the inheritance shall be ours. And laying hold of him, they killed him and cast him out of the vineyard."

Thus do some men believe that if they could drive God from the earth the inheritance of sin would be there without remorse; and if they could but silence conscience, they could inherit peace without justice. It was just this mentality which sent Our Lord to the Cross. If the voice of God could be stifled, they believed they could enjoy the voice of Satan in peace.

Now, take a different outlook on the world. How many, even of those who have killed conscience can say: "I am happy, there is nothing I want." But if you are not brave enough to say that, then why not seek? And why not seek in the one direction in which you know happiness lies?

At death you will leave everything but there is one thing you will not leave—your desire to life. You want the one thing the Cross brings you:—Life through death.

In its effulgence the mystery of existence becomes clear. The Cross refers to me, personally and individually as if no one else in the world ever existed. On the cross He has traced for me in sacrifice, which is the sublimest of gestures, a programme of life; submission to the Divine Will. He went down the dark road of Gethsemane to Calvary's death out of devotedness to God's glory and my salvation.

For my culpable self-indulgence, He atones by surrender of Himself. "He was wounded for our iniquities; He was bruised for our sins. The chastisement of our peace was upon him." (Isais 5, 3-5).

If this Master of the world's symphony would miss my single note of virtue in the harmony of the universe; if this Captain of Wars would miss my spear in His battle for Goodness; if this Artist would miss my little daub of color in the masterpiece of redemption; if this Cosmic Architect would note the absence of my little stone in the building of His temple; if this Tree of Life would feel the fall of but my little leaf to the sinfulness of earth; if this the Heavenly Father would miss me in the empty chair at the banquet spread for the millions of the children of God; if this Orator from the Pulpit of the Cross would note my inattention as I turned to glance at an executioner; if God cares that much for me, then I must be worth something since He loves me so!

> *But if Himself He come to thee, and stand*
> *Beside thee, gazing down on thee with eyes*
> *That smile, and suffer; that will smite thy heart,*
> *With their own pity, to a passionate peace;*
> *And reach to thee Himself and the Holy Cup*
> *(With all its wreathen stems of passion-flowers*
> *And quivering sparkles of the ruby stars),*
> *Pallid and royal, saying 'Drink with Me';*
> *Wilt thou refuse? Nay, not for Paradise!*
> *The pale brow will compel thee, the pure hands*
> *Will minister unto thee; thou shalt take*
> *Of that communion through the solemn depths*
> *Of the dark waters of thine agony,*
> *With heart that praises Him, that yearns to Him*
> *The closer through that hour. Hold fast His hand,*
> *Though the nails pierce thine too! take only care*
> *Lest one drop of the sacramental wine*
> *Be spilled, of that which ever shall unite*
> *Thee, soul and body to thy living Lord!*

Harriet Eleanor Hamilton-King.

Way To Happiness

[1953]

Introduction
Plan And Purpose

THESE articles are written with a particular purpose, a special method, a deliberate spirit. The purpose will be to bring solace, healing and hope to hearts; truth and enlightenment to minds; goodness, strength and resolution to wills. The method will be the application of eternal moral and spiritual principles to the basic problems of individual and social life today. The spirit will be that of charity: love of God and love of neighbor.

And this preface will declare the basic assumptions of this book.

First: The over-emphasis on politics today is an indication that people are governed, rather than governing. The complexities of our civilization force us to organize into larger and larger units; we have become so intent on governing what is outside of us that we neglect to govern our own selves. Yet the key to social betterment is always to be found in personal betterment. Remake man and you remake his world. We gravely need to restore to man his self-respect and to give him his appropriate honor: this will keep him from bowing cravenly before those who threaten to enslave him, and it will give him the courage to defend the right, alone if need be, when the world is wrong.

Second: As society is made by man, so man, in his turn, is made by his thoughts, his decisions and his choices. Nothing ever happens to the world which did not first happen inside the mind of some man: the material of the skyscraper merely completes the architect's dream. Even the material of our physical selves is the servant of our thoughts: psychologists recognize the fact that our bodies may become tired only because of tiredness in the mind. Worry, anxiety, fear and boredom are felt as physical: mind-fatigue appears to us as bodily fatigue.

One basic reason for tiredness of mind is the conflict in all of us between ideal and achievement, between what we ought to be and what we are, between our longing and our having, between our powers of understanding and the incomprehensible mysteries of the universe. A house divided against itself cannot stand; this perennial tension in man can be accepted and made bearable only by a surrender of the self to God. Then whatever happens is welcomed as a gift of love: frustration cannot happen to us for we have no clamorous, selfish will.

Society can be saved only if man is saved from his unbearable conflicts, and man can be rescued from them only if his soul is saved. Once, not so long ago, men put their hope of happiness in material advance; now that mood of shallow optimism has ended; the heavy burden of worry and anxiety about the future of the race and of the individual has made men conscious of their souls.

Third: Our happiness consists in fulfilling the purpose of our being. Every man knows, from his own unfulfilled hunger for them, that he was built with a capacity for three things of which he never has enough. He wants life—not for the next few minutes, but for always, and with no aging or disease to threaten it. He also wants to grasp truth—not with a forced choice between the truths of mathematics or geography, but he wants all truth. Thirdly, he wants love—not with a time-limit, not mixed with satiety or disillusionment, but love that will be an abiding ecstasy.

These three things are not to be found in this life in their completion: on earth life is shadowed by death, truth mingles with error, love is mixed with hate. But men know they would not long for these things in their purity if there were no possibility of ever finding them. So, being reasonable, they search for the source from which these mixed and imperfect portions of life, love, truth derive.

The search is like looking for the source of light in a room: it cannot come from under a chair, where light is mixed with darkness and shadow. But it can come from the sun, where light is pure with neither shadow nor darkness dulling it. In looking for the source of love, light, truth, as we know it here, we must go out beyond the limits of this shadowed world—to a Truth not mingled with its shadow, error—to a Life not mingled with its shadow, death—to a Love not mingled with its shadow, hate. We must seek for Pure Life, Pure Truth and Pure Love—and that is the definition of God. His Life is personal enough to be a Father; His Truth is personal and comprehensible enough to be a Son; His Love is so deep and spiritual that it is a Spirit.

When enough men have found this way to happiness, they will find one another in brotherhood. Social peace will then ensue.

Chapter 1

Contentment

Contentment is not an innate virtue. It is acquired through great resolution and diligence in conquering unruly desires; hence it is an art which few study. Because there are millions of discontented souls in the world today, it might be helpful for them to analyze the four main causes of discontent, and to suggest means to contentment.

The principle cause of discontent is egotism, or selfishness, which sets the self up as a primary plant around which everyone else must revolve. The second cause of discontent is envy, which makes us regard the possessions and the talents of others as if they were stolen from us. The third cause is covetousness, or an inordinate desire to have more, in order to compensate for the emptiness of our heart. The fourth cause of discontent is jealousy, which is sometimes occasioned through melancholia and sadness, and at other times by a hatred of those who have what we wish for ourselves.

One of the greatest mistakes is to think that contentment comes from something outside us rather than from a quality of the soul. There was once a boy who only wanted a marble; when he had a marble, he only wanted a ball; when he had a ball, he only wanted a top; when he had a top, he only wanted a kite, and when he had the marble, the ball, the top, and the kite, he still was not happy. Trying to make a discontented person happy is like trying to fill a sieve with water. However much you pour into it, it runs out too rapidly for you to catch up.

Nor is contentment to be found in an exchange of places. There are some who believe that if they were in a different part of the earth they would have a greater peace of soul. A goldfish, in a globe in water, and a canary in a cage, on a hot day, began talking. The fish said: "I wish I could swing like that canary; I'd like to be up there in that cage." And the canary said: "Oh, how nice to be down in that cool water where the fish is." Suddenly a voice said: "Canary, go down to the water! Fish, go up to the cage!" Immediately, they exchanged places, but neither was happy, because God originally had given each a place according to his ability, one that best suited his own nature.

The condition of our contentment is to be contained, to recognize limits. Whatever is within limits is likely to be quiet. A walled garden is one of the quietest places in the world; the world is shut out, and through its gates one can look upon it with the affection of distance, borrowing enchantment from it. So, if the soul of man is kept within limits (that is to say, not avaricious, greedy, over-reaching nor selfish), it, too, is shut into a calm, quiet, sunny contentment. Contented man, limited and bound by circumstances, makes those very limits the cure of his restlessness. It is not to the point whether a garden has one acre or three, or whether or not it has a wall; what matters is that we shall live within its bounds, whether they be large or small, in order that we can possess a quiet spirit and a happy heart.

Contentment, therefore, comes in part from faith—that is, from knowing the purpose of life and being assured that whatever the trials are, they come from the hand of a Loving Father. Secondly, in order to have contentment one must also have a good conscience. If the inner self is unhappy because of moral failures and unatoned guilt, then nothing external can give rest to the spirit. A third and final need is mortification of desires, the limitation of delights. What we over-love, we often over-grieve. Contentment enhances our enjoyment and diminishes our misery. All evils become lighter if we endure them patiently, but the greatest benefits can be poisoned by discontent. The miseries of life are sufficiently deep and extensive, without our adding to them unnecessarily.

Contentment with our worldly condition is not inconsistent with the desire for betterment. To the poorest man, Christianity says not to be merely content, but "be diligent in business." The contentment enjoined is for the time being. Man is poor today, and for this day, faith enjoins him to be satisfied; but deliverance from his poverty may be best for tomorrow, and therefore the poor man works for his increased prosperity. He may not succeed; if his poverty continues for another day, he accepts it, and then proceeds until relief comes. Thus, contentment is relative to our present state, and is not absolute in respect to the entire demands of our nature. A contented man is never poor though he have very, very little. The discontented man is never rich, let him have so very much.

Chapter 2

Reducing Ego to Zero

THE chief cause of inner unhappiness is egotism or selfishness. He who gives himself importance by boasting is actually showing the credentials of his own worthlessness. Pride is an attempt to create an impression that we are what we actually are not.

How much happier people would be if instead of exalting their ego to infinity, they reduced it to zero. They would then find the true infinite through the rarest of modern virtues: humility. Humility is truth about yourselves. A man who is six feet tall, but who says: "I am only five feet tall," is not humble. He who is a good writer is not humble if he says: "I am a scribbler." Such statements are made in order that there might be a denial and thus win praise. Rather he would be humbler who says: "Well, whatever talent I have is a gift of God and I thank Him for it." The higher the building the deeper the foundation; the greater the moral heights to which we aspire the greater the humility. As John the Baptist said when he saw Our Lord: "I must decrease; He must increase." Flowers humbly depart in the winter to see their mother roots. Dead to the world, they keep house under the earth in humble humility, unseen by the eyes of men. But because they humbled themselves, they are exalted and glorified in the new springtime.

Only when a box is empty can it be filled; only when the ego is deflated can God pour in His blessings. Some are already so stuffed with their own ego that it is impossible for love of neighbor or love of God to enter. By seeking their own constantly, everyone disowns them. But humility makes us receptive to the giving of others. You could not give unless I took. It is the taker that makes the giver. So God, before He can be Giver, must find a taker. But if one is not humble enough to receive from God, then he receives nothing.

A man possessed by the devil was brought to a Father of the Desert When the saint commanded the devil to leave, the devil asked: "What is the difference between the sheep and the goats whom the Lord will put at His right and His left Hand the day of Judgment?" The saint answered: "I am one of the goats." The Devil said: "I leave because of your humility."

Many say: "I have labored for years for others and even for God, and what did I get out of it? I am still nothing." The answer is, they have gained something; they have gained the truth of their own littleness— and of course, great merit in the next life. One day two men were in a carriage. One said: "There is not enough room for you here in this seat." The other said: "We will love each other a little more, and then there will be room enough." Ask a man: "Are you a saint?" If he answers in the affirmative, you can be very sure that he is not.

The humble man concentrates on his own errors, and not upon those of others; he sees nothing in his neighbor but what is good and virtuous. He does not carry his own faults on his back, but in front of him. The neighbor's defects he carries in a sack on his back, so he will not see them. The proud man, on the contrary, complains against everybody and believes that he has been wronged or else not treated as he deserves. When the humble man is treated badly he does not complain for he knows that he is treated better than he deserves. From a spiritual point of view, he who is proud of his intelligence, talent or voice, and never thanks God for them is a robber; he has taken gifts from God and never recognized the Giver. The ears of barley which bear the richest grain always hang the lowest. The humble man is never discouraged, but the proud man falls into despair. The humble man still has God to call upon; the proud man has only his own ego that has collapsed.

One of the loveliest prayers for humility is that of Saint Francis: *"Lord, make me an instrument of Thy peace. Where there is hatred, let there be love; where there is injury, pardon; where there is doubt, faith; where there is despair, hope; where there is darkness, light; where there is sadness, joy. O Divine Master, grant that I may not seek so much to be consoled as to console; to be understood as to understand; to be loved as to love. For it is in giving that we receive, it is in pardon that we are pardoned, it is in dying that we are born to Eternal Life."*

CHAPTER 3

JOY

Joy is the delightful experience of the feelings of pleasure at a good gained and actually enjoyed or the prospect of good which one has a reasonable hope of obtaining. There can be both natural joys and spiritual joys. Natural joys would be the joy of youth before disappointment has stretched the soul, or the joy of health when food is pleasant and sweet, or the joy of success when the battle has been won, or the joys of affection when the heart is loved. All these natural joys are intensified by spiritual joys and put upon a more enduring basis. No earthly happiness would be permanent or thorough if it were not associated with a good conscience.

Spiritual joy is a serenity of temper in the midst of the changes of life, such as a mountain has when a storm breaks over it. To a man who has never rooted the soul in the Divine every trouble exaggerates itself. He cannot put his full powers to any one thing because he is troubled about many things.

A joy is not the same as levity. Levity is an act, joy a habit. Mirth is like a meteor, cheerfulness like a star; mirth is like crackling thorns, joy like a fire. Joy being more permanent makes difficult actions easier. Soldiers after a long day's march would hardly walk as nimbly as they do, if they did not march to music. A cheerful heart always finds a yoke easy and a burden light.

Certainly no nurse is helpful in a sick room unless she has the spirit of cheerfulness. Every nurse really ought to have two things before she enters a sick room: an incision and a sense of humor. An incision in order that she may know the value of pain; a sense of humor in order that she may know how to diffuse happiness. This incision need not be physical but it should at least be symbolic, in the sense that there should be a deep appreciation of the woes and sufferings of others. There is nothing that so much adds to the longevity of sickness as a long face.

Joy has much more to do with the affections than with reason. To the man with a family his wife and children call out and sustain his delights much more than his intellect could ever stimulate. Standing before a cradle a father seems face to face with the attributes of the everlasting Being Who has infused His tenderness and love into the babe. The power of rejoicing is always a fair test of a man's moral condition. No man can be happy on the outside who is already unhappy on the inside. If a sense of guilt weighs down the soul no amount of pleasure on the outside can compensate for the loss of joy on the inside. As sorrow is attendant on sin, so joy is the companion of holiness.

Joy can be felt in both prosperity and adversity. In prosperity it consists not in the goods we enjoy but in those we hope for; not in the pleasures we experience but in the promise of those which we believe without our seeing. Riches may abound but those for which we hope are the kind which moths do not eat, rust consume, nor thieves break through and steal. Even in adversity there can be joy in the assurance that the Divine Master Himself died through the Cross as the condition of His Resurrection.

If joy be uncommon today it is because there are timid souls who have not the courage to forget themselves and to make sacrifices for their neighbor, or else because the narrower sympathies make the brighter things of the world to come, appear as vanities. As the pull from the belief in God and the salvation of the soul fade from life, so also joy vanishes and one returns to the despair of the heathens. The old Greeks and Romans always saw a shadow across their path and a skeleton at their feet. It was no surprise that one day a Roman who had nothing to live for, nothing to hope for, entered his bath and opened a vein and so bled quietly and painlessly to death. A famous Greek poet once said of life that it was better not to be born, and the next best thing was to quit life as soon as possible. All this is at the other extreme from St. Paul, who said: "Rejoice in the Lord always and again I say, Rejoice."

Chapter 4

Is Modern Man Far From Peace?

No one is dangerously unhappy except the individual who does not know what happiness means. Life is unbearable only to those who are ignorant of why they are alive; men in such a condition of soul equate happiness with pleasure (which is a very different matter) and identify joy with a tingling of the nerve-endings (which it is not). But things which are external to us never bring us inner peace. The more persistently anyone looks for satisfaction and a goal to serve in something outside of his control, the less stable he will find it, the more subject he will be to disappointments.

There are two movements towards happiness. The first of these is our withdrawal from the outside ... from too great an absorption in the things of the world. The second movement is far more profound: it is an ascension from what is inferior within us to what is its superior, from our egotism to our God. Modern man has experienced the first movement; exterior things have become so many sources of misery to him. Wars, depressions, the insecurity and emptiness of life have so terrified men that they have tried to close off their contacts with the outside world and have begun to seek for satisfactions in their own limited selves. That is why psychiatry is having such a field-day: the modern soul, alarmed at what it finds without, has drawn down the shades and begun to look for contentment in analyzing its own unconsciousness, anxieties and fears, its doldrums and frustrations.

But such self-containment can prove a prison if one is locked into it with his own ego alone, for there is no more confining strait-jacket in the world than that of the self left to itself. The cure never lies in using a psychoanalytic scalpel to release the inner moral pus and watch it flow; that is a morbid act for both the patient and the doctor. The cure, rather, consists in discovering why one is lonely, and afraid of solitude—for most people have a dread of being alone, without knowing why the prospect frightens them.

The problem of our day is this problem of finding interior peace, and it is in this that the twentieth century is marked off from the nineteenth. A hundred years ago men looked to the exterior world for the answers to their problems: they worshipped science or nature, expected happiness to come from progress or politics or profits. The twentieth century man is worried about himself: he is even more concerned over the problem of sex than by sex itself—is interested in the mental attitude he should take towards it, rather than in its physical satisfaction and the begetting of children. His own values, moods and attitudes absorb him.

Although a great deal of nonsense has been written about the interior life of men in our day, it is still true that the twentieth century is closer to God than the nineteenth century was. We are living on the eve of one of the great spiritual revivals of human history. Souls are sometimes closest to God when they feel themselves farthest away from Him, at the point of despair. For an empty soul, the Divine can fill; a worried soul, the Infinite can pacify. A self-concerned, proud soul, however, is inaccessible to Grace.

Modern man has been humiliated: neither his proud expectations of progress nor of science have turned out as he hoped. Yet he has not quite reached the point of humbling himself. He is still imprisoned in the self, and able to see nothing else beyond. The psychoanalysts may be allowed to bore into his thoughts for a few years more; but the time is not far off when modern men will utter a frantic appeal to God to lift them from the empty cistern of their own egos. St. Augustine knew it well: he said, "Our hearts are restless until they rest in Thee."

That is why—although a catastrophic war may threaten us—the times are not as bad as they seem. Modern man has not yet returned to God; but he has, at least, returned to himself. Later he will surpass and transcend himself with God's grace, which he is seeking, even now. No one ever looked for something unless he knew that it existed; today the frustrated soul is looking for God, as for the memory of a name he used to know.

The difference between those who have found God in faith and those who are still seeking Him is like the difference between a wife, happy in the enjoyment of her husband's companionship, and a young girl wondering if she will ever find a husband, and perhaps trying to attract men by the wrong approach. Those who search for pleasure, fame and wealth are all seeking the Infinite, but the seekers are still on the outskirts of the Eternal City. Those with faith have penetrated to their real home within the Infinite and have found the "peace which the world cannot give." As 6ne can see a figure far off and not yet recognize him as a long-lost friend, so one can sense the need of the Infinite and desire the endless ecstasy of love, but not yet know that it is God.

It makes no difference how wicked a soul may be, there is no one subjecting himself to illicit pleasures who does not have a consciousness of his subjection and his slavery. Perhaps that is why alcoholics are often liars; their lips deny a slavery which their lives so visibly witness. Such individuals, unwilling to admit themselves mistaken, still refuse to be convinced of Divine Truth; but their sadness and their emptiness will eventually drive them to the God of Mercy.

Our exterior world today is in desperate straits, but the inner world of man is far from hopeless. The world of politics and economics lags behind the psychological development of men themselves. The world is far from God, but human hearts are not. That is why peace will come less from political changes than from man himself, who, driven to take refuge within his own soul from the turmoil without, will be lifted above himself to the happiness for which he was made.

Chapter 5

Joy From The Inside

Each of us makes his own weather, determines the color of the skies in the emotional universe which he inhabits. We can, by a creative effort, bring such sunlight to our souls that it makes radiant whatever events may come our way. We can, on the other hand, permit ourselves to slump into a state of inner depression so deep and filled with gloom that only the most intense outward stimulations of the senses are able to rouse us from our apathy.

Everyone must have pleasure, the philosophers tell us. The man who has integrated his personality in accordance with its nature, and oriented his life towards God knows the intense and indestructible pleasure the saints called joy. No outward event can threaten him or ruffle his happiness. But many men look outward for their pleasure and expect the accidents of their lives to provide their happiness. Since nobody can make the universe his slave, everyone who looks outward for pleasure is bound to disappointment. A glut of entertainment wearies us; a realized ambition becomes a bore; a love that promised full contentment loses its glamour and its thrill. Lasting happiness can never come from the world. Joy is not derived from the things we get or the people we meet; it is manufactured by the soul itself, as it goes about its self-forgetful business.

The secret of a happy life is the moderation of our pleasures in exchange for an increase of joy. But several contemporary practices make this difficult for us. One of these is the type of merchandising which tries to increase our desires in order that we shall buy more goods. Allied with this, is the spoiled-child psychology of modern man, which tells him that he is entitled to get anything he wants, that the world owes everyone the satisfaction of his whims. Once the ego has become the center around which everything else revolves, we are vulnerable

: our peace can be destroyed by a draft from an open window, by our inability to buy a coat made of some exotic fur so rare that only twenty women in the world can wear it—by our failure to get invited to a luncheon, or our failure to pay the biggest income-tax in the nation. The ego is always insatiable, if it is in command; no indulgences and no honors quiet its craving, either for "madder music and for a stronger wine," or for the heady delights of testimonial dinners and 72-point headlines.

The ego-centered men view as calamities the denial of any of their wishes: they want to dominate their world, to pull its puppet-strings and force those about them to obey their will. If such an ego's wishes are crossed and checked by another ego, its owner is in despair. Occasions for despondency and sadness are thus multiplied, for all of us are bound to be denied some of the things we want—it is our choice whether this loss shall be accepted with a cheerful good grace or taken as an outrage and an affront to us.

Today millions of men and women consider that their happiness is destroyed if they must get along without a few things of which their grandfathers had never dreamed. Luxuries have become necessities to them; and the more things a man needs in order to be happy, the more he has increased his chances of disappointment and despair. Whim has become his master, trivia his tyrant; he no longer is self-possessed, but he has become possessed by outward objects, trumpery toys.

Plato in his "Republic" wrote of the man whose life is run by his whims and fancies; his words were written 2,300 years ago, but they are still pat today: "Often he will take to politics, leaping to his feet, and do or say whatever comes into his head; or he conceives an admiration for a general and his interests turn to war; or for a man of business, and straightway that is his line. He knows no order or necessity in life; he will not listen to anyone who tells him that some pleasures come in the gratification of good and noble desires, others from evil ones, and that the former should be fostered and encouraged, the latter disciplined and chained. To all such talk, he shakes his head and says that all enthusiasms are similar and worthy of equal attention."

Pleasures must be arranged in a hierarchy if we are to get the greatest enjoyment out of life. The most intense and lasting joys come only to those who are willing to practice a certain self-restraint, to undergo the boredom of a preliminary discipline. The best view is from the mountain-top, but it may be arduous to reach it. No man ever enjoyed reading Horace without drilling himself with the declensions of his grammar first. Full happiness is understood only by those who have denied themselves some legitimate pleasures in order to obtain deferred joys. Men who "let themselves go," go to seed or go mad. The Saviour of the world

Himself told us that the best joys come only after we have purchased them by prayer and fasting: we must give up our copper pennies first, out of love for Him, and He will pay us back in pieces of gold, in joy and ecstasy.

Chapter 6
Love Is Infinite

THERE is a profound difference in quality between the possessions that we need, and use, and actually enjoy, and the accumulation of useless things we accumulate out of vanity or greed or the desire to surpass others. The first kind of possession is a legitimate extension of our personalities: we enrich a much-used object by our love, and it becomes dear to us. We can learn about the two kinds of ownership in any nursery: a child who has only a single toy enriches it with his love. The spoiled child, with many play-things spread out for him, quickly becomes blase and ceases to take pleasure in any one of them. The quality of his love diminishes with the number of objects offered for his love ... as a river has less depth, the more it spreads over the plains.

When we visit a large mansion, inhabited by only two people, we feel the coldness of such a house, too vast to be made a home by human love. Each of us, by his presence, can ennoble a few cubic feet ... but no more. The more people own beyond the limit of things they can personalize and love, the more they will suffer boredom, ennui and satiety.

Yet men and women are forever trying to add to their possessions far beyond the limit of enjoyment. This is because of their mistaken belief that their hunger for Infinity can be satisfied by an infinity of material things: what they really wish is the Infinity of Divine Love.

Our imaginations are easily misled into desiring a false infinity, when once we begin to long for "wealth". For "wealth" and "money" are things that appeal to the imagination, which is insatiable in its wishes. Real goods, such as those our bodies need, have not this quality: there is a narrow limit to the amount of food our stomachs will hold and when that is reached, we do not wish for more. Our Lord fed the five thousand in the desert with fish and bread, and all of them had their fill. But if

He had given them, instead, $20,000 war bonds, no single person would have said, "One is enough for me."

Credit-wealth ... stocks, bonds, bank-balances ... have no set limit, at which we say, "No more". They have in them a caricature-infinity, which allows men to use them as false religions, as substitutes for the true Infinity of God. Like money, love and power can become ersatz religions: those who pursue these things as ends will never find satisfaction. Such men are all in pursuit of God, but they do not know His name, nor where to look for Him.

Since every increase in quantity among the things we love brings a decrease in the quality of love, there are two ways by which we may hope to keep love pure. One is to give away in proportion as we receive: this habit reminds us that we are merely trustees of God's riches, not their rightful owners. Yet few people risk doing this: they are afraid to touch their "capital", and every cent they add to it becomes part of the sacred pile which must not be disturbed. They become identified with what they love; if it is wealth, they cannot bear to part with any portion of its accumulated burden.

The second way of preserving ourselves from an unseemly greed is the heroic way ... the way of complete detachment from wealth, as practiced by St. Francis of Assisi and all those who take the vows of poverty. There is a paradox in such a renunciation, for the man who has given up even the hope of "security" is the richest man in the world; he is the most secure of all of us, for he wants nothing ... and that is a boast that no millionaire can make. Everyone's power of renunciation is greater than anyone's power to possess: no man can own the earth, but any man can disown it.

The misers may fill their wallets, but never their hearts, for they cannot obtain all the wealth they are able to imagine and desire. But the poor in heart are rich in happiness. God gave us love enough to spend in getting back to Him so that we could find Infinity there; he did not give us love enough to hoard.

Chapter 7

The Philosophy
Of Pleasure

We all want happiness. We should all take the sensible step of learning that there are three laws of pleasure which, if followed, will make the attainment of happiness immeasurably easier.

The first law. If you are ever to have a good time, you cannot plan your life to include nothing but good times. Pleasure is like beauty; it is conditioned by contrast. A woman who wants to show off her black velvet dress will not, if she is wise, stand against a black curtain, but against a white curtain. She wants the contrast. Fireworks would not delight us if they were shot off against a background of fire, or in the blaze of the noonday sun: they need to stand out against the darkness. Lilies bring us a special pleasure because their petals rise, surprisingly, on the waters of foul ponds. Contrast is needed to help us see each thing as being vividly itself.

Pleasure, by the same principle, is best enjoyed when it comes to us as a "treat," in contrast to experiences that are less pleasurable. We make a great mistake if we try to have all our nights party-nights. No one would enjoy Thanksgiving if every dinner were a turkey dinner. New Year's Eve would not delight us if the whistles blew at midnight every night.

Fun rests on contrast, and so does the enjoyment of a funny situation. If a Bishop has a mitre thrust on the side of his head by an errant master of ceremonies, it makes us laugh; it would not be funny if all Bishops always wore their mitres askew.

Our enjoyment of life is vastly increased if we follow the spiritual injunction to bring some mortification and self-denial into our lives. This practice saves us from being jaded; it preserves the tang and joy of living. The harp-strings of our lives are not thin, made slack by being pulled until they are out of tune; instead, we tighten them and help preserve their harmony.

Self-discipline brings back to us the excitement of our childhood, when our pleasures were rationed—when we got our dessert at the end of the meal and never at the start.

The second law. Pleasure is deepened and enhanced when it has survived a moment of tedium or pain: this law helps us to make our prized pleasures last for a whole lifetime. To do so, we must keep going at anything we do until we get our second wind. One enjoys a mountain climb more after passing through the first moment of discouraged exhaustion. One becomes more interested in a job of work after the first impulse to drop it has been overcome.

In the same way, marriages become stable only after disillusionment has brought the honeymoon to an end. The great value of the marital vow is in keeping the couple together during the first quarrel; it tides them over their early period of resentment, until they get the second wind of true happiness at being together. Married joys, like all great joys, are born out of some pain. As we must crack the nut to taste the sweet so, in the spiritual life, the cross must be the prelude to the crown.

The third law. Pleasure is a by-product, not a goal. Happiness must be our bridesmaid, not our bride. Many people make the great mistake of aiming directly at pleasure; they forget that pleasure comes only from the fulfillment of a duty or obedience to a law—for man is made to obey the laws of his own nature as inescapably as he must obey the law of gravity. A boy has pleasure eating ice-cream because he is fulfilling one of the "oughts" of human nature: eating. If he eats more ice-cream than the laws of his body sanction, he will no longer get the pleasure he seeks, but the pain of a stomach ache. To seek pleasure, regardless of law, is to miss it.

Shall we start with pleasure or end with it? There are two answers to the question: the Christian and the pagan. The Christian says, "Begin with the fast and end with the feast, and you will really savor it." The pagan says, "Begin with the feast and end with the morning-after headache."

Chapter 8
Work

VERY FEW people in this age do the kind of work they like to do. Instead of choosing their jobs from choice, they are forced by economic necessity to work at tasks which fail to satisfy them. Many of them say, "I ought to be doing something bigger," or "This job of mine is only important because I get paid." Such an attitude lies at the bottom of much unfinished and badly-executed work. The man who chooses his work because it fulfills a purpose he approves is the only one who grows in stature by working. He alone can properly say,- at the end of it, "It is finished!"

This sense of vocation is sadly lacking nowadays. The blame should not be placed on the complexity of our economic system, but on a collapse of our spiritual values. Any work, viewed in its proper perspective, can be used to ennoble us; but a necessary prelude to seeing this is to understand the philosophy of labor.

Every task we undertake has two aspects—our purpose, which makes us think it worth doing, and the work itself, regarded apart from its end purpose. We play tennis to get exercise; but we play the game as well as possible, just for the joy of doing the thing well. The man who argued that he could get as much exercise by sloppy technique on the courts would have missed an understanding of the second aspect of all activity: the accomplishment of the task in accordance with its own standards of excellence. In the same way, a man working in an automobile factory may have, as his primary purpose, the earning of wages; but the purpose of the work itself is the excellent completion of the task. A workman should be aware of the second purpose at all times—as the artist is aware of the aim of beauty in his painting and the housewife is aware of the need for neatness when she dusts.

Today the first aspect of working has become paramount, and we tend to ignore the second ... so that many workmen lead half-lives in their laboring hours. They are like gardeners, ordered to grow cabbage to give them sauerkraut juice, but indifferent as to whether their plots are weeded properly or their cabbages are healthy vegetables. This is a mistaken attitude: God Himself worked when he made the world and then, viewing it, He called it "good."

The legitimate pride in doing work well relieves it of much of its drudgery. Some people, who have held to this craftsman's standard, get a thrill from any job they do. They know the satisfaction of "a job well done" whether they are engaged in caning a chair or cleaning a horse's stall or carving a statue for a Cathedral. Their honor and their self-respect are heightened by the discipline of careful work. They have retained the old attitude of the middle ages, when work was a sacred event, a ceremony, a source of spiritual merit. Labor was not then undertaken merely for the sake of economic gain, but was chosen through an inner compulsion, through a desire to project the creative power of God through our own human effort.

No task should be undertaken in a spirit which ignores either of these two primary aspects of work. To link together the two things ... the joy of making a table well with the purpose of making it at all, which is to earn a living ... the following principles should be kept in mind:

(1) Work is a moral duty and not, as many men imagine, a mere physical necessity. St. Paul said, "The man who refuses to work must be left to starve." When work is seen as a moral duty, it is apparent that it not only contributes to the social good, but also performs further services to the worker himself: it prevents the idleness from which many evils can arise and it also keeps his body in subjection to the reasoned will.

(2) "To work is to pray." The well-regulated life does not defer prayer until work has been accomplished; it turns the work itself into a prayer. We accomplish this when we turn to God at the beginning and completion of each task and mentally offer it up for love of Him. Then, whether we are nursing a child or making carburetors, turning a lathe or running an elevator, the task is sanctified. No amount of piety in leisure hours can compensate for slipshod labor on the job. But any honest task, well done, can be turned into a prayer.

(3) A medieval economist, Antonio of Florence, summed up the relationship of work to life in the happy formula: *"The object of making money is that we may provide for ourselves and our dependents. The object of providing for self and others is that one may live virtuously. The object of living virtuously is to save our souls and attain eternal happiness."*

Work should, in justice, receive two kinds of reward—for it is not only individual, but also social. John Jones, who works in a mine, is tired at the end of the day: this is his individual sacrifice. For it he receives his wages. But John Jones has also, during the day, made a social contribution to the economic well-being of the country and the world. For this social contribution, John Jones today is given nothing ... although he has a moral right to a share of the social wealth his work creates. We need a modification of the wage system, so that the worker may share in the profits, ownership or management of his industry. When labor leaders and capitalists thus agree together to give labor some capital to defend, there will no longer be two rival groups in industry; labor and management will become two cooperating members working together, as the two legs of a man cooperate to help him walk.

Chapter 9
Repose

NEVER BEFORE have men possessed so many time-saving devices. Never before have they had so little time for leisure or repose. Yet few of them are aware of this: advertising has created in modern minds the false notion that leisure and-not-working are the same—that the more we are surrounded by bolts and wheels, switches and gadgets, the more time we have conquered for our own.

But this division of our days into working and not-working is too simple; in practice, for most men, it leaves out the very possibility of real leisure. They waste precious hours away from work in aimless loafing, in negative waiting-around for something interesting to come along.

True repose is not a mere intermission between the acts of the working-life. It is an intense activity, but of a different kind. Just as sleeping is not a cessation of life, but living of a different sort from wakefulness, so repose is an activity no less creative than that of our working hours.

Repose—true leisure—cannot be enjoyed without some recognition of the spiritual world. For the first purpose of repose is the contemplation of the good ... its goal is a true perspective one, the small incidents of everyday life in their relation to the larger goodness that surrounds us. Genesis tells us that after the creation of the world, "God saw all that he had made, and found it very good." Such contemplation of his work is natural to man, whenever he, too, is engaged in a creative task. The painter stands back from his canvas, to see whether the details of the seascape are properly placed. True repose is such a standing back to survey the activities that fill our days.

We cannot get a real satisfaction out of our work unless we pause, frequently, to ask ourselves why we are doing it, and whether its purpose is one our minds wholeheartedly approve. Perhaps one reason why so many of our economic and political projects miscarry is because they are in the hands of men with eyes so tightly glued to what they are doing that they never stop to question whether it should be done at all. Merely keeping busy, merely getting paid can never satisfy man's need for a creative work.

A job of any kind can be lifted up and given Divine purpose, if it is seen in the perspective of Eternity. The sweeping of a floor, the driving of a garbage-truck, the checking of a list of box-car numbers—all these can be "made good" through a simple act of the will which directs them to the service of God. The simplest task can be given spiritual significance and made divine.

If we direct our work towards God, we shall work better than we know. The admission of this fact is another of the tasks for which we need repose. Once a week man, reposing from work, does well to come before his God to admit how much of what he did during the week was the work of his Creator; he can remind himself, then, that the material on which he labored came from Other hands, that the ideas he employed entered his mind from a Higher source, that the very energy which he employed was a gift of God.

In such a mood of true repose, the scientist will see that he himself was not the author of his research volume on nature's laws, but only its proof-reader. It was God who wrote the book. In such repose, the teacher will confess that every truth he passed on to his students was a ray from the sun of Divine Wisdom. The cook who peels potatoes after such a period of repose will handle them as humble gifts of God himself.

Repose allows us to contemplate the little things we do in their relationship to the vast things which alone can give them worth and meaning. It reminds us that all actions get their worth from God: "worship" means admitting "worth." To worship is to restore to our workaday life its true worth by setting it in its real relationship to God, who is its end and ours.

Such worship is a form of repose—of an intensely active and creative contemplation of Divine things, from which we arise refreshed. For the promise of the Gospel of St. Matthew is still waiting for those who are willing to hear it: *"Come to me, all you that labor and are burdened; I will give you rest."*

Chapter 10

The Idle in
The Marketplace

A GREAT and distinguished psychologist once said that the tragedy of man today was that he no longer believed he had a soul to save. To such a group Our Lord addressed His beautiful parable of the laborers in the vineyard. Toward the close of the day the master of the vineyard went to the marketplace and said: "Why stand you here all the day idle?" In certain places of the East this custom still prevails, men gathering in front of Mosques and public places with shovels in their hands, waiting to be hired.

This story has a spiritual application and refers to various kinds of idlers. In addition to those who idle in the literal sense, there are mere loafers with nothing to do. Many are idle in the sense of being industrious triflers, wearied with toils that accomplish no real worth. Many are idle because of constant indecision, and others become frustrated and worried, not knowing the purpose of life. To the human eye, there are not many idlers, but as the Eye of Heaven looks down to earth it must be like a vast marketplace wherein few labor. To the Divine, all such activity as the acquiring of wealth, marrying and giving in marriage, buying and selling, studying and painting, are all means to the supreme and final end which is the saving of one's soul. Every expenditure of human strength which makes what is a means an end, which isolates living from the goal of living, is a busy idleness, a sad and mournful unreality.

Despite this new and harsh definition of idleness which Our Divine Lord gives, there is nevertheless much hope in the story, for some were hired at the eleventh hour, and they received just as much as those who had labored all the day. It is never too late for God's grace. It is a peculiar psychological fact that those who turn to God late in life generally consider all their previous life wasted. St. Augustine reflecting on his wasted youth said: "Too late, O ancient Beauty have I loved Thee." There are no hopeless cases; no life is too far spent to be recouped; no life long idleness precludes a few minutes of useful work in the vineyard of the Lord even the last few hours of life, as was the case with the penitent thief.

When the Lord gave everyone at the end of the day the same wages, those who had borne the heat and burdens of the sun complained that those who came in at the eleventh hour received just as much. To which Our Divine Lord retorted: "Does your eye see evil because I do good?" The thought of reward does not enter into the heavenly service. Those who lead a moral life for forty years and then protest the late-comers' salvation have the spirit of the hireling. With all the true acts of the spiritual man, the inspiration is love and not a desire of reward. One can not speak of the rewards of a true love in marriage without insulting the husband and wife. One can not associate compensation with the affection that twines a child's arms about a mother's neck, or that keeps her waiting in vigils that outwatch the patient stars. One can not associate reward with the heroism of a man who would risk his life to save another. In like manner the servitors of daily piety and religion are as full of the charm and fascination and glory of self-forgetting devotion as any of these.

Physical idleness deteriorates the mind; spiritual idleness deteriorates the heart. The joint action of air and water can turn a bar to rust. Therefore at every hour in the marketplace, man must ask himself: "Why stand I here idle?"

Chapter 11
The Three Causes Of Love

EVERY LOVE rests on a tripod. Every love has three bases or supports: goodness, knowledge and similarity.

Take goodness first: a man may be mistaken in his choice of what seems to him to be good, but he can never desire anything unless he believes in its intrinsic goodness. The prodigal son was seeking something good for him— something to satisfy his hunger—when he tried to live on husks; he was wrong only in his judgment, in thinking husks a fit food for a man. All of us are in the same predicament as he. We are forever trying to fill our lives, our minds, our bodies, our homes with "goods," and we accept nothing unless it seems, at the moment, to have some good in it. But our estimates are not always correct; we may mistake an apparent for a real good, thus injuring ourselves.

Without this reaching-out towards goodness, there would be no love: neither love of country, nor of pleasures, of friend, nor of spouse. Through loving, each heart tries to acquire a perfection which it lacks, or to express the perfection it already owns. All love springs out of goodness, for goodness, by its nature, is lovable to man.

The goodness which we love in other people is not always a moral goodness; it may be physical goodness, or utilitarian goodness. In such cases, an individual is loved because of the pleasure that he gives us, or because he is useful to us, or because he can "get it for us wholesale," or for some other reason in which selfishness is involved. But even then, there is a good we seek in our loving and unless something somehow seems good to us, we simply cannot care for it.

But knowledge is also involved in every love: We cannot love what we do not know. "Introduce me to her," is the phrase of a man who seeks the knowledge of a woman which, he knows, must precede the possibility of his really loving her. Even the "dream girl" of the bachelor has to be built up from fragments of knowledge in his mind. Hatred comes from want of knowledge, as love comes from knowledge; thus, bigotry is properly related to ignorance.

Knowledge, in the early stages, is a condition of love; but as the relationship deepens, love increases knowledge. A wife and husband who have lived together many years possess a new kind of knowledge of each other, deeper than any spoken word or any analysis of motives could provide. This knowledge (impossible in the honeymoon weeks) comes gradually from love-inaction, as a kind of intuitional understanding of what lies in the mind and heart of the other. It is thus possible for us to love beyond our knowledge, to allow faith to fill up the insufficiency of our intellectual understanding. A simple person in good faith may therefore have a greater love of God than a theologian, and this love can give him a keener understanding of the ways of God with human hearts than any psychologist will possess.

One of the reasons why decent people shrink from vulgar discussions of sex is that the knowledge two people gain of one another in so intimate a relation is, by its very nature, incommunicable to others. The whole exchange is so personal that those involved shrink from sharing it with outsiders—the knowledge thus gained is too sacred to be profaned. And it is a psychological fact that those whose theoretical knowledge of sex has been realized in the unifying love of marriage at least inclined to bring the matter out of its twilit realm of shared mystery to the glaring light of public discussion. This is not, at all, because they are "disillusioned" about sex, but because sex has now been changed by the transcendent alchemy of love, so that its nature can no longer be understood by those who stand outside the shared experience. On the other hand those whose knowledge of sex has not been sublimated into the mystery of love (and who are therefore frustrated) are the ones who like to talk about sex. Husbands and wives whose marriages are marred by infidelity seek such discussions; fathers and mothers who are happy in their relation never want to mention it.

When knowledge has been transmuted to love, it fills the heart so full that no outsider could contribute anything further, and the matter need never be aired. People who talk about their intimate relations confess, by doing so, that they have not raised their love high enough to turn it into a mystery, or transformed it into the only kind of love between the sexes that deserves the name.

The third leg of the tripod on which love rests is similarity: similarity between two persons, leading to love, need not indicate that they are both alike in actual fact. It can mean merely that one possesses in actuality what the other owns potentially. Because the human heart, itself imperfect, desires perfection, we seek, through love, to make up for our own deficiencies. The homely young man will wish to marry a beautiful girl: the potential beauty (which he does not possess himself, but for which he has a hunger) attracts him to that which is beautiful beyond himself.

Similarity underlies even the most vulgar and tawdry of our loves. The woman who is a social climber cultivates "important" people because they possess, in actuality, what she would like to have, but lacks. On a much higher level, saints love sinners—not because they share developed qualities of soul, but because the saint is able to apprehend the possible virtue in the sinner. It was thus that the Son of God Himself became the Son of man: He loved what man might be and, in the words of St. Augustine, "He became man that man might become like God."

Chapter 12

When Lovers Fail There Is Love

MARRIAGES FAIL when love is regarded not as something transparent like a window pane which looks out on the heavens, but as something opaque like a curtain which sees nothing beyond the human. When couples do not see that the love of the flesh is the preface to the love of the spirit, one of the partners is often made the object of worship in place of God. This is the essence of idolatry, the worship of the image of the reality; the mistaking of the copy for the original, and the frame for the picture.

Human love promises something only God can give. When God is ignored in love, the one who was worshipped as a deity is discovered not to be a God, or even an angel. Because he or she did not give all that was promised, being incapable of giving it, because not Divine, the other feels betrayed, deceived, disappointed and cheated. The stem of the rose is blamed for not bearing what it could not bear, the marble bust of deity. The result is that erotic love turns to hate when the other is discovered to have feet of clay—to be a woman instead of an angel, to be a man instead of an Apollo. When the ecstasy does not continue, and the band stops playing, and the champagne of life loses its sparkle, the other partner is called a cheat and a robber. And then finally called to a divorce court on the grounds of incompatibility.

Then begins the search for a new partner, on the assumption that some other human being can supply what only God can give. Instead of seeing that the basic reason for the failure of marriage was the refusal to use married love as the vestibule of the Divine, one thinks that husks can satisfy, when one was meant to eat only the bread of angels. The very fact that a man or a woman seeks a new partner is a proof that there never was any love at all, for though sex is replaceable, love is not. Sex is for a pleasure; love is for a person.

Cows can graze on other pastures, but a person admits of no substitution. As soon as a person becomes equated with a package to be judged only by its wrappings, it will not be long when the tinsel turns green and the package will be discarded. This arrangement enslaves a woman, because she is much more a creature of time than man, and her security becomes less and less through the years. She is always much more concerned about her age than a man, and thinks more of marriage in terms of time. This is because a man is afraid of dying before he has lived, but a woman is basically afraid of dying before she has begotten life. A woman wants the fulfillment of life more than a man, and it is less the experience of life that she craves, than the prolongation of life. Whenever the laws and the customs of a country permit an arrangement whereby a woman can be discarded because she has dishpan hands, it ends by making her the slave not of dishpans but of man.

Life is not a snare nor an illusion. It would be that only if there were no Infinite to satisfy our yearnings. Everyone wants a Love that will never die and one that has no moments of hate or satiety. That Love lies beyond humans.

Human love is a spark from the great flame of Eternity. The happiness which comes from the unity of two in one flesh is a prelude to that greater communion of two in one spirit. In this way, marriage becomes a tuning fork to the song of the angels, or a river that runs to the sea. Then it is evident that there is an answer to the elusive mystery of love and that somewhere there is a reconciliation of the quest and the goal, and that is in final union with God, where the chase and the capture, the romance and the marriage fuse into one. For since God is boundless, Eternal Love, it will take an ecstatic eternal chase to sound its depths.

Chapter 13

True Love

THERE ARE two kinds of love: love for its own pleasure, or love for the sake of another; the first is carnal love, the second is spiritual. Carnal love knows the other person only in a biological moment. Spiritual love knows the other person at all moments. In erotic love, the burdens of the other are regarded as impairing one's own happiness; in spiritual love, the burdens of others are opportunities for service.

Somewhere along the line, the modern world has been duped and fooled into giving the name of love to some vague obsession which parades itself in every billboard advertisement, reigns in the film industry, puzzles dramatists who must solve triangles short of suicide, makes novels best sellers, perfumes so exotic as to be unfit for a tyro's concupiscence, and humor more spicy. Love has become so vulgarized, so carnalized, that those who really love are almost afraid to use the word. It is used now almost exclusively to describe one of the opposite sex, rather than a person; it is made to revolve around glands, rather than a will, and is centered in biology instead of personality. Even when it disguises itself as infatuation for another, it is nothing else than a desire to intensify its own self-centeredness.

Purely human love is the embryo of the Love of the Divine. One finds some suggestions of this in Plato, who argues that the purpose of love is to make the first step toward religion. He pictures love for beautiful persons being transformed into love for beautiful souls, then into a love of justice, goodness and finally God who is their source. Erotic love is, therefore, a bridge which one crosses, not a buttress where one sits and rests; it is not an airport but an airplane; it is always going somewhere else, upwards and onwards. All carnal love pre-supposes incompleteness, deficiency, yearning for completion, and an attraction for enrichment, for all love is a flight for immortality. There is a suggestion of

Divine Love in every form of erotic love, as the lake reflects the moon. The only reason there is love for creatures in human hearts, is that it may lead to the love of the Creator. As food is for the body, as body is for the soul, as the material is for the spiritual, so the flesh is for the eternal. That is why in the language of human love, there can often be detected the language of Divinity, such as "worship," "angel," "adore."

The Saviour did not crush and then extinguish the flames that burned in Magdalene's heart, but transfigured them to a new object of affection. The Divine commendation that was given to the woman who poured out the ointment on the feet of her Saviour, reminded her that love which once sought its own pleasure can be transmuted into a love that will die for the beloved. For that reason He referred to His burial at the very moment her thoughts were closest to life.

Because it is in the Divine plan to use the love of the flesh as a stepping stone to the love of the Divine, it always happens in a well regulated moral heart, that as time goes on, the erotic love diminishes, and the religious love increases. That is why in true marriages the love of God increases through the years, not in the sense that husband and wife love one another less, but that they love God more. Love passes from an affection for outer appearances, to those inner depths of personality which embody the Divine Spirit.

There are few things more beautiful in life than to see that deep passion of man for woman which begot children as the mutual incarnation of their love, transfigured into that deeper "passionless passion and wild tranquility" which is God.

Chapter 14
The Effects
Of Want Of Love

Most People in the world are unloved. Some do not make themselves lovable because of their selfishness; others do not have enough Christian spirit to love those who do not love them. The result is that the world is full of lonely hearts. Here we speak not of love in the romantic or carnal sense, but in the higher sense of generosity, forgiveness, kindness and sacrifice. Perhaps it would help some to know some of the psychological effects of not loving others in a really noble and unselfish way.

The first effect of not receiving love because one is generous and loving toward others is cynicism and even hostility. Never a good word can be said for anyone. Because one is unloved one tries to make everyone else unlovable. Characters are assassinated, the noblest motives reduced to the basest, and slanders believed and propagated. When others do show them kindness they look "for the catch in it"; even gifts are viewed with suspicion and the sincerest of compliments acknowledged with a charge of insincerity. Because such egotists are so miserable they seek to make everyone else miserable. Never once do they see that they are the cause of their own unhappiness. Someone else is always to blame. "I bumped into the other car, because you made me nervous this morning at breakfast by asking about my bank balance." "I have a cold now because you did not give me a mink coat like the wives of the other officials have."

And the effect of want of love is the martyrdom complex, which is a morbid attempt to get pity or sympathy when real love is gone. Feigning sickness is one of the tricks. Because good health does not win the affection of others, one pretends to be wounded in the firm hope that someone else will bind the wounds. The "pain" which is in the mind is loss of love. That "pain" is translated into the body and becomes sickness. If one could put into words what goes on inside of such a person it might be this: "I really want to be well. But if I become sick, then others must love me." Just as headaches can be caused by a desire to escape responsibility, so disease can be caused by a desire to win affection. This reaches a point in some where they become bed-ridden for years or unable to walk. In the San Francisco earthquake it was said that over thirty people who had not walked in over a period of twenty years, got up and walked. These were mental, not physical cripples.

Another type of reaction is in those who admit that they need love, but say: "I will pretend from now on that I do not need it." As a result they develop a false spirit of independence, become quarrelsome, oppose every idea and suggestion regardless of how good it is, develop anti-social instincts, smoke in front of no-smoking signs, and park in front of no-parking signs. Hardness and roughness and a certain toughness and boorishness of character is many times nothing other than a bold front for want of love.

It is very likely that the over-emphasis on security in society today is due to a want of love. In other generations people wanted to be happy, and many of them were happy in the framework both of a family and of a permanent marriage bond, or in the embrace of religion. Now the instability of the home through divorce is increasing. A substitute must be found for married love, and it comes out in a ruthless quest for power and security which is only one of the lesser ingredients of happiness. The business man who is completely lost in his business and stays at the office late hours rather than go home may sometimes be doing that to compensate for his want of love at home. Some doctors are now tracing some skin diseases to mental causes. It has been said that some people who are afraid to "face the world" develop skin blemishes. A "Stained mind" becomes a "stained body." Whatever be the medical evidence to support this view, it is true that no group of women seem to have complexions like nuns. Most of them never look into a mirror, but they have one incomparably fine beauty aid which many other people lack, namely, a good conscience and peace of soul. The skin of those who suffer with a hidden sense of guilt almost tells the story of the diseases going on inside the soul. One person who had repressed guilt and kept saying to herself: "I am a moral leper," developed a skin infection which vanished when reconciliation was made with her husband.

There is no cure for want of love but love. There will always be love for the lovable, but there will never be love for the unlovable unless we begin to love them for God's sake. Thus we are brought back again to religion and to God whose New Testament definition of His essence is: "God is love."

Chapter 15

Reflections On Love

THE EGO has a peculiar way of disguising the real reasons of its love. It can pretend to be interested in another's welfare while actually it is seeking its own pleasure.

There are some people who love to boast of their tolerance, but actually it is inspired by egotism; they want to be left alone in their own ideas, however wrong they be, so they plead for a tolerance of other people's ideas. But this kind of tolerance is very dangerous, for it becomes intolerance as soon as the ego is disturbed or menaced. That is why a civilization which is tolerant about false ideas instead of being charitable to persons is on the eve of a great wave of intolerance and persecution.

The egotist always considers his ego in terms of not having or wanting something. His principle action is drawing something to himself like the mouth which absorbs food. There is no outgoing, no service, and never a sacrifice, because he interprets sacrifice as the diminishing of himself.

True love, on the contrary, feels that the need to give is more imperious than the need to receive. At the beginning of love there is a feeling that one can never give enough. Regardless of how precious the gift, it still seems to fall short of what one would offer. Price tags are torn off, because we want no proportion established between the gift and the need of giving. The tragedy of love when it begins to die, is that then people do not even give what they have. No longer is there a question of not being able to give enough; there is rather no giving at all.

In real love there is pity and need. Pity in the sense that one feels the need of expansion and of giving to the point of exhaustion; need, because of a void that one would see filled. True love receives without ever interpreting what is given. It never seeks another motive than that of love itself. He who asks "Why" something is given does not trust.

One of the tragedies of our time is that freedom is interpreted in terms of freedom from something instead of in terms of love. The man who loves everybody is the free man; the man who hates is the man who has already enslaved himself. The man who hates is dependent on that which he cannot love—and therefore he is not free. To hate one's next door neighbor is a restriction of freedom. It demands walking around the block so one will not see him, or waiting until he leaves the house before leaving oneself.

It is our loves and desires that determine our pains. If our supreme love is the pleasure of the body, then our greatest pain is loss of health; if our supreme love is wealth, then our deepest worry is insecurity; if our supreme love is God, then our greatest fear is sin.

The great mystery is not why we love, but why we are loved. It is easy to understand why we love because of our incompleteness and our radical dissatisfaction apart from goodness. But why anyone should love us is the mystery, for we know when we look at our real selves how very little there is to love. Why creatures should love us is not too great a mystery, for they are imperfect too. But for God to love us— that we will never understand. The soul that has finally come to love God is worried by the thought that he has already lost so much time. As St. Augustine said: "Too late O ancient beauty have I loved thee." But, on the other hand, this regret is compensated for by the knowledge that it was always in the Divine plan that we should eventually come to know God.

We love to see ourselves idealized in the minds of others. That is one of the beautiful joys of love. We become fresh, innocent, brave, strong in the mind of the beloved. Love covers up the corruption of the soul. The winter of discontent is forgotten by being clothed in the blossoms of a new spring. After a while the lover begins to substitute what he really is in his own mind, with what he is in the mind of the other. It is this idealization which pleases in love. That is why love gives an incentive to betterment. When the other thinks well of us, we try to be worthy of that opinion. The fact that others assume us to be good is a great incentive to goodness. That is why too, one of the basic principles of life ought to be to assume goodness in others; thus we make them good.

Chapter 16

The Mystery Of Love

There Comes a moment in even the noblest of human * loves when the mystery has gone. One has now grown "used to" the best, and has come to take it for granted, as jewelers may casually handle the most precious stones without troubling to admire them. What we completely possess, we can no longer desire. What we have already attained, we cannot hope for. Yet hope and desire and, above all, mystery, are needed to keep our interest in life alive.

When wonder has vanished from our days, then they become banal. Our minds were made to function at the stretch and to reach out, forever, towards the solution of some lofty problem that forever eludes us. It is possible that the popularity of mystery novels in our day is occasioned by the fact that so many people have ceased to dwell on the mysteries of faith and are looking, in any cheap substitute that comes to hand, for something to replace what they have lost. Readers of mystery stories spend all their wonder on the method by which someone was killed; they do not, as the contemporaries of Dante and of Michaelangelo would have done, wonder about the eternal fate of those who die.

Man cannot be happy if he is satiated; our zest comes from the fact that there are doors not yet opened, veils not yet lifted, notes that have not been struck. If a "love" is only physical, marriage will bring the romance to an end: the chase is ended, and the mystery is solved. Whenever any person is thus taken for granted, there is a loss of the sensitivity and delicacy which are the essential condition of friendship, joy and love in human relations. Marriage is no exception; one of its most tragic outcomes is mere possession without desire.

There is no love left when one hits bottom, or imagines that he has; the personality we have exhausted of its mystery is a bore. There must be always something unrevealed, some mystery we have not probed, some passion that we cannot glut ... and this is true even in the arts. We do not want to hear a singer constantly reiterate her highest note, nor have an orator tear a passion to tatters.

In a true marriage there is an ever-deepening mystery and, therefore, an ever-enchanting romance. At least four of the mysteries of marriage can be tabulated. First comes the mystery of the other partner's physical being, the mystery of sex. When that mystery has been solved, and the first baby is born, a new mystery begins: the husband sees in his wife a thing he never saw before—the beautiful mystery of motherhood. She sees in him the sweet mystery of fatherhood. As other children come to revive their strength and beauty, the husband never seems older to his wife than on the day they met, and the wife appears to him as freshly beautiful as when they first became engaged.

When the children reach the age of reason, a third mystery unfolds: that of mother-craft and father-craft — the disciplining of young minds and hearts in the ways of God. As the children grow to maturity this mystery continues to deepen; each child's personality is something for the parents to explore and then to form closer to the likeness of the God of love.

The fourth mystery of the happily married involves their social living, the contribution that they jointly make to the well-being of the world. Here lies the root of democracy, for in the family the individual is not valued for what he is worth, nor for what he can do, but for what he is. His status, his position in the home, is granted him by virtue of merely being alive. If a child is dumb or blind, if a son has been maimed at the war, he is still loved for himself and for his intrinsic worth as a child of God. No parent mitigates his love because of changes in a child's earning power or worldly wisdom, or troubles about the class to which his off-spring may belong. This reverence for personality for its own sake in the family is the social principle on which the wider life of the community depends and is a potent reminder of the most important of all political principles: the state exists for the person, and not the person for the state.

Chapter 17

Love And Ecstasy

Ecstasy means to be "carried out of oneself" and, broadly speaking, the very fact of loving carries the lover out of himself by leading him to center his thoughts, beyond himself, on the beloved. Adolescent boys and girls are often surprised to find that their elders know they have fallen in love; they give themselves away by their dreamy inattention, by staring into space and by indifference to such things as mealtimes. Love has "carried them away."

Love, again, is at the bottom of all the stories about the absent-minded professors, who, on rainy nights, put the umbrella to bed and stand themselves in the sink; the things of the mind they love have "carried them out" of their surroundings. Any great love has a similar effect: it makes the lover indifferent to physical hardships and sordid surroundings. The hovel of a man and wife who love each other is a far more joyous place than the rich apartment of the couple who have lost their love. Love of God begets an even greater indifference to our environment: a saint like St. Vincent de Paul was so carried away by his love for God's poor that he forgot to feed himself. As Edna St. Vincent Millay wrote of the Christian life: "If you pitch your tent each evening nearer the town of your true desire, and glimpse its gates less far, then you lay you down on nettles, you lay you down with vipers, and you scarcely notice where you are."

But there is one great difference between human love and the love of God, although both of them "carry us away." In human love, the ecstasy comes at the beginning. But when it is a matter of loving God, the ecstasy is attained only after one has passed through much suffering and agony of soul. In bodily enjoyments, we encounter first the feast and then the fast, and maybe the headache, as well. But the spirit encounters first the fast, and perhaps the headache, only as a necessary prelude to the feast. The ecstatic pleasures enjoyed by a young husband and wife at the commencement of their marriage are, in a sense, a "bait," inducing them to fulfill their mission of parenthood. The honeymoon is a kind of Divine credit extended to those who, later on, will have to pay the costs of rearing a family. But no great ecstasy, either of the spirit or of the flesh, is given us as a permanent possession without our having to pay for it. Every ecstasy carries a price tag with it.

"First fervor is false fervor" in marriage as in religion. The earliest ecstasy is not the true, lasting love we seek to find and hold. That may come to us—but only after many purging trials, fidelities under stress, perseverance through discouragement and a steady pursuit of our Divine destiny past all the allurements of this earth. The deep, ecstatic love of some Christian fathers and mothers is a beautiful thing to see: but they have won it after passing through their Calvaries. Theirs is the true ecstasy, which belongs less to youth than to old age.

The first ecstasy of love is a thrill, but a somewhat selfish thrill: in it, the lover seeks to get from the beloved all that he will give. In the second ecstasy, he tries to receive from God all that both of them can give. If love is identified with the early ecstasy alone, it will seek its prolongation in another person's presence; if it is identified with a unifying, enduring and eternal love, it will seek the deepening of its mystery in the Divine, Who put all loves into our hearts.

Too many husbands and wives expect their partners in marriage to give what only God can give: eternal ecstasy. Yet if any man or woman could do that, he would be God. We are right to want the ecstasy of love; but if we expect to enjoy it through the flesh, which is merely on pilgrimage to God, we prepare ourselves for disappointment. The first ecstasy of love is not an illusion; but it is only a kind of travel-folder, a foretaste, a pre-view, urging body and soul to start the journey towards eternal joys. If the first ecstasy passes, this change is not an invitation to love another person, but to love in another way — and the other way is the Christ Way, the way of Him Who said: "I am the Way."

Chapter 18

Motherhood

Human Motherhood is twofold in its essence, and is a more complex thing than motherhood among the animals. There is, first, the physical act of giving birth, which women share with all of nature. As the tree bears fruit and the hen hatches her eggs, so every mother, by the act of birth, is bound up with the life of all living things, and of her it may be rightly said, "Blessed is the fruit of thy womb."

But human motherhood has a second and far lordlier aspect — that of the spirit. The soul of a child does not emanate from the mother's soul or body, but is freshly created by God Himself, Who infuses it into the body of the unborn child. Physiological motherhood is glorified by this cooperation with God Himself, Who fathered the baby's soul and then permitted a woman to clothe it in her flesh. The human mother does not bear a mere animal but a man, made to the image and likeness of the God Who created him.

Every child born of woman has, then, two fathers: his earthly father, without whom he could not have life, and his Heavenly Father, without Whom he could not possess a personality, a soul, an irreplaceable "I." The mother is the essential partner through whom both fathers work. Her own relationship to the child has two resulting aspects: there is the mother-baby aspect, wherein the child is physically and almost absolutely dependent on the mother. But there is also the mother-person relationship (expressed at baptism, when the child is given its own name). This confirms the dignity and separate selfhood of even the smallest infant and foreshadows his right eventually to lead his own life and to depart from his parents to cling to a wife of his own.

Every birth requires a submission and a disciplining. The earth itself must undergo harrowing before it passively accepts the seed. In woman, the submission is not passive: it is sacrificial, consciously creative, and for this selflessness her whole nature has been formed. It is well known that women are capable of far more sustained sacrifice than men; a man may be a hero in a crisis, and then slip back to mediocrity. He lacks the moral endurance which enables a woman to be heroic through the years, months, days and even seconds of her life, when the very repetitive monotony of her tasks wears down the spirit. Not only a woman's days, but her nights—not only her mind, but her body must share in the Calvary of motherhood. That is why women have a surer understanding of the doctrine of redemption than men have: they have come to associate the risk of death with life in childbirth, and to understand the sacrifice of self to another through the many months preceding it.

In a mother two of the great spiritual laws are united into one: love of neighbor and co-operation with God's grace — and both of them are applied in a unique way. For love of neighbor, to anyone except a mother, is love of a nonself; a mother's neighbor during pregnancy is one with herself, yet to be loved differently from the self. The sacrifice sometimes involved in neighborly love now takes place within her flesh: the agent and the object of her sacrifice are both contained within her.

And the co-operation with grace in a mother, although it may be unconscious on her part, yet makes her a partner of Divinity: every human mother is, in a sense, "over-shadowed by the Holy Ghost." Not a priest, and yet endowed with a kind of priestly power, she, too, brings God to man, and man to God. She brings God to man by accepting her mother's role, and thus permitting God to infuse a new soul into her body for it to bear. She brings man to God in childbirth itself, when she allows herself to be used as an instrument by which another child of God is born into the world.

If motherhood is seen as a matter involving only a woman and a man it is seen too astigmatically, and without the honor that is its due. For to comprehend the real significance of motherhood, we must include the spiritual element that goes to make a child—we must see the human woman co-operating with her husband, the father of the human baby, and with God, the Father of a soul that is eternal, indestructible and unlike any other ever formed throughout the history of the world. Thus every human motherhood involves a partnership with the Divine.

Chapter 19

Parents And Children

There Are no juvenile delinquents; there are only delinquent parents. The Fourth Commandment, "Honor thy father and thy mother," is hardly ever quoted today as the means of restoring domestic peace. If discipline in the home is neglected, it is rarely made up for later. As Coleridge said: "If you bring up your children in a way which puts them out of sympathy with the religious feelings of the nations in which they live, the chances are that they will ultimately turn out ruffians and fanatics, and one as likely as the other." The effects of the conduct of children on their parents vary. Mothers suffer more at their evil ways than fathers enjoy their good ways.

The duty of parents to children is to rule while avoiding exasperating severity on the one hand and excessive indulgences on the other. God gives parents a child as so much plastic material that can be molded for good or evil What if God placed a precious diamond in the hands of parents and told them to inscribe on it a sentence which would be read on the Last Day, and shown as an index of their thoughts and ideals? What caution they would exercise in their selection! And yet the example parents give their children will be that by which they will be judged on the Last Day. This tremendous responsibility never means that parents, when their children do wrong, should provoke them to wrath, for wrath leads to discouragement. Parents hold the place of God in the house. If they act as tyrants they will develop unconsciously anti-religious sentiments in their children. Children love approbation and can be easily cast down into despair when blamed excessively for trivial faults. With great difficulty can children ever be taught the Love and Mercy of God, if His vice regents in the home act without it and are so difficult to please. When good intentions are rated low, and children are put under the ban of dishonor, they are likely to show they are no better than their parents think they are.

Children came into their own with Christianity when its Divine Founder said: "Suffer the little children to come unto Me, and forbid them not for such is the Kingdom of Heaven." He consecrated childhood by becoming a child, playing on the green hills of Nazareth and watching the mother eagles stir among their young. From that day it became eternally true: "Train up the child in the way he should go; and when he is old he will not depart from it." As the twig is bent, so is the tree. It is interesting, when one sees children, to speculate from the way they act as to the kind of homes from which they come. As one can judge the vitality of a tree from the fruit it produces, so one can tell the character of the parents from their children. One knows that from certain homes there will never be an errant child, while a glance at a mother or father will reveal a future full of fears for the child.

The present tendency is to shift responsibility to the school. But it must be remembered that education will make as much difference to a child as soil and air and sunshine do. A seed will grow better in one soil and climate than in another, but the kind of tree that grows depends on the kind of seed that is sowed. Then too, one must inquire if education is of the mind alone, or also of the will. Knowledge is in the mind; character is in the will. To pour knowledge into the mind of a child, without disciplining his will to goodness, is like putting a rifle into the hands of a child. Without education of the mind a child could be a stupid devil. With education of the mind, but without love of goodness, a child could grow up to be a clever devil.

The nation of tomorrow is the youth of today. They are the assurance of progress; the fresh arrows to a better future; the wings of aspiration. Even in war the strength of a nation is not in its bombs, but in the soldiers who defend it. In peace, it is not economics or politics that save, but good economists and good politicians—but to be that, they must be good children. To be that, there must in the first place be the grace of God; in the second place, in the home lessons of love and truth; in the schools, knowledge and self-control. Even in their early failures, the parents are not to be discouraged, remembering that fifteen centuries ago when the heart of a mother was broken for her wanton boy, St. Ambrose said to her: "Fear not, Monica; the child of so many tears cannot perish." That vain and wanton boy grew up to be the great and learned St. Augustine, whose "Confessions" everyone ought to read before he dies.

Chapter 20
Blood, Sweat And Tears

RECENTLY a woman at a Forum asked an important politician this question: "Why is it that our political leaders never speak of blood, sweat, tears and sacrifice, but only of how much they will give the farmers and the manufacturers and the labor unions if they are elected?" The politician answering quoted another politician, but it seemed as if he missed the deep significance of the woman's question. Actually, she was a spokesman of a large segment of the American people who know enough about history and psychology to know that no nation, as an individual, ever achieves anything worth while except through sacrifice and self denial.

Toynbee pointed out that sixteen out of nineteen civilizations which have decayed from the beginning of history to the present, have rotted from within; only three fell to attacks from without. Very often an attack from the outside solidifies a nation and strengthens its moral fibers. Lincoln once said he never feared that America would be conquered from without, but that it might fall from within. Lenin once said that America would collapse by spending itself to death, an eventuality that is not too distant with a national debt of a little less than three hundred billion dollars.

Was Walter Whitman speaking of our age as well as his own when he wrote: "Society in these days is cankered, crude, superstitious and rotten ... Genuine belief seems to have left us.... The great cities reek with respectable as well as non-respectable robbery and scoundrels. In fashionable life, flippancy, tepid amours, weak infidelities, small aims, or no aims at all, only to kill time.... It is as if we were somehow endowed with a vast and thoroughly appointed body, but then left with little or no soul."

Whitman's worry was in the woman's mind for she was disturbed about our indifference, tepidity and moral apathy. If there is anything that is becoming clear in our national life, it is that so-called progressive education is extremely unprogressive. Juvenile delinquency, crime, racketeering, political scandals—all these illegitimate children are dropped on the door step of an educational theory that denied a distinction between right and wrong and assumed that self-restraint was identical with the destruction of personality. Every instinct and impulse in either a child or an adult, does not, if left to itself, necessarily produce good results. Man has a hunting instinct which is good when directed to deer in season, but bad when directed to the police in season or out of season. The disrespect for authority which is the outgrowth of the stupidity that every individual is his own determinant of right and wrong has now become an epidemic of lawlessness.

Someday our educators will awaken to several basic facts about youth: 1) Youth has an intellect and a will. The intellect is the source of his knowledge; the will the source of his decisions. If his choices are wrong, the youth will be wrong regardless of how much he knows. 2) Education through the communication of knowledge does not necessarily make a good man; it can conceivably make learned devils instead of stupid devils. 3) Education is successful when it trains the mind to see the right targets, and disciplines the will to choose them rather than the wrong targets.

At present two currents manifest themselves in our American way of life: one is in the direction of a great development of moral character both in individuals and in the nation; the other is toward the surrender of morality and responsibility through a socialist state in which there will be no morality but state-morality, no conscience but state-conscience. Of the two the first is by far the stronger, though neither politics nor economics has seen it. Some of our educators are turning away from the spoiled child psychology, in which the child was called progressive if he did whatever he wanted; now the return is toward doing a little bit of thinking and working in order to wrest us out of our juvenile delinquency and moral flabbiness.

Youth particularly is yearning for something hard; it no longer believes its teachers who say that good or evil is a point of view and it makes no difference in which you believe. They now want to believe that something is so evil that we ought to fight against it, and something is so good that we ought, if necessary, to steel and discipline ourselves and even die to defend it. This latent power of blood and sweat and tears in our American youth will be captured within the next generation by one of the other forces: either by some political crackpot who will turn that desire for sacrifice into something like Nazism, Fascism or Communism, or by our leaders, political, educational and moral who will first show self-discipline and moral courage in their own lives and thus give an example to others.

The greatest responsibility falls on religious leaders whose message ought to be the message the woman wanted from politicians—the clarion call to restraint on evil influences and the showing forth of altruism and love of God.

Chapter 21

The Teen-Agers

ADOLESCENCE, or "teen-age," is the short hour between the springtime and the summer of life. Before the teen-age is reached, there is very little individuality or personality, but as soon as the teens begin, the emotional life takes on the character of its environment, like water takes its shape from the vessel into which it is poured. The adolescent begins to be conscious of himself and others, and for that reason begins to live in solitude. The youth is more lonely than many parents and teachers know; perhaps the teen-ager agonizes in a greater solitariness of spirit than at any other time in life until maturity when the sense of unrequited guilt begins to weigh down the human soul.

As the teen-ager projects his personality to the world round about him, he seems to get further away from it. Between his soul and the world there seems to be a wall. There is never a complete self analysis. As it takes an infant a long time to coordinate his eyes and his hands, so it takes the teen-ager a long time to adjust himself completely to this great broad world to which he feels so strangely related. He cannot yet take it in stride; novelty, new emotional experiences, great dreams and hopes flood his soul, each demanding attention and satisfaction. He does not confide his emotional states to others; he just lives. It is hard for the adult to penetrate the shell into which the teen-ager crawls. Like Adam after his fall, he hides from discovery.

Along with this loneliness, there goes a great desire to be noticed, for egotism is a vice that has to be mastered early in youth. This craving for attention accounts for the loudness in manner of some teen-agers. Not only does it attract the gaze of others, but it also experiences a latent sense of rebellion against others, and affirms that he is living for himself in his own way and as he pleases.

Along with this quality of impenetrability the teen-ager becomes an imitator almost like the Japanese. Being in rebellion against the fixed and being governed largely by fleeting impressions, he becomes like a chameleon, which takes on the colors of the objects upon which it is placed. He becomes a hero or a bandit, a saint or a thief, depending on the environment or his reading or his companions. This spirit of imitation reveals itself in the dress. Overalls, shirts sticking out of trousers and overhanging like the flag of a defeated army, hair cuts fashioned after the savages of Oceania—all these become universal among youths who are afraid to march "against the grain."

There are few natural leaders among teen-agers, most of them being content to follow others. In this unconscious mimicry of others is a moral danger, for character is dependent on the ability to say "No". Unless education can give to teen-agers a training of the will, many of them will slip into adulthood and become slaves of propaganda and public opinion the rest of their lives. Instead of creating, they imitate. To create is to recognize the spirit in things; to imitate is to submerge personality at the lowest level of the mass.

Elders must not be too critical of the teen-agers, particularly when they rebel against them. From one point of view they are not in rebellion against restraint, but against their elders for not giving them a goal and purpose of life. The teen-ager's protest is not conscious. He does not know why he hates his parents, why he is rebellious against authority, why his fellow teen-agers are becoming more and more delinquent. But the real reason is under the surface; it is an unconscious protest against a society which has not given him a pattern of life. The schools he attends have never stressed restraint, discipline or self control. Many of the teachers have defined freedom and even democracy as the right to do whatever you please. When this temporary phase of rebellion is past, the teen-agers will look for some great cause to which they can make a total dedication. They must have an ideal. In many instances today, they have no greater object of worship than to wrap their emotional lives around a movie hero, a movie star, a band leader or a crooner. This sign of decaying civilizations will pass when the catastrophe comes. Then youth will look for a different type to imitate, namely, either heroes or saints. A sad commentary it is on our civilization that the teen-agers have never rallied around our war heroes. This is because they are not yet ready for the more solid ideal. But it will come. And when it does, education must be careful lest in reacting against "progressive" education devoid of discipline, they follow the false sacrificial gods, such as the youths of Europe in prostrating before Nazism, Fascism and Communism. The latent capacity for doing the brave and heroic which is in every youth will soon come to the surface, and when it does, please God, it will be both for heroes and saints that they center their affection. The ascetic ideal has passed away from the elders, but God sends fresh generations into the world to give the world a fresh start. Our teenagers will one day find their right ideals, in love of country and love of God, and particularly the latter, for it is the function of religion to make possible to men sacrifices which in the face of reason or egotism would never come to the surface.

Chapter 22
More About Teen-Agers

What Americans call "teen-agers," or adolescents, covers that period midway between springtime and summer. As what happens to the trees and the blossoms during March determines the fruit, so the experiences of teen-agers help mould their maturity. Some youths, like some fruits, ripen too soon, and others never seem to ripen, but there are others who fulfill the best aspirations of an older generation.

The psychology of teen-agers is as important as it is interesting. The three dominant characteristics are: inferiority, imitation and restlessness.

Inferiority: A trait often missed because of the energy of youth is its consciousness of solitude and its sense of aloofness born of the realization that a kind of barrier is thrown up between itself and the world. Boys try sometimes to overcome this barrier by shaving before their time, thus leaping the wall between adolescence and manhood; girls affect it in dress or other mannerisms in order to bridge the gap. Gestures are clumsy, uneasy, ungraceful; arms seem too long and always in the way; words have little value for exchange purposes with adults in establishing contact with the grown world. There are more images than ideas in the interior world, which may account in part for the inability to establish rapport with others. Sometimes this very ineptitude increases interiority and drives the youth back into himself or herself. Because exterior actions do not always give release to the inner world, the teen-ager often has recourse to an inner world of images where he or she has an interior adventure, picturing himself as a hero on a football field, or herself as married to a prince. Movies are popular because they are a good feeder for such day dreams and hopes. The general picture, however, is of one who has suddenly arrived at a growing interior depth but, not knowing its value, expresses himself or herself badly.

Imitation: There is a profound philosophical reason for imitation. The ego is under the imperative and need of emerging from itself as a chrysalis; the interior is bursting to affirm its personality. Imitation becomes a substitute for originality; originality commits the youth to effort, labor, pain, perseverance and sometimes the scorn of others; but imitation gives one the needed exteriorization through a kind of social conformism. Locked up in itself, youth must emerge. Since it is harder to be oneself, and at that age one does not quite know what is oneself, it becomes a hero-worshipper; hence the fan clubs, fanaticism for players of percussion instruments, the idolizing of some so-called movie star.

That is why in the high school age one finds very few who ever dress outside of the pattern set by a few. The creative minority in adult life is few; therefore the youth must not be taken to task for imitation. This mimicry could be dangerous if what was idolized were low; but it can be also one of the ennobling influences of youth if those who are imitated are noble, good and patriotic. Youth imitates because it wants to create and creation marks the end of inferiority in a constructive way.

Restlessness: Perhaps a better description of restlessness would be a mercurial affection. There is extreme mobility in youth, due to the multitude of impressions which flood the soul. Life is multiple; there is little harmony because of the great variety of appeals from the external world. Hence the appeal of certain youths of a certain type of jitter bug music; it provides a muscular outlet for sense energy which has not yet been rationalized. Because of this agitation, it is difficult for a youth to fix his or her attention on any one object; perseverance in study is hard; the impulsions of the moment solicit with a loud voice. This could end in delinquency if the activity never found a target. But at the same time, like the other characteristics, it can also be the salvation of the youth, for he is really running around the circumference of human experience in order to decide on which particular segment he will settle for life; he tours the world of professions, avocations and positions and then decides in which he will repose. Once this energy becomes canalized, focused and rationalized, it becomes the beginning of a life's work and an adolescent begins to be what God intended him to be— a man who in loving virtue knows how to love a woman, a friend and his country.

Chapter 23

The Loves Of Youth

EVERY YOUTH is full of incertitude and a latent anxiety. This is because life has not yet been brought to unity. What is immediate and present solicits him with such force that there is little thought of over-all goal and purpose. To cover up this uneasiness, a youth often imagines what a psychologist might call a Super-self. It is not another image of himself, but rather the image of something that will complete himself and bring him to unity. This Super-self is what we desire to be to complete our personality and what we sometimes fear we never will be. It is almost like the acorn imagining the oak, the bud imagining the flower, and the foundation the roof. It is the completion of all aspirations, the realization of our dreams. *"The young men dream dreams, the old men see visions."* The young look ahead, the aged look back. The young, like the rivulet look forward to the sea which will immerse them in joy; the old, like the sea look backwards to the rivulets.

Hence in the love of youths there is a tendency to admire those who complete its incompleteness. Basically, this is nothing else than a love of God Who alone can satisfy all the aspirations of the heart. He, therefore, who believes himself completely satisfied, who never reaches out for a perfection which he has not at this moment, is incapable of loving. Every youth falls in love with the image of the possible, that is, with his dream walking, his emptiness filled, and his yearnings realized. Gustave Thibon once said that *"every woman promises that which only God can give."* By this he meant that the love every heart wants is the infinite; woman seems to give this to man, but actually what man wants is not the lovable but Love which is Divine. In literature, it is not uncommon to find women described as the image of the possible, for example, Beatrice for Dante. No one really knows if Beatrice ever existed. But certainly her influence was greater because she remained as the possible ideal. Everyone carries within himself a blueprint of his ideal. Some day this ideal is seen and though it is called "love at first sight" it could conceivably be that which was always loved, but never seen before. Our ideal, or Super-self may even induce us to put ourselves in situations favorable to seeing it realized, as a man who loves dueling seeks out the company of those who duel. Youth seeks out the person who will complete the interior circuit, who will fulfill a desire which is basically for God, but which for a time substitutes for Him. Everyone loves the whole more than the part. Therefore everyone loves God more than His lover reflected in creatures. In most, however, this love is unconscious rather than conscious.

The great mystery of life is really not that we want to be loved, but that we are loved. We need love because we are imperfect; but why anyone should love the imperfect is not easy to understand. That is why all lovers consider themselves unworthy. The beloved is on a pedestal, the lover is on his knees professing his unworthiness. Love always comes as an undeserved gift. To abandon or be unfaithful to that love is to hurt the whole personality, for it destroys the image that was first there. The destruction of the image of the possible is to condemn oneself to a heartache as one feels the truth of the cruel words of Ovid: *"I cannot live either with you or without you."*

This Super-self, or ideal, or image of the possible manifests itself in different ways in a young man and a young woman. In the former, there is a delight found in giving reasons why she is the ideal. Thus does he rationalize his ideal proving to himself and to others that the ideal has come to life. In the latter, however, she strives to intensify the idea that she is the ideal by seeming flight. To attract she appears to fly, thus making her more of an ideal to the pursuer. But in each case the true and absolute ideal is not found. That is God. But it is only later on in life that youth realizes that what he wanted was *"the love we fall just short of in all love"*—the love of the Infinite with *"passionless passion and wild tranquility!"*

Chapter 24

"Getting Away With It"

Behind every attempt to "get away with it" is the belief that one will never be found out. If there is only one check on the books, one can be reasonably secure that there will be no discovery of the theft, but if there is a second check by a master bookkeeper, one is less inclined to commit the crime. Nothing so much conduces to evil as the belief that this world is all, and that beyond there is not a further judgment on the way we have lived and thought. If this world is all, then why not get all you can out of it and at any cost, providing you can "get away with it."

Contrary to this philosophy is that of Our Lord which said: "What is veiled will all be revealed, what is hidden will all be known." (Luke 12/2) Everything tends from darkness to the light where it may stand in its true judgment. Seeds that are buried seek to pierce their grave; trees in a thick forest bend to more readily absorb the light; shells deep in the sea grope their way to the shore. So the lives of men, however deeply they bury their crimes, will one day push themselves to the Light of Judgment where "each man will be judged according to his works."

Modern psychology is based on the assumption that even in this world man really "gets away" with nothing. His secret hates, his hidden sins, his flippant treading upon the laws of morality—all of these leave their traces in his mind, his heart and his unconsciousness. Like the boy in the ancient fable who concealed in his blouse a fox which he had stolen. While denying his guilt, the fox ate away his entrails. The thousands of people stretched out on psychoanalytical couches may deny morality and guilt, but even while making their denial a real psychologist can see their mind being eaten away. There is nothing hidden that will not be revealed.

Inside of every heart are passions and wishes, hopes and fears, hatreds and lusts, evil intents and hidden guilts; one day all of these shadowy dwellers of the mental underworld will work their way up either to a confession of guilt or else to mental and physical signs of the denial of that guilt. Anyone is free to deny morality, but he is not free to escape the effects of its violation. Sin is written on faces, in the brain, it is seen in the shifting eyes and the hidden fears of night.

If a man knows that his thefts will one day be discovered, he will take every possible means to make recompense before discovery. If a man knows that one day every thing he did will not only be revealed to God but also to fellowman, he will purge himself of them, that what was before a debit may now be a credit. To such a soul there is nothing more foolish than trying to "get away with it."

Psychiatry is not as much a modern discovery as it is a modern need. Its method has been known for centuries, but there was never the occasion to apply it, because in other ages men knew they could not "get away with it." Their purgations, reparations and amendments were settled on their knees in prayer, rather than on their back on a couch. But at that moment when the Divine and morality were denied, society came face to face with handling the mental effects which that very denial entailed. The crimes were not new, for people could snap their fingers just as much against the moral law in the days of faith as now. In those days when they did wrong, they knew it was wrong. They lost the road, but they never threw away the map. But today when men do wrong they call it right. This creates in addition to the moral problem which is denied, a mental problem. And that is where much psychiatry comes in. There is nothing new about the discovery that the reality we refuse to face we bury in our unconscious mind. What is new is the need to treat those who break the law and deny the law; who live by freedom and refuse to accept its consequences. Every soul that violates a law of God sooner or later turns states-evidence against himself. The long tongue of wrong doing will not be quiet. Deny though he may the Divine Judge, his anxieties and fears reveal that there is already a judge seated in his own conscience, condemning even when society approves, and reproving when he himself would deny. There is no secrecy for wickedness. The fear of God may have vanished from modern civilization, but the fear of man has taken its place and therefore made us unhappy. To fear God is to dread hurting one we love, like a child before a devoted father. To fear man is to shrink from threats and cruelty. One day a Great Book will be opened and there even every idle word we uttered will be recorded. Whatever is spoken in darkness will be brought to light, for in the final analysis no man "gets away" with anything.

Chapter 25
Self-Discipline

THE PHILOSOPHY of self-expression is so much taken for granted today that few there are who analyze its meaning. Self-expression is right when it means acting according to reason and our higher nature; it is wrong when it means acting in accordance with our instincts and lower nature. A hunter is self-expressive in the right way when he hunts animals in season; he is wrong when he goes hunting mothers-in-law, in season or out of season. Those who identify self-expression with license, or the right to do whatever they please, think that self-discipline is self-destruction, but actually it is only taming the lower for the sake of the higher. The violinist does not break the string when he tunes it to concert-pitch; the sculptor does not destroy the marble when he chisels it to produce the image.

When the chastening of self comes from the outside, it is affiliation; when it comes from the inside by an act of our own will, it is self-discipline. In either case, its purpose is the emergence of a truer and better character. God never permits an affliction except for the purposes of purification. Scripture goes so far as to say that "Whom the Lord loveth tenderly He chasteneth." A young man who loves a young woman wants to see her dressed in a most becoming manner; she, too, suits the color of her dress and the fashion of her hair to his taste. All egotistic wishes are expunged for the sake of the beloved. God, too, sometimes shakes all the leaves off the trees which surround our self-existence in order that we may see the heavens.

Sometimes even the death of a child is God's way of making parents look beyond this world to the next. When a shepherd finds that his sheep have exhausted the lower pastures, but refuse to climb to greener pastures, he will take a young lamb in his arms to the heights of the mountain side, and the other sheep will follow. The mother eagle gets her young to fly by pecking away pieces of the nest bit by bit, until finally the young have to leave the temporary security. God, too, sometimes has to disturb man in his economic security, lest he think that it is the only security there is.

But over and above the passive discipline from without, there is the active discipline. There is no evil propensity of the heart that is so powerful that it cannot be subdued by discipline. Every man is like an onion. His superficial self has many layers of skins, and at the center of them all is his real self. Self-abnegation tears off all the outer deceptions and finally reveals our true character. One of the reasons why so few know God is because they do not know themselves. They live in a world of make-believe where nothing is real, and thus miss the Ground of all Reality.

We of the Western World have begun to falsely believe that a character is made by external works, and that it matters little what a man does or thinks or wills on the inside. But this can be an escape, for a man can plunge into work to try to forget himself, just as a man can plunge into alcohol to forget himself. When anything goes wrong, the undisciplined blames things—as the golfer blames the clubs for the poor shot, or the clumsy carpenter the tools for inferior work. Actually the fault lies within the disordered and selfish self.

If a man gives up his wealth, his time, and his energy to others, but actually does not give up himself, he has given up nothing. But he who has had some wealth and some honor, but has denied himself, then he is most free. When Our Blessed Lord said that a man must hate himself, He did not mean those qualities in him which make for God-likeness, but rather those barnacles of selfishness which prevent him from becoming all that love has destined for him. There has been no greater secret of inner peace ever given than in the words of John the Baptist when he saw Our Lord Coming: "He must increase; I must decrease."

Chapter 26

Kindness

MANY PEOPLE who are very kind in their own homes and offices can become very unkind and selfish once they get behind the steering wheel of an automobile. This is probably due to the fact that in their own home they are known; in the automobile they have the advantage of anonymity and hence can be almost brutal without the fear of discovery. To be kind out of fear of others thinking we are unkind is not real kindness, but rather a disguised form of egotism.

The word "kindness" is derived from kindred or kin, and therefore implies an affection which we bear naturally to those who are our flesh and blood. The original and archetypal kindness is that of a parent for a child and a child for a parent, an idea which is preserved in the German language where Kind means child. Gradually the word gained in extension until it embraced everyone whom we are to treat as a relative. Unkindness is therefore unnaturalness.

Because kindness is related to love, it follows that the kind person loves another not for the pleasure the other person gives, nor because the other person can do us a kindness in return, but because the other person is lovable in himself. The basic reason why everyone is lovable is because God made him. If we were evolved from the beast, none of us would bp deserving of any love.

Since God finds us lovable because He put some of His love into us so we can find others lovable, because we put some of our love into them. But to do this implies a basic kindness which is always prepared to be pleasant with other people. If we start with the belief that most people in the world are crooks, it is amazing how many crooks we find. If, however, we go into the world with the assumption that every one is nice, we are constantly running into nice people. To a great extent the world is what we make it. We get back what we give. If we sow hate, we reap hate;

if we scatter love and gentleness we harvest love and happiness. Other people are like a mirror which reflects back on us the kind of image we cast. The kind man bears with the infirmities of others, never magnifies trifles and avoids a spirit of fault finding. He knows that the trouble with most people in the world is that they are unloved. No one cares for them either because they are ugly or nasty, or troublesome, or so-called bores. To a great extent their character is made by the resentment they feel to others who are unkind. One of life's greatest joys comes from loving those whom no one else loves. Thus do we imitate Our Heavenly Father Who certainly cannot see much in any of us creatures that is very attractive. It is curious that most people are more kind to the blind than they are to the deaf. Aristotle commented upon this fact, saying that sight is the most spiritual of all the senses and hearing the most material. For that reason we are moved by sympathy towards those who are afflicted in the most spiritual way. This psychological explanation, however, in no way justifies a want of kindness to either.

Kindness towards the afflicted becomes compassion, which means a suffering with, or an entering into the distress and the pains of others as if they were our own. It enlarges the interest of the heart beyond all personal interest and prompts us to give either what we have in the form of alms, or the giving of one's talent as a doctor may treat a poor patient, or the giving of one's time which is sometimes the hardest thing of all to give. The truly compassionate and kind man who gives up his time for others manages to find time. Like the bread, miraculously multiplied, he gives, and yet he gathers up for himself more than he gave.

Many psychiatrists today know very well that all they have to do to help certain distressed minds is to listen to their stories. Convince the anxious heart that you know the secret of his anxiety and he is already half cured. Even if we can convince the enemy that we have no bitterness in our heart against him, his arm will fall helpless at his side. All mental abnormalities have their roots in selfishness, all happiness has its roots in kindness. But to be really kind, one mut see in everyone an immortal soul to be loved for God's sake. Then everyone is precious.

Chapter 27

Fear And Ethics

Most neuroses are bulwarks against fear. Many psychologists and physicians have come to adopt this thesis inasmuch as fear does provoke some kind of self defense. It is actually not fear that is feared; the enemy is the tension between the conscience and what has happened. Fear is like the gauge on a steam boiler. It merely registers pressure.

The simplest way but the worst way to remove fear from the conscious mind is to repress it—that is, to relegate it into unconsciousness. When unexpected visitors come to the house, a housewife will take old linen and dirty shirts which lie about the front room and toss them into the cellar. The mind does the same thing; it defends itself against tormenting sensations by throwing them into the unconsciousness.

The effects of suppressing fear are manifold. First on the physical side they may be palpitation, migraine, cramps, convulsions, etc. On the mental side the repressed fear comes out as anger, depression and surliness. One psychologist tells the story of a small boy who wept copiously whenever he heard bells tolled for a funeral. He had often wished that his parents were dead, but he repressed the wish. He had fear as a result of the wish and he escaped it by weeping. His fear resulted from the guilt of wishing his parents dead and he sublimated it by tears.

Lady Macbeth had induced her ambitious husband to murder the King, their guest, while he slept, and then to assume the crown. When her husband is shaken by the act she reminds him:

> "These deeds must not be thought
> After these ways, so it will make us mad."

This is an excellent description of the pathological effects of the murderer's endeavor to escape fear. She is trying to drown conscience by saying that one must not think of the deed in terms of right and wrong. Yet all the while that she is repressing it she is inducing her own madness. She tells her husband to wash his hands and then to smear the grooms with blood. Since he is afraid to do so, she kills the grooms herself and then smears their bodies with the blood. Then she exclaims:

> *"My hands are your color, but I shame*
> *To wear a heart so white....*
> *A little water clears us of this deed."*

Here she tries to convince herself and her husband again that one must not seek to have a clean heart; that there is no judge within the human breast, and that all one has to do is to clear oneself of the external consequences.

Conscience still produces its effects; she who tried to deny it now has a compulsion neurosis which expresses itself in the constant washing of hands:

> *"Who would have thought the old man*
> *To have so much blood in him...*
> *Will these hands ne'er be clean?"*

First she thought that the guilt of the murder could be cleansed by washing away the blood; now she has to wash away the fear of guilt, as she admits with her husband that all the waters of the seven seas are not enough to wash the blood from her hands.

There are some people who wash their hands after touching door knobs and who repeat this process as much at ten times before they get out of the house. This signifies a need of cleansing and it is thought that the external washings will be a substitute for the moral and inner washing which is denied because of repressed guilt. This does not mean to say that all those who suffer from guilt have violated some moral principle; but it does mean that those who have done so can never expect to have their fears lifted by mere treatment of the external symptoms.

Medical treatment in dealing with fear should never neglect the moral principles which may possibly be behind fear and their manifestations in body and mind. Even Freud has admitted that from a medical point of view the unscrupulous method of satisfying every instinct may make the patient worse. Ethics is the very essence of sound medical treatment.

Chapter 28

Rest And Mediation

MODERN MAN would be far happier if he would take a little time off to meditate. As the Old Testament prophet said: "Peace, peace and there is no peace, but no man considereth in his heart." The Gospel tells us that Our Blessed Lord withdrew Himself from the crowds into the wilderness and prayed. Martha, who was too busy about many things, was told that only one thing was necessary. A life of faith and with peace of soul can be cultivated only by periodical isolation from the cares of the world.

There are various kinds of weariness: weariness of the body, which can be satisfied under any tree or even on a pillow of stone; weariness of the brain, which needs the incubation of rest for new thought to be born; but hardest of all to satisfy is weariness of heart, which can be healed only by communion with God.

Silence helps speech; retirement helps thinking. A contemporary of Abraham Lincoln tells us that he spent three weeks with Lincoln just after the Battle of Bull Run: "I could not sleep. I was repeating the part that I was to play in a public performance. The hour was past midnight. Indeed, it was coming near to dawn, when I heard low tones coming from the room where the President slept. The door was partly open. I instinctively walked in and there I saw a sight which I shall never forget. It was the President, kneeling beside an open Bible. The light was turned low in the room. His back was turned toward me. For a moment I was silent, as I stood looking in amazement and wonder. Then he cried out in tones so pleading and sorrowful: 'O thou God that heard Solomon in the night that he prayed for wisdom, hear me; I cannot lead this people, I cannot guide the affairs of this nation without Thy help. I am poor and weak and sinful. O God, who didst hear Solomon when he cried to Thee, hear me and save this nation'."

One wonders how many of our public officials in the great burdens that are laid upon them ever cry to God for help. When the United Nations held its first meeting in San Francisco, fearful that we might offend the atheists, it was decided to keep a minute of silence instead of praying fearlessly to God to illumine and guide the nations. It was in the moment of Peter's failure in fishing that Our Lord said: "Launch out into the deep." It is in the times of our failures that the soul must draw away from the shores.

What the Saviour promises in the retirement is "rest for your souls." Rest is a gift; it is not earned; it is not the payment for finishing a job; it is the dowry of grace. Greed, envy, wealth and avarice think of rest in terms of the good things of the world; true rest is the stilling of passions, the control of wavering ambitions, the joy of a quiet conscience. There is no rest until life has been made intelligible. Most of the restlessness of souls today comes from not knowing why they are here, or where they are going, and they refuse to take time out to solve that problem. Until it is solved, nothing is solved. There is not even much sense in going on living unless one knows why he is living.

Driving power is always associated with inner repose; otherwise energy is explosiveness and imprudent action. They that wait upon the Lord shall renew their strength. The renewals of strength are less physical than they are spiritual. A tired soul makes a tired body more often than a tired body makes a tired soul. The rest which Christianity enjoins is less cessation from work than it is freedom from the anxieties that come from guilt and avarice. Spiritual refreshment in prayer, retreat, meditation are the most potent influences for restoring harmony to the thousands of nervous patients. Life, like music, must have its rhythm of silence as well as sound.

The rest which retirement and contemplation give is not just a rest from toil, but it is even a rest in toil. The peace of Christ is not a hothouse plant; it raises its head for the storms; it is peace for the battle and joy of conscience for those who assail conscience. The world cannot give it; the world cannot take it away. It is not given by outward circumstance; it rules in the heart; it is an inward state. To be spiritually minded is to have rest.

Chapter 29
Better To Give
Than Receive

THE VAST majority of the people in Western civilization are engaged in the task of getting. Strange as it may seem, the Christian ethic is founded on the opposite principle, that it is more blessed to give than to receive. Both the opportunity and the burden of filling this Divine mandate falls principally upon those of us who live in a civilization that has been abundantly blessed by God. The per capita income of the United States is about $1,500 a year, and yet the per capita income of one third of the world's population is less than $50 a year, while two thirds of the world's population is living on less than $200 a year. In the United States $28 out of every $100 is paid into the government as taxes. We pay more in taxes than most people of the world earn to keep body and soul together.

We are, of course, a nation helping the socially disinherited people of the world; we have even given an example of loving our enemies in war by helping their economic restoration. But here our concern is less with the national spirit of giving, than it is with the personal spirit. The reason it is more blessed to give than to receive is because it helps to detach the soul from the material and the temporal in order to ally it with a spirit of altruism and charity which is the essence of religion. Cicero once said that "men resemble gods in nothing so much as in doing good to their fellow creatures." Aristotle says that by narrowness and selfishness, by envy and ill will, men degenerate into beasts and become wolves and tigers to one another; but by goodness and love, by mutual compassion and helpfulness, men become gods to one another.

The history of the Jews reveals how much their temporal blessing was consecrated to the service of God and to aiding the poor. In the best days of their history, their tithes and offerings, their thank-offerings and their free will offerings, were on a scale of splendid munificence; nor did they lose thereby for they were constantly thanking God for their many blessings. Even today that same spirit of generosity has characterized these people, not only to their own brethren, but also to Protestants and to Catholics.

On a smaller scale, it will be found the unity of a community depends to a great extent upon the services and kindnesses of one individual to another. The farming population of any country in the world is a perfect example of this altruism. At harvest time, each farmer helps every other farmer, and when there is a death in the family, willing hands are always found to pick the corn and cut the wheat.

There is not always the same spirit in the large cities, partly due to the anonymity of the masses, and partly due to competition. Where most people we meet are strangers, there is a tendency to lock one's self in his shell. One notices this particularly in driving an automobile. Men who are very gentle at home and kind to friends, become like raging beasts growling at the stupidity of every other driver once they get behind a wheel where anonymity protects them.

Giving is really a divinely appointed way of acknowledging the mercies of God. We have indeed nothing to offer anyway that we have not received, and yet He is pleased to accept our offerings as tokens of our gratitude. Egotism makes the self the center; altruism and charity make the neighbor the center. Only on the principle of giving can the inequalities of the human race be adjusted, can the strong help the weak, and social peace reign among men. Many a man when he was poor had a heart that was open to every call of pity, but as riches increased he set his heart more upon them. The massing of wealth has a peculiar effect on the soul; it intensifies the desire of getting. What is often lust in youth is avarice in old age. Could they but expose themselves to the great joy of giving and respond to pity's claim, they would sense the great thrill in benevolence. Great as the pleasure is in receiving, greater is the pleasure in benevolence.

There is an old story about a Scotsman, Lord Braco, who was very rich and miserly and who had great stores of gold and silver in his vaults. One day a farmer said to him: "I will give you a shilling if you will but let me see all your gold and silver." Braco consented. The farmer gave him the shilling saying: "Now I am as rich as you are. I have looked at your gold and silver, and that is all you can do with it."

There is more happiness in rejoicing in the good of others, than in rejoicing in our own good. The receiver rejoices in his good; the giver in the joy of others and to such comes the peace nothing in the world can give.

Chapter 30
The Spirit Of Service

THE DESIRE for distinction is one of the most radical principles of our nature; even though it be crucified and buried in an unexpected moment it revives and rises again in power. The subtle passion is strongest in the middle period of life. It comes in between the love of pleasure which besets youth and the love of gain which besets old age. Opposed to all egotism and selfishness is the ideal of usefulness and service. He only is great of heart who floods the world with great affection; he only is great of mind who stirs the world with pure thoughts. Our Divine Lord gave the key to greatness when He said that He came not to be ministered unto, but to minister. Such service of fellowman as He inspired must be loving in the sense that out of no fountain save that of love can such amazing and endless acts of helpfulness flow.

Loving and serving are inseparable. Such service, too, is self-denying and ego-effacing. To continue helping day after day in the midst of reproach and opposition and rejection means that one is governed by a higher law than the desire of applause of fellowman. Such service cannot be bought, for no gold could purchase it, neither does it need to be bought, for it is freely rendered.

Unless a man sets out to help his neighbor in the spirit of love he will never overcome those faulty tendencies in his nature which constantly try to drag it down. Over 2,000 years ago Aristotle remarked that all of our degrading tendencies arranged themselves under two heads of temper and desire—bad temper and ill-regulated desire. When one is not present the other is, and sometimes one and sometimes the other appear at different periods in the life of the same man. Inasmuch as service is a voluntary undertaking of a work in obedience to the Higher Will, it is a corrective of these tendencies.

It is corrective first of all of temper in its every day form of self-assertion and pride. The man who serves from his heart cannot indulge in egotism. He represses self in order to make his service the more kindly. Each five minutes of conscientious service has the effect of keeping the ego disciplined and of bidding it submit to a Higher and more Righteous Will. Self asserting man always tries to make an inferior feel the full weight of his petty importance and thus, sooner or later, self assertion becomes tyranny. Helpfulness, on the other hand makes the ego appear inferior in order that the neighbor may be exalted.

Irregulated desire is also crushed by affectionate helpfulness. Desire is irregulated when it makes self the center of all things and even the law to which all others must submit. This evil can be cured radically only by making God the object of desire. One then sacrifices many of his luxuries and pleasures in order to assist the needy and the less fortunate. In doing this, character is incidentally improved inasmuch as it detracts one from sensuous and effeminate ease which leads to the spoiling of character.

Even upon material works God has stamped the law of sympathetic service. It is written out in the clouds of the sky to seek to die in the service of rain. The little streams flee decaying self-content by emptying themselves into the vastness of the ocean. The mountains too are in service. They are like giant hands raised to catch and re-distribute the moisture, sending it down across the plains in healthful and life-giving streams. Not a drop of water leads a selfish life; not a wind blast is without its mission. What God has imposed upon nature by law He intended we should impose upon ourselves in virtue of our free will. The waters and the clouds and the mountains and even the earth itself which spends itself in giving life to the seed—all of these rebuke the man who refuses to live for his fellow man. In doing good, everything in God's universe gets good. Service of others is the highest service of self, and the best way for any man to grow in grace is to move forward in helpfulness. The mill wheel will cease to revolve when the waters of the rushing stream are cut off; the moving train stops when the glowing heat cools within the hidden chamber; and charity in this world will degenerate into mere professional schedules and statistical averages without inspiration, without power and without love as men forget the inspiration of Him Who said: "Greater love than this no man hath, that he lay down his life for his friend."

Chapter 31
How To Give

"**M**AKE TO YOURSELF friends with the Mammon of iniquity" is one of the mysterious words of Our Lord to those who do not understand its meaning. "Mammon" is a Syrian word meaning money, and it is called the "Mammon of iniquity" because those to whom Our Lord spoke too often used it for the purposes of injustice and iniquity. A dollar bill in our pocket, if it could speak, might scandalize us in telling us the things for which it was spent, the transactions it had assisted, and the sinful pleasures it had bought. Our Lord tells us that there is a time when it fails, for the man who has money is only a steward. Death says to every man: "Give an account of thy stewardship for thou canst be steward no longer." Money simply cannot be transferred to the world beyond.

Here we come to the purpose of money according to the Saviour. Give away money to those who are in need, for by relieving their necessity you will make friends of those who will intercede for the salavation of your soul. Money will not buy heaven; but it will make friends for us that will help us when we fail. "Inasmuch as you do it to the least of these my brethren, you did it unto me." Those who have been helped by our charity will lead us before the throne saying: "This is he of whom we have spoken and who did so much for us in the life below."

A traveler in a foreign country exchanges his own currency for that of the other land. So too the wealth we have here can be exchanged for spiritual wealth in the next world which "rust does not consume, moths eat, nor thieves break through and steal."

What is the psychology of those who will never touch their capital for charity? They keep piling up more and more reserves, each new addition becoming as sacred as the one before. The answer is that every man is made for the infinite, which is God. But his reason becomes blinded through prejudice or sin, so he substitutes another infinite which is money. He then wants more and more of having, instead of more and more of being which is life in God. No matter how many hairs a man has in his head, it hurts to have even one pulled out. No matter how much capital a man has, it hurts to touch even a cent of it. He knows "he can't take it with him" so he denies there is any place to go.

The Christian way is to use money that those who are helped may be our intercessors for heaven. A wealthy man once told his maid to give away fruits in his garden to his neighbors, in order that she might make friends of them. Wealth thus becomes worthy of its name, which is weal.

A wealthy woman once got into heaven where St. Peter pointed out the mansion of her chauffeur. She said: "If that is my chauffeur's home, think what mine will be.", St. Peter pointed out to her one of the more humble bungalows of heaven saying: "That is your home." "Oh," she said, "I could never live there." St. Peter answered: "Sorry, Madam, but that is the best I could do with the materials you sent me."

There is much money given away, but little of it is used for the soul. Some give it away in order to have their name glorified on the door of a hospital or a university. Men who have had very little education are conspicuous for endowing libraries, that they might create the impression of being learned, which they are not. Our Lord said: "Let not your left hand know what your right hand gives." This was followed by the second principle of giving: The gift must be offered for a Divine reason. The cup of cold water will be given a reward a hundred fold if it is given in Christ's name.

Some years ago the cloister of Carmelite nuns was opened to the public on the feast of St. Theresa. Many curious people poured in to see those women who led a life of silence, prayer and penance. One man who could not understand their life called the attention of a young and beautiful nun to the finest residence in the city which stood on the opposite hill. He said to her: "Sister, if you could have had that home, with all the wealth, luxury and pleasure that went with it, would you have left it to enter the Carmelites?" She answered: "Sir, that was my home."

There is so much giving that is wasted because it is not done for the soul. The world thinks that the highest things must be used for the lowest, for example, the intellect to make surplus wealth. The man of God believes that the lowest must be used for the highest, that is, money must be spent to help spread Divine Truth, to solace the afflicted and to cure the sick that their souls may be free to work out their salvation. The truest answer to "You can't take it with you" is: "You can, provided you give it away." Then it is stored up as merit in the next life.

Chapter 32

Progress

G. K. Chesterton once said: "There is one thing in the world that never makes any progress and that is the idea of progress." By this he meant that unless we have a fixed concept of what progress really means we can never know that we are making any headway. Unfortunately, there are many who, instead of working toward an ideal, change it, and call it progress. One would never know he was making progress from Chicago to San Francisco if San Francisco became identified with New York. Only when the goal is fixed and definite do we ever have a target and the energy to shoot the arrow.

Everything in earth's geology and everything on the earth's surface point to a future: the impulse of a river is forward into the sea; the little child tells what he intends to be when he is a man; thoughts fly on wings toward the tomorrow; all these impulses which carry us onward imply a future under God. Those who lose sight of the goal often concentrate on mere motion and try to derive pleasure from it. They delight in turning the pages of a book, but never finish the story; they pick up brushes, but never finish a picture; they travel the seas, but know no ports. Their zest is not in the achievement of a destiny but rather in gyration and action for the mere sake of movement.

Perfection is being, not doing; it is not to affect an act but to achieve a character. There is nothing that makes life unhappier than its meaninglessness, and life is devoid of meaning only when it is without purpose. There are tens of thousands of minor purposes, but the one great purpose is the perfection of our character from a moral point of view. Infinite as are the varieties of life, he who has not found out directly how to make everything converge to the sanctification of his own soul has missed the meaning of life.

The son of Confucius once said to him: "I apply myself with diligence to every kind of study, and neglect nothing that could render me clever and ingenious, but still I do not advance." To which Confucius answered: "Omit some of your pursuits and you will get on better." The life of a man is vagrant, changeful, desultory, like that of children chasing butterflies, until he has discovered for himself why he is here and where he is going. Rivers do not grow shallower as they roll away from their sources, and the heart's river need not be any exception. It should flow on, widening and deepening until it meets the great ocean of Divine Love for which it is destined, and mingles with it.

Dissatisfaction sometimes can be the motive of true progress. Dissatisfied with the pen, man invented the printing press; dissatisfied with the chariot and the locomotive, he invented the airplane. There is implanted in everyone an impulse which drives the spirit to beat its wings like an imprisoned eagle in the cages of this earth until there is blood on its plumes. Did hearts but analyze this urge that is within them, which drives them away from the actual to the possible and makes them dig in the desert of their lives for new living springs, and climb every mountain to get a better look at heaven, they would see that they are being drawn back again to God, from Whom they came.

To stay complacently where we are in our spiritual life is to be as a tree that might congratulate itself that it is higher than the shrubs, or to be like a caterpillar that should stay exultant with its spots and stripes whilst the glorious life of the butterfly is untasted. No man is living who is resting on his own laurels, as no one is happy who says that he lives on his memories. Past laurels must be put aside as man must press forward to that supernal vocation to which he is called, forgetting the things that are behind. The bird must forget its nest, the sea its husk, the flower its bud, and unless these are forgotten we can never reach the goal. Both brooding and boasting are alike to be discouraged, for the happiness of life is in the prospect of the best and the holiest.

Chapter 33
The Mass-Man

A NEW TYPE of man is multiplying in the modern world, and if there be any reader who recognizes his own portrait herein, let him take pause, reflect, and change. The new man is the mass-man, who no longer prizes his individual personality, but who seeks to be submerged in the collectivity or crowd.

This mass-man may be recognized by the following traits:

1) He is without originality of judgment; does no other reading except what is found in a daily newspaper, or picture magazine, or an occasional novel. He has only a different point of view to give on a common subject, but no new principle or solution.

2) He hates tranquility, meditation, silence or anything which gives him leisure to penetrate into the depths of his soul. He needs noise, crowds, and the radio, whether he listens to the latter or not.

3) Evasion or escape from self is a necessity. Alcohol, cocktails, detective stories, or movies are taken in steady doses to fill up the emptiness of the hour. As the genius loves concentration, he seeks dispersion, particularly sex, in order that the excitement of the moment may dispel consideration of the problem of life.

4) He seeks to be influenced rather than to influence, is sensitive to propaganda, to the excitations of publicity and generally has one favorite columnist who does his thinking for him.

5) He believes that every instinct should be satisfied, regardless of whether or not its exercise is in accordance with right reason; he cannot understand self-denial, or self-discipline; he regards self-expression as identical with freedom, and at no vital points is he master of himself.

6) His beliefs of right and wrong change like the weathercock; he maintains positions which are nothing but a succession of contradictions, lays down mental tracks one month and the next month pulls them

up. He is going nowhere, but he is sure he is on the way. He has no sense of gratitude toward the past and no sense of responsibility to the future. Nothing matters but distractions, so that life becomes cut up into a crazy pattern of successive instants none of which add up to make sense.

7) He identifies money and pleasure, and hence seeks to have much of the first in order to have much of the second. But the money must be obtained with as little effort as possible. The ego is the center of everything and everything is to be related to it through the intermediary of money.

8) To break his solitude he has recourse to an ersatz communion with others, through night clubs, parties and collective distractions. But from each of these he returns more lonely than before, finally believing with Sartre that "hell is others."

9) Being a mass-man completely standardized, he hates superiority in others, either real or imagined. Scandals he loves because they seem to prove that others are no better than he. Religion he dislikes, the real reason being that by denying it he thinks he could then go on living as he does without remorse of conscience.

10) He might just as well go by a number as by a name he is so immersed in the crowd mind. Even the authority he invokes is anonymous. It is always "they." "They say," or "they are wearing," or "they are doing this." Anonymity becomes a protection against the assuming of responsibilities. In the big cities he feels more free because he is less known, but at the same time he hates it because it cancels his personal distinction. The perfect symbol of the impersonal mass-man is the social security number, which completes his alienation from himself.

These are the ten marks of the mass-man who is the raw material of every form of Totalitarianism from Fascism to Communism. Psychologically, he is also the unhappy man, full of despair, anxiety, fear, and afraid of the meaninglessness of life. But he is not hopeless if he would but enter into himself. The only reason he wants to be lost in the crowd is because he cannot bear his inner misery. It follows that he must detach himself from the masses and come to grips with himself. Flight is cowardice and escapism, especially flight into anonymity.

It takes a brave man to look into the mirror of his own soul to see written there the disfigurements caused by his own misbehavior. It is no truism to say men must be men, not atoms in a mass. Once man sees his self-inflicted wounds, the next step is to take them to the Divine Physician to be cured. It was to such tired mass-men that He made His appeal: "Come to Me all ye who labor and are heavily burdened and find rest for your souls."

Chapter 34
A Recall To
The Inner Life

A FATHER GAVE his little son a cut-up puzzle of the world and asked him to put it together. The boy finished the picture in an amazingly short time. When the astonished father asked him how he did it, the boy answered: "There was a picture of a man on the other side; when I put the man together, the world came out all right." Such is the key to the understanding of all the political and economic problems of our day. Nothing ever happens to the world which does not first happen inside man. Wars are not made by politics, but by politicians with a certain philosophy of life. No explanation of war has ever been as clear as the Biblical one which declares that wars are punishments on man for his sin. Not a punishment in the sense that God sends a war as a father spanks a child for an act of disobedience; but rather that a war follows a breakdown of morality, as thunder follows lightning, and as blindness follows the plucking out of the eye.

Those who are in middle age have lived through an era where war is more "normal" than peace. There has been literally fulfilled what Nietszche prophesied, namely, that the twentieth century would be a century of wars. War is a symptom of the breakdown of civilization. There are only different degrees of guilt among the combatants. All is not black on one side, and all is not white on another. When a body becomes diseased, the germ does not localize in one organ to the exclusion of all others; it infects the whole blood stream. So the evil of our day is the evil not of the East or the West, but of the world. It is of the world because men generally have become estranged from the true center of their spiritual life. Having ceased to fear God, in the sense of filial fear such as a child has for a father, they have begun to fear man with a servile fear, such as a slave has for a tyrant.

Modern man has become passive in the face of evil. He has so long preached a doctrine of false tolerance; has so long believed that right and wrong were only differences in a point of view, that now when evil works itself out in practice he is paralyzed to do anything against it. Political injustice, chicanery in high office, and organized crime leave him cold. While keeping very busy and active on the outside, he is passive and inert on the inside, because he rarely enters into his own heart. Remedying the evil therefore falls to agencies and mechanical realities external to man. No government or state can put the screws on personal freedom, unless the citizens have already abdicated in themselves the basis of that freedom, namely, their responsibility to God.

Having lost his inward unity, man is more and more compelled to seek the unity outside himself in the unity of organization. Disclaiming all responsibility, he surrenders it more and more to the State. The sheep that will not obey the shepherd must be retrieved by a dog barking at their heels. The citizen who will not obey the moral laws of God, must be organized by a dictator snapping at their souls. The weakening of the inner spiritual life is the basic cause of the disharmony and discord which prevail throughout the world. The forcible organization of the chaos created by the enfeeblement of the moral sense always calls forth some dictator who makes law personal rather than a reflection of the Eternal harmony that rules in the heavens.

A great burden is thrust upon men who call themselves religious. In this fatal hour, all of their energies should be spent recalling man to his spiritual destiny and summoning him to invoke the God Who made him. Instead of that there are some who would accuse their neighbors who also believe in God, of being disloyal to their country, or else of trying to impose their faith by force on their fellow citizens. Such lies do a disservice both to God and to country. And their supposed faith in God is to be questioned, because no one who loves God hates his neighbor, nor does he try to incite citizen against citizen through slander. Let those who call themselves Catholics, or Protestants, or Jews recall that the function of their religion is to intensify the spiritual life of man and not to empty the vials of bitterness into hearts, stirring up one against another. It is not to the politicians and the economists and the social reformers that we must look for the first steps in this spiritual recovery; it is to the professed religious. The non-religious can help by repudiating those who come to them in the name of God or America and say that their neighbor does not love either. Religion must not be a cloak covering the dagger of hate!

Chapter 35
Why We Are Not Better

THE REASON why we are not better than we are is that we do not will to be better: the sinner and the saint are set apart only by a series of tiny decisions within our hearts. Opposites are never so close as in the realm of the spirit: an abyss divides the poor from the rich, and one may cross it only with the help of external circumstances and good fortune. The dividing line between ignorance and learning is also deep and wide: both leisure to study and a gifted mind would be required to turn an ignoramus into a learned man. But the passage from sin to virtue, from mediocrity to sanctity requires no "luck," no help from outer circumstances. It can be achieved by an efficacious act of our own wills in cooperation with God's grace.

St. Thomas tells us that, "We are not saints because we will not to be saints." He does not say, mind you, that we do not want to be saints: many of us do. But mere wanting is the wish that something shall come to pass without our acting to bring it about. Willing means that we plan to pay the necessary cost in effort and in sacrifice.

We often delude ourselves into imagining that we have willed to be better, when we have made actually many reservations, have determined there are many present practices we will not change; then the willing is merely an idle wish. The key to spiritual advancement is to be found in the Creed: "He descended into hell; the third day He arose again." Each of us, too, must make a descent into the subconsciousness, to the portions of our minds which we keep dark, for it is here that the unspoken reservations hide. These reservations are not easily seen by us, but they color everything that we do see; they act like so many colored windows, changing the truth of external reality as it reaches our conscious minds. Reality is distorted if we have such reservations as prejudice, habits of sin, pride, avarice and jealousy; any of these can make honest judgment impossible for us. The truth is then twisted to fit our imperfections; we lie to ourselves in order not to have to change, not to abandon these prized habits of evil.

Most of us live out our lives with a false picture of ourselves which we will not surrender; we dread the pain of finding ourselves less noble than we like to believe. We strain reality through a sieve of self-love, keeping out whatever truth would hurt us. Using this private measurement of truth is as misguided as it would be to let our own preferences decide which key on the piano is middle C.... and as useless. We might pretend that a key easier to reach was Middle C, and act accordingly; but we should make discords, instead of harmonies. Reality cannot be cowed to fit our wishes.

These reservations to which we cling .... these attitudes we insist we will not surrender or change .... affect our conscious judgments and make them untrue. Before we can ever emerge into the gladness of God's reality, we have to go down into the hell in which we hide these unadmitted faults. This requires us to make a thoroughgoing analysis of ourselves in the light of God's unchanging laws.

The "Don't kid yourself!" of slang is sound spiritual advice. Nothing so stands in the way of our progress towards God as egotism, and the egotist is always full of self-deceit, of "sacred" faults he will not renounce, nor even admit he has. That is why the egotist in all of us requires a pitless searching-out of every hidden nook and corner of our minds. We need to see the self as it really is, and not as we pretend it is. We must love Truth more than we love self; we must be willing to surrender all our unguessed faults, if we are ever to be able to see the Truth, as it is.

Nothing so cripples the spiritual life as these hidden "bugs" in the motor of our soul. They may be any one of several common faults such as self-seeking, bitterness towards others, jealousy and hate. Those who are trying to grow closer to God without self-analysis wonder why they suffer such frequent defeats: invariably it is because of the Trojan Horse within them, the unrecognized dominant fault. Until that is dug out and admitted before God, with a desire to destroy it, there will be no real spiritual progress. As St. Augustine has said, *"He is Thy best servant who looks not so much to hear that from Thee that he himself willeth; as rather to will that which he heareth from Thee."*

Chapter 36
Revolution
Starts With Man

THERE ARE ANY number of social and economic theories under discussion today, but all plans for changing the world boil down to two: we may reform institutions, or we may reform man.

Most of the blue-print-for-perfection writers begin with the assumption that all the ills of humanity can be charged against an institution, a thing: change that, they tell us, and all will be well. Some of their programs blame private property for our troubles, and would "reform" it into collective ownership. Others blame our parliamentary systems, and offer to "reform" them into dictatorships. Others blame the gold policy, and tell us to "reform" it into a silver policy. But in every instance the revolution is to be waged against something outside of man; the blame is placed, and the solution sought, in property, or government, or finance. Present-day reformers never blame man himself for the world's debacle, nor try to reform the individual.

This emphasis on institutions as the cure-alls of the world has become so great that many reformers draw up a plan for peace and prosperity... and then demand that man himself shall change his nature to fit their plan. Human personality has become insignificant to them; the State is no longer seen as existing for man, but man is told he gains his meaning only in the service he can give the State. Man, under such a system, is de-humanized, de-personalized, poured into a dictatorial pattern, so that he will be molded into a mere servant of a nation, a race or a class.

This stubborn worship of a theory has had most appalling consequences in our day. To the theorist, it does not seem to matter that whole nations are deprived of liberty, that millions starve, that thousands are purged... so long as the theory is maintained in power. Instead of making the hat of governmental policy fit the head of man, the modern tendency is to cut off the head if it does not fit the hat ... to demand that institutions, political schemes and social theories must prevail, no matter if their cost proves to be the destruction of man himself.

But there is a second method of reforming the world. This method is based on the belief that reform must begin with man. It holds that his nature must, indeed, adapt itself ... but to a larger plan than any temporal theory, than any government or institution or blue-print for world order. This second method agrees that there must be a revolution ... but not a revolution against something outside of man. It urges a revolt against the evil within man; his pride, his egotism, his selfishness, his envy and his avarice.

The second kind of revolutionary reform does not place the blame for our troubles on institutions but on humanity ... not on how man handles his property, but on how man handles himself. This is a less popular method of reform than the first: we all prefer to blame something other than ourselves for our difficulties. The child kicks the door on which he bumped his head; the golfer breaks his club because he did not make the hole. Yet it was the golfer's fault he missed ... not that of the club, nor of the God Whom he may curse, in his irritation. The world is like the golfer: man forever throws the blame for his troubles away from the one place where it belongs—himself.

Projecting the blame for our difficulties brings no solution, and it never will. For the trouble with the world lies in man. There is no point in transferring the title to property from a few capitalists to a few commissars, if you leave both groups greedy and dishonest. There is no point in tinkering with the rules of parliamentary institutions, when the troubles lies, not in the rules, but in the selfishness of the men who administer them. If we would remake the world, we must being by remaking the individual man; then the institutions will be good enough, for they will resemble the good men who made them.

And that is why institutions and plans must be supple and elastic enough to fit the free, aspiring spirit of the men who grow and enlarge their vision as they reach toward God. No lesser goal than God Himself is great enough to demand of any man that he transform his nature ... no human institution has the right to cramp his powers. Man is the highest creature on earth: he matters more than every theory, every government, every plan, for the world and all that it contains are not worth one immortal soul. Let institutions crumble, blueprints go up in smoke, and governments decay. These are mere trivia, compared to the vast question asked of all of us: "How is a man the better for it, if he gains the whole world at the cost of losing his own soul?"

Chapter 37
There Is Hope

OUR WORLD is full of prophets of gloom, and I would be one of them if I did not practically believe in God. Thirty years ago the one word on everyone's lips was "progress." Now everyone speaks of defeat and the atomic bomb. This attitude of pessimism varies in direct ratio and proportion to the frequency with which one follows world news. This is not necessarily because world news is depressing, but because one seldom allows time for counterbalancing war news with other factors. As a result people lead political lives, not spiritual lives.

It would be interesting to see a commentator take the medical reports of sick patients in hospitals and broadcast them; or to read the headlines after one detail of the report was selected to the exclusion of others. We might read something like this: "Appendix lost! Life despaired!" Tremendous disproportions are created by headlines and news reports, as too often the startling is identified with the true. Parents who live in love and affection for one another, and rear their children for the triple piety of God, neighbor, and country make no headlines. But let Glamorous Glamor separate from her husband after eighteen months of biological unity, and it becomes news. The worst is taken; the good is forgotten.

So it is with the war and the world situation. Times are bad! They have never been worse; for never before has a world civilization turned against the Divine Light. We are indeed witnessing the transfer of the Christian heritage from the West to the East. Not that the West will lose it, but that the East will begin to do with it what the West did with it in its Springtime. But despite these facts, this is not the end of civilization; nor are we to be without hope. We have simply reached a moment in history where God is permitting us to feel our inadequacy, so long as we trust only in ourselves. Very often a father will allow his son, who "thinks he knows all about it," to fumble and to err in building his playhouse, until in humility he calls upon the father to help him.

Instead of this being a time of disaster, it is rather a period of humiliation. We are being left to ourselves, to our own devices, to our own conceits. Day by day we are learning that Scriptural truth: "Woe to them that go down to Egypt for help, trusting in horsemen because they are many and in horses because they are strong, and have forgotten the loving God."

A farmer went with his son into a wheat field to see if it was ready for the harvest. The son pointed to the stems that held up their heads, saying: "Those that let their heads hang cannot be good for much." The father replied: "See here, foolish child. This stalk that stands so straight is lightheaded, and almost good for nothing, while these that hang their heads so modestly are full of beautiful grain." In national life, as in nature, humility, with a head bowed before God, is the beginning of greatness.

Our greatest days are ahead, though in between intervenes the purging, where we will learn that as the rays cannot survive without the sun, so neither can we prosper without God. This hope can be translated into victory in either of two ways: by prayerful remaking our hearts, or by being brought within an inch of disaster, until from the depths of our insufficiency we cry out to the Goodness of God. The world, and in particular our own country, is filled with thousands and thousands of good people; there is an intensification of spiritual life that is inspiring; intercession has multiplied; the young are craving for spiritual sacrifice. We are not lost! We are only losing our pride. God never puts the crown of victory on a swollen head. As the shadows of the sun are longest when its beams are lowest, so we are greatest when we make ourselves least. Pride slays thanksgiving. Our next greatest victory in making peace will be celebrated by a solemn national act of thanksgiving to God. How far away is it?

Way to Inner Peace

[1954]

PART 1

INNER PEACE

Chapter 1

Egotism—The Enemy of Inner Peace

Here is a psychological suggestion for acquiring peace of soul. Never brag; never talk about yourself; never rush to first seats at table or in a theatre; never use people for your own advantage; never lord it over others as if you were better than they.

These are but popular ways of expressing the virtue of humility, which does not consist so much in humbling ourselves before others as it does in recognizing our own littleness in comparison to what we ought to be. The modern tendency is toward the affirmation of the ego, the exaltation of selfishness, riding roughshod over others in order to satisfy our own self-centeredness. It certainly has not produced much happiness, for the more the ego asserts itself the more miserable it becomes.

Humility which gives preference to others is not very popular today, principally because men have forgotten the Greatness of God. By expanding our puny little self to the infinite, we have made the true Infinity of God seem trivial. The less knowledge we have of anything the more insignificant it seems. Our hatred of a person often decreases as we learn to know him better. A boy graduating from high school is generally not as humble as when he graduates from medical school. At eighteen he thought he knew it all; at twenty-eight he feels himself ignorant in the face of the medical science he has yet to acquire. So it is with God. Because we do not pray or contemplate or love Him, we become vain and proud; but when we know Him better we feel a deep sense of dependence which tempers our false independence. Pride is the child of ignorance, humility the offspring of knowledge.

A proud man thinks himself better than he is, and when criticized always believes his neighbor is jealous or has a grudge against him. The humble man knows himself as he really is, for he judges himself as he judges time, by a standard outside himself, namely, God and His Moral Law. The psychological reason for the modern fondness for news which deflates others or brings out the evil in their lives, is to solace uneasy consciences which are already laden with guilt. By finding others who apparently are more evil, one falsely believes he becomes better. It used to be that the most popular biographies were the lives of good men for the sake of imitation, rather than scandals for the sake of making ourselves believe we are more virtuous. The pagan Plutarch said; "The virtues of great men served me as a modern mirror in which I might adorn my own life."

Humility as it relates to our fellowman is a golden mean between a blind reverence of others on the one hand and an overbearing insolence on the other. The humble man is not a rigid exacter of things to which he has no undoubted right; he is always ready to overlook the faults of others knowing that he has so many. Neither is he greatly provoked at those slights which put vain persons out of patience, knowing that as he shows mercy to others so shall he receive mercy from God. Before undertaking a task great or small, before making decisions, before beginning a journey, the humble man will acknowledge his dependence on God and will invoke His guidance and His blessing on all his enterprises. Even though he be placed above others by vocation, or by the will of the people, he will never cease to recognize that God has made of one blood all the nations that dwell on the earth. If he is very rich he will not be a "defender of the rights of the poor" without unloading his riches in their aid. Our modern world has produced a generation of rich politicians who talk love of the poor, but never prove it in action, and a brood of the poor whose hearts are filled with envy for the rich and covetousness of their money. The rich man who is humble helps the poor rather than the revolutionists who use the poor to bomb their ways to Stalinist thrones.

Another evidence of want of humility is in regard to knowledge. Scripture bids us "be wise unto sobriety." Humility moderates our estimate of what we know and will remind us that God gave to the wise more talents than others and more opportunities for developing those talents. But of him who has received much, much also will be expected. The intellectual leader has a tremendous responsibility thrust upon him and woe to him if he uses his office of teaching to lead the young into error and conceit. Notice how often today authors will have their picture taken with their book in their left hand, the title in full view of the camera, so that the photograph may tell the story: "Look Ma! My Book!" Television commentators have books on their desks with the title toward the audience so that the audience may be impressed. No man who reads books at a desk ever has the titles turned away—but toward himself. Perhaps someday when there are diaphanous walls, the intelligentsia will keep the titles on their bookshelves turned toward the wall so their next door neighbor will know how smart they are.

In the face of Divine Wisdom, all that we have, or do, or know, is a gift of God, and is only an insignificant molehill compared to His Mountain of Knowledge. Well indeed then may those who enjoy any relative superiority ask with Paul: "What have you that you have not received? If so, then why glory as if you had not received."

Chapter 2

Faithfulness in Little Things

Faithfulness in great things is not uncommon; faithfulness in little things is rare but most indicative of true character. Almost any husband would leap into the sea or rush into a burning building to rescue his perishing wife. But to anticipate the convenience or happiness of the wife in some small matter, the neglect of which would go unnoticed, is a more eloquent proof of tenderness.

Our lives for the most part are made up of little things, and by these our character is to be tested. There are very few who have to take a prominent place in the great conflicts of our age; the vast majority must dwell in humbler scenes and be content to do a more humble work. The conflicts which a man has to endure either against evil in his own soul or in the moral circle where his influence would seem to be trivial are in reality the struggle of the battle for life and decency; and true heroism is shown here as well as in those grander scales in which others win the leader's fame or the martyr's crown. Little duties carefully discharged; little temptations earnestly resisted with the strength which God supplies; little sins crucified; these all together help to form that character which is to be described not as popular or glamorous, but as moral and noble.

From God's point of view nothing is great, nothing is small as we measure it. The worth and the quality of any action depends upon its motive and not at all upon its prominence or any of the other accidents which we are apt to adopt as standards of greatness. Nothing is small that can be done from a mighty motive, such as the mite which the widow dropped into the Temple treasury. Conscience knows no such word as "large" or "small"; it knows only two words, "right" and "wrong." "He who welcomes a prophet because he is a prophet shall receive the reward given to prophets," because though not gifted with the prophet's tongue he has the prophet's spirit and does his small act of hospitality from the very same prophet-impulse which in another and one more loftily endowed leads to burning words and mighty deeds.

Man is much more inclined to concentrate his moral actions in one great moment and thereby often wins the merit of a hero. The woman, on the contrary, scatters her tiny little sacrifices through life and multiplies them to such an extent that very few give her the credit for sacrifice because it has been so multiplied.

In the spiritual order it is much easier to do some mighty act of self-surrender than daily and patiently to crucify the flesh with all of its inordinate affections. The smallest duties are often harder, because of their apparent insignificance and their constant recurrence. Unfaithfulness in little things can also prepare for unfaithfulness in the great. By a small act of injustice the line which separates the right from the wrong is just as effectively broken. Infidelity in little things deteriorates the moral sense; it makes man untrustworthy; it loosens the ties that bind society together, and it is a counteracting agency of that Divine Love which ought to be the cement of good human relationships.

Men in public life who are accused of confiscating great sums of money or else profiting by their office to secure gifts or enrich themselves in any manner whatsoever, began with unfaithfulness in the minor details of life. Somewhere and somehow the wall and partition between right and wrong had to be broken down, and what is tragic about our national situation is that there is no longer a moral indignation against such infractions of the law of honesty.

Little things make up the universe. The clouds gather up the rain and moisture and part with them in drops; time is so precious that it is given out second by second; stars do not leap about in their orbits but keep a measured pace. In like manner, humans will find little to do if they save their energy for great occasions. In every direction the great is reached through the little. The turning of a tiny needle steadily toward a fixed point is a little common thing, but it guides navies along the uncharted seas. The most insignificant trifle becomes a great thing if the alternative of obedience or rebellion is involved in it. To live by the day and to watch each step is the true pilgrimage method, for there is nothing little if God requires it.

Chapter 3
Knowledge But No Truth

Never Before in the history of the world was there so much wealth, and never before so much poverty; never before was there so much power, and never before so little peace; never before so much education and never before so little coming to the knowledge of the truth. This latter discrepancy is the Scriptural sign of "perilous times."

This does not mean that our generation is not studious, nor an uninterested inquirer, nor wanting in a thirst for knowledge. As a matter of fact, there is not a university professor in the country who does not use many times in the course of the year, the hackneyed phrase that he is interested in "extending the horizons of knowledge." We are all bent on attaining the new, but not sufficiently concerned with utilizing what we already possess. Everyone boasts that he loves to knock at the door of truth, but the sad fact is that if the door opened, many would die of the shock. They much prefer to hear the sound of their knuckles on the portals, rather than to accept responsibilities which truth implies. We do not even want to hear truth about ourselves.

Knowing many things is different from knowing truth, just as a crazy quilt is different from a blueprint. Ten thousand isolated bits of knowledge do not make for understanding, any more than the mixture of all the bottles on the shelves of a druggist makes for health. A corpse has chemical elements as well as a live body, but a corpse lacks unity which only the soul can supply. What the soul is to the body, that truth is to knowledge; what the architect and his plan are to a building, that truth is to an education.

One of the most dangerous effects of reducing education to the amassing of knowledge rather than the acquisition of truth, is that it forgets the relationship between truth and character. If a man does not know the true purpose of an explosive, he may hurt himself. The same effects do not follow from one point of view about the contents of a bottle as from another. If the bottle is filled with poison, it will do little good to the one who takes it to maintain that he was sincere in his belief that it contained bourbon. A boxer can be very "sincere" about his belief that he ought always to lead with his right, but all may not be right in the end. A farmer may be sincere in planting thistles, but he will not raise corn.

On the other hand, because a man knows the truth, his conduct will not necessarily be good. But at any rate, he has a map: he knows where he ought to go. If he gets off the road he will not blame his ductless glands or his grandmother. Even though he is off the road, he knows there is a right road. The tragedy of today is that the world is not only tearing up the photographs of a good society, but also tearing up the negatives. By denying truth the world gives up the search for it, just as the man who believes that blindness is normal will never even seek a cure.

It does not make a whale of a difference what a man believes about party politics, for parties in a democracy generally represent indifferently good means to a good end, namely the preservation of the common good. It makes little difference in the moral character of a man whether he believes golf is better exercise than tennis, but it makes all the difference in the world whether he believes that a man is a creature of God or a beast. It may take a few years for his wrong philosophy to work itself out in action, just as it takes time for cockle sown instead of wheat to appear in the harvest field, but eventually it does appear. If we are wrong in the purpose of life, we are wrong on everything. The soul is dyed with the color of its beliefs. A popular bromide is to say: "If I do my best, it will be all right." The Income Tax Bureau will not accept that philosophy. Neither will it console a man if he misses a train or has failed in his bar examination.

Education is presently directed to help students answer the question: "What can I do?" If a pencil were endowed with consciousness, it would not first ask itself: "What can I do?" but rather: "What am I?" "What is my purpose?" Once that was established, then the pencil would be prepared for writing. When our youth has discovered the Truth about life, two conclusions will follow: courage to be oneself, and humility to recognize his creatureliness; that being a product, a result, a creature of the Power that made him, he will seek with the help of that Power to be a man—aye, more than a man—a child of God!

Chapter 4
No Truth
Without Humility

Whenever a new scientific theory is born there are not wanting intelligentsia who set it to music so that every other kind of knowledge in the world dances to its tunes. When Comte developed sociology, then everything was socialized, even God; when Darwin developed evolution, then everything was revolutionized, including morals; now that relativity has been established, non-scientists make everything relative, saying there is no such thing as Truth or Goodness—these are relative to your point of view. Quite apart from the fact that the theory of relativity does not deny an absolute—for it is based on the absoluteness of the spread of light—it is rather absurd to apply the methods of one branch of knowledge to all other branches of knowledge. Relativity, for example, does not mean that we have six toes on one foot counted one way, and four toes on the other foot counted another way.

The denial of Truth is just as fatal to the mind as the denial of light is to vision. Truth in its fulness is not easy to attain, even if one does admit its existence. There are certain psychological and spiritual conditions which are essential for its discovery, and the most important of these is the virtue of humility.

Humility is not a want of moral force; rather humility is a recognition of the truth about ourselves. To explore the Truth in all its complexity there must come moments when we confess ignorance, when we frankly admit that we were mistaken or bigoted, or prejudiced. These admissions are painful, but they actually enrich character just as much as all approximations to falsehood forfeit it. If we are proud, covetous, conceited, selfish, lustful, constantly wanting our own way, it is far better to come face to face with our own ugliness than to live in a fool's paradise. The basis of all criticism of neighbor, the source of false judgments, slander, jealousies and pulling down the reputation of others is our refusal to look into our own soul. Since the sense of justice in us is so deep and ineradicable, if we do not make ourselves just by conforming to truth, we find fault with others in the vain hope of establishing justice in them. Every man is stronger for knowing the worst he can about himself and then acting on that knowledge. When we explain away our conceits by psychological jargon we increase our inner mental discomfort, as the denial of a physical illness gives random speed to the disease.

The growth of democracy has done much to do away with a false social snobbishness and to keep men humble in their external relations. But it has also, from another point of view, weakened the respect for Goodness and Truth, inasmuch as the masses of people are generally inclined to equate morality with the general level of society at any given moment. Numbers become the measure of goodness. If a sufficient number can be counted who violate a certain Commandment of God, then it is argued: "Fifty million adulterers cannot be wrong. We have to change the Commandments." The excellence of moral excellence does not reside in any external conformity to a conventional standard, but in an inward disposition under the control of a recognized principle to which we submit whether we agree with it or not.

Humility is required to challenge mediocrity; one must be ready to brave the taunts of those who knock anyone in the head who raises himself above the level of the masses. Mediocrity can be a terrific form of tyranny, and it has a thousand and one penalties for those who forsake the external standards for an inward change of heart to a line of conduct above the level. When a thousand people are walking to the edge of an abyss, he who is seen walking in the opposite direction is taunted for not following the mob. A man must be prepared to be humble to bear up under these reproaches and dare to be right when the majority is wrong.

Thus, humility is the pathway to Truth and inner peace is grounded on the recognition of two dimensions beyond the flatness of the mass level: one is the recognition of the dimension of height, which is the Sanctity above; the other is the dimension of depth, which is the existence of evil within the human heart.

Chapter 5
Desire

Desire is to the soul what gravitation is to matter. When we know our desires, we know the direction our soul is taking. If desire is heavenly, we go upwards; if it is wholly earthly, we go downwards. Desire is like raw material out of which we fashion either our virtues or vices. As Our Lord said: "Where your treasure is, there is your heart also."

Very few people ever withdraw enough from the world to ask themselves what is their basic desire. There are some who live a seemingly good life, who pay taxes, contribute to advertised welfare needs, but their basic desires are evil. Their goodness is often a want of opportunity for doing what is sinful. They are like the Elder Son in the Parable of the Prodigal Son who accuses his brother of "wasting his substance on harlots." There was nothing of this kind in the story. But the accusation revealed that the elder son would have done this very thing if he had been his brother.

On the other hand, there are some people who do very evil things, but who have a basic desire to be good, and are waiting for the day when a helpful hand will lift them from the pit. It was of such a group that Our Lord said: "The harlots and the publicans will enter the Kingdom of Heaven before the Scribes and the Pharisees."

Contentment depends upon the control of our desires. Advertising serves many needs but it has also made the luxuries appear as necessities, and created a desire for goods which the individual cannot possibly possess in their fullness. The Eastern World has struck on the secret of inner peace by suggesting that inner happiness is dependent on the control and limitation of desires. St. Paul said: "I have learned in whatever state I am to be content." Contentment is not indifference though the ignorant sometimes make that identification. Contentment does not mean immunity from trial, for it can know sighs and tears, but its feelings are never allowed to run into fretfulness. If it cannot have what it wants, it never broods over its disappointments but brightens them by sweet submission. It has no kinship with fatalism which refuses to plan or act in the belief that nothing can be altered. It is such fatalism which characterizes certain Eastern philosophies and makes progress impossible. In contentment one does not submit before he has prayed and acted, but after one has done all he can, accepting the event as the will of the Lord.

There is a world of difference between submitting to the Divine Will from sullenness and submitting to it knowing that God is Supreme Wisdom, and that someday we will know all that happened, happened for the best. There is a marvelous peace that comes into the soul if all trials and disappointments, sorrows and pains are accepted either as a deserved chastisement for our sins, or as a healthful discipline which will lead us to greater virtue. The violin strings, if they were conscious, would complain when the musician tightened them, but this is because they do not see that the sacrificial strain was necessary before they could produce a perfect melody. Evils actually become lighter by patient endurance and benefits are poisoned by discontent.

Contentment is based on the idea that "our sufficiency is not from ourselves but from God." The soul does not desire or lack more than what God has supplied him. His will suits his state after he has exhausted his resources and his desire does not exceed his power. Hence everything that happens is judged to be as good and worthy of Divine appointment. As Socrates observed: "He is nearest to God who needs the fewest things."

Contentment is not inconsistent with our endeavor to have our condition improved. We do everything we can, as if all depended on us; but we trust in God as if everything depended on Him. The talents we have must be put to work, but if they yield only a certain return, we do not murmur because the return is not greater. When we really examine our consciences, we have to admit that we have received more than we morally deserved! The discontent is far greater among the overprivileged than the underprivileged. The rich need the psychoanalysts more than the poor. Few European minds cracked under two wars. Many American minds have. The first learned not to expect anything. This lesson America has yet to learn.

PART 2

GOODNESS

Chapter 6

Goodness Needs Publicity

An Organ can produce a thunderous outburst of discordant sounds but it can also, when played properly, give forth the most soothing and peaceful melodies. So it is with the passions of man. They can be used without regard to law or they can be governed to foster joy and affection.

A man may have the knowledge of music and yet not enjoy it, as Nietzsche did before his madness as he thumped the keys of the piano with his elbows. So too we may have a knowledge of love and yet not show love to others.

One wonders if an apology for want of love is not the effect of sampling one person out of every ten thousand, and then writing a history of their passions. Would it not tend to substitute statistical average for a noble emotion? Then, too, is it scientific? Suppose we decided to write a history of the United States, and took only one day out of every ten thousand days. That would be writing one event every twenty-seven years.

What one sets out to find, one generally finds. Those who are critical by nature, almost always find faults in others. If we start with the assumption that most people are dishonest, are we not constantly bumping up against "crooks"? On the contrary, if we believe people to be kind and good-hearted, these are about the only kind of souls we ever meet. They who are afraid of accidents most generally have them; their first principle of always looking for the worst makes the worst appear. Sometimes it is possible to tell a person to hide something in a room, and later discover the hiding place by taking hold of his hand and following its instinctive motions. When one begins with the idea that infidelity is. common and that one ought to search for it, it is very likely that one will instinctively go to those areas and persons where infidelity is most likely to be found, and avoid those other groups or people where infidelity is less likely to be manifested. Tramps coming to New York, even for the first time, land in the Bowery, not on Park Avenue. What a man believes is to a great extent a determinant of where he will go, like an alcoholic to a bar, and a Christian to a church.

The mood of our century is critical, partly because of its own uneasy conscience. "Misery loves company," it is said, but so also does evil. The good has but few publicists. Most newspaper editors love murders, graft and scandals, but how few ever headline virtue. And yet the world is so full of good people, heroic deeds, generous hearts. Take the sublimest act of love that is possible in this world, namely, dying as a martyr rather than deny the God of Love. Never in history have there been as many martyrs as there are today. The martyrdoms of the first 250 years of Christian history are trivial in comparison to the unnumbered heroes of the soul who have died for the faith today. This is loyalty! This is fidelity! And any civilizations that can produce martyrs on such a high level must necessarily produce them on a lower level even in the home. What heat is to the natural universe, that love is to the moral universe.

It is love that needs sampling today, mostly because love does so little advertising of its own. Being humble by nature, like the violet, it is served by few propagandists. Cities report births as well as deaths; why then should not publicists be as interested in those who love as well as those who betray? It is part of the perversity of human nature to give more space to an ancient or a modern Benedict Arnold who betrayed his country than to ten thousand patriots who died for it. But the solemn fact remains that faithfulness, honor, control of errant impulses and love keep the world at peace. It would be well for us, in these days when men look for evil and find it, to look for good and diffuse it—in particular among the millions of cases of disinterested love where others are served, with no hope of ever receiving even an empty hand in grateful clasp.

Chapter 7
Perfection Is Not Automatic

Whenever anyone hears of a new psychological theory such as the ability to see the future in a dim way, or reads of a drug which retards old age, there is almost a cosmic rush to the conclusion that in a few years humanity will be free from error and immune from disease. This urge to perfection is right and good, for there is no reason why the evolutionary process should stand still once it comes to man.

But the fallacy is that man always thinks of this perfection as coming to him without his own effort or the exercise of his own will. Perfection is regarded as available without cost, but not like the crown of effort such as playing the piano, which is born of a thousand acts of the will and the tediousness of exercises. Perfection is thus taken out of the moral order and reduced to the physical order; it is something that is given to us, rather than something we acquire; it comes like a surprise legacy which we did not earn nor merit, rather than as a prize which was won by blood and sweat and tears. The truth is that perfection has something to do with becoming what we are not, and that this becoming is achieved through willing, self-discipline and even suffering, and implies an ideal above us and one toward which we strive.

Perfection is the plenitude of goodness, or the uniting within ourselves of goodness and happiness. This in turn demands distinction and comparison. For example, suppose a man wished to be a good archeologist, such as one of the greatest of them all, Heinrich Schlieman. Three factors were required: 1) A recognition of the fact that there was much to learn; 2) A realization of an ideal and the working toward it as the task of his life; 3) A sense of his own imperfection. This sense of imperfection came to him as a boy of seven, when his father told him about the heroes of Homer and how the mighty city of Troy was levelled and burned. The idea of perfection, from the point of view of Greek archeology, would be to discover the city of Troy. When his father told him that nobody knew where the city of Troy stood, to him perfection was expressed in the sentence: "When I am big, I shall go to Greece and find Troy and the King's Treasure." The third stage was the development of that idea. He learned many modern languages, studied Greek history and Homer until he knew him by heart. Finally, in the year 1783, after digging up 325,000 cubic yards of earth, he found Troy and the King's Treasure.

But there is not only archeological perfection, there is also human perfection, that is, our growth in goodness as human beings. This too implies three terms: 1) The first two are correlative—a sense of our own imperfection and an idea of perfection which is God. The more a man believes he knows it all, and that he has never done anything wrong for which he has to expiate his guilt, the less is his impulse toward anything better. That is why subjectively, though not objectively, the more we inflate our ego the less important God seems to be. The sick man recognizes the need of a physician; the ignorant mind senses the need of a teacher; and the soul which recognizes his own unworthiness yearns for God to complete his personality.

In between these two correlatives, namely the thirst and the fountain, hunger and the Bread of Life, there comes the third essential for moral perfection, namely, an act of the will by which one begins to lop off imperfections through restraint, sacrifice, self-discipline, and begins the positive achievement toward the Divine goal. What impels a man toward this perfection is love, for when we love perfection, we eliminate everything which offends the Loved One. For example, a girl will wear red, even though she does not like it, because she knows it pleases her beloved. Michael Angelo once was asked how he carved his statues. He said that it was very easy. Inside of every block of marble is a beautiful form. All you have to do is cut away the marble and the form will appear. In like manner, in every person there is a possible new self, the Ideal self. All one has to do is first to have an image of the model before one and trust in His grace, and then cut off huge chunks of selfishness and egotism until the Divine Image appears.

Chapter 8
Our Neighbors
In Distress

In the parable of the Good Samaritan it is said that a priest and a levite passed by the wounded man and help was given him by one of another race—namely, the Samaritan. We do not know whatever happened to the priest and the levite, but it is very likely that they went into Jerusalem and reported the condition of the dying man to a social service agency. The point of the parable is that some neighbors have to be helped in their emergency at the cost of our convenience. The neighbor is not the one who lives next door, nor the one with whom we have a nodding acquaintance. What makes a man a neighbor is love in the heart. When this is wanting it avails nothing that a man lives in the same block, or belongs to the same club, for none of these external bonds can supply the place of love.

No doubt those who saw the Samaritan aid the wounded traveler would have said that he was a neighbor or an old friend, but the truth of the matter is that the Samaritan did not know the wounded man at all; it was his genuine compassion and affection that made the Samaritan his brother and his neighbor and a friend.

The story of the Good Samaritan was told in answer to the question of a lawyer: "Who is my neighbor?" The answer of the parable is: "Every man in distress is your neighbor." Sometimes that neighbor is the one who is least capable of making known his condition. Not long ago one of the nationally known picture magazines had a photograph of a man prostrate on subway stairs. For thirty minutes many people passed him by without ever a helping hand. The editorial comment was about the coldness of the modern man in the face of distress. What was forgotten was that the photographer of the picture magazine did nothing for thirty minutes for the afflicted individual except to snap pictures and make his own living. The unfortunate traveler on the road between Jericho and Jerusalem could make no importunate supplications for relief, could not even ask for help. The need is often greatest where the least is asked. How many forms of misery are there lying within our knowledge as we journey through the bloodstained road of life. We pass them by because they do not bar our progress or because it is possible for us to put them out of our mind and live as if they were not in it.

The best way to help a man is by identifying ourselves with his affliction, getting into him and feeling his pains as our own. It is not enough merely to have an intellectual understanding of another man's difficulty; we need to go a little farther to feel it as our own burden, as the Samaritan put the wounded man upon a beast of burden and took him to an inn. On the other hand, if we have a trial and want to get mastery over it, the best person to go to is the one who has gained a victory over the same temptation. If one has marital difficulties and is inclined to leave the spouse, the worst person to go to is a psychiatrist who is already divorced and re-married. The best man to convert a drunkard is a converted drunkard. Power to appreciate temptation is the fine condition of being able to help others out of temptation. The first step God took toward making us become like Him was to become as far as He could like us.

The powerful are always under obligation to the weak. Advantage of any kind is not a personal possession but a trust. St. Paul said: "I am a debtor both to the Greeks and the barbarians; both to the wise and unwise." He owed the Greeks nothing; they had persecuted him; the barbarians he had never seen, but Paul was conscious that God had conferred upon him great gifts and he was bound to make others partake of them.

It is such willing generosity that marks the true lover of mankind. There are two kinds of liquors and juices, those that pour themselves out and drop of their own accord, and those that have to be squeezed and pressed out by violence. The latter give but grudgingly; the former are generally found more sweet. Those who help others reluctantly are like the reluctant juices. It is a long time before the purse can be found and before the hand can get in it to find change; when they give they do it in such a manner as if to indicate that the hand had stolen from the heart unaware, and that the eye was displeased with the discovery of the theft.

Love that desires to limit its own exercise is not love. Love that is happier if it meets only one who needs help than if it met ten, and happiest if it met none at all, is not love. One of love's essential laws is expressed in the words of Our Lord that the Apostles fondly remembered after He ascended: "It is more blessed to give than to receive." Our nation will be happier and our hearts will be gayer when we discover the true brotherhood of man, but to do this we must realize that we are a race of illegitimate children unless there is also the Fatherhood of God.

Chapter 9
The Problem
Of Giving

"To have" is the opposite of "to give," yet each of these things is good in its proper place. To have is to extend our personalities: we do not contain within ourselves all the essentials for human living, therefore our "being" must be completed by also "having." Existence implies the right to have sufficient food and clothing and a place to live; it does not, however, imply the right to have a sea-going yacht. Our rights to own property, to have things, decrease as the objects are farther and farther removed from our personal necessities.

The virtue of giving is dependent upon having ... for unless we possess something we cannot give it away. (This is true even of our time.) But having does not, to most people, appear as an opportunity for giving ... they look upon giving as a loss, because having is, in itself, so dear to them. This is short-sighted; if you give away half a loaf, another half-loaf remains to you, and you have had the happiness of being a donor, too.

Many people, especially among the rich, estimate the value of their own personalities in terms of owning more and more unessential things. They refuse to cut into their capital, increasing it each year, until it seems to them another self without which they would not be complete. To slice off a portion of this capital through alms would seem to them like cutting off an arm or a leg.

One woman has lived in history because she did not fear cutting into her capital. The story is told in the Gospel: *"As He was sitting opposite the treasury of the temple, Jesus watched the multitude throwing coins into the treasury, the many rich with their offerings; and there was one poor widow, who came and put in two mites, which makes a farthing. Thereupon He called his disciples to Him, and said to them, 'Believe me, this poor widow has put in more than all those others who have put offerings into the treasury. The others all gave out of what they had to spare; she, with so little to give, put in all that she had, her whole livelihood.'"*

Our Divine Lord was interested in studying the alms-givers and it was the quality of their giving which arrested Him, far more than the quantity they gave. He had once said that where our treasure is, there our heart is, also. Now He tells us that where the heart goes, there the treasure follows. Few of us have His attitude towards alms; we do not trouble to read the list of donors in fine type under the heading, "Amounts less than ..." But probably that would be to Him the most important section of the list; on that occasion in the temple He immortalized a gift of two of the smallest coins in the ancient world.

Probably the poor woman at the temple did not see her Judge nor know that she had pleased Him, nor guess that, in the scales of Divine Justice, she *"gave more than all those others who put offerings in the treasury."* They gave of their superfluity: she gave all she had, "her own livelihood." She was poor, yet she gave to the poor. She emptied herself to fill the emptiness of others. The jingle of her two small coins as they fell cried out to refute the whole base philosophy of materialism, which would teach men to acquire as much as they can—as if this earth were our only home.

And the widow's tiny gift has another meaning: it reminds us that Our Lord wants everything from us. He was the first "Totalitarian" of the spirit: He asks that we hold nothing back from Him. He demands total love: "with thy whole mind, thy whole heart, thy whole spirit, and thy whole strength." Only those who have given their whole hearts to God can give Him their whole capital, as well.

Nothing that is given in such a spirit of generosity is ever lost. In the materialist's reckoning, what is renounced is lost forever. In the realm of the spirit, this is not true. For what we give to God is not only recorded to us for eternal merit—it is even returned in this life. One of the most practical ways of assuring that we shall always have enough is to give and give and give in the Name of the Lord. Similarly, the most rapid increase in love of God can be obtained by being totally generous to our neighbors. *"Give and the gifts will be yours; good measure, pressed down and shaken up and running over, will be poured into your lap; the measure you award to others is the measure that will be awarded to you."* (Luke 6:39.)

The use to which we put what we have is closely related to what we are, to our "being," and to what we will become. He who keeps everything he has for himself, must lose it all at death; he who has given it away will get it back in the coin of immortality and joy.

Chapter 10
Hospitality

GREAT virtues are apt to pass out of civilization because the structure of society changes. When there were few cities and journeys were long and arduous, hospitality was one of the most frequently practiced virtues. Herodotus, the Greek historian, tells us of being shipwrecked on a sparsely settled shore, and how a whole family went without food to care for him. One of our missionaries in the Pacific stated that he would never tell the natives of the island that he had even so much as a headache; otherwise they would sit up outside his tent the whole night boiling water and herbs, and holding themselves at attention in case of need.

Hospitality has not passed out of the world today, but to a large extent it has become corporate or organized. Institutions are set up to care for the traveler or the needy, as the care becomes less personal and the responsibility less individual. A few decades ago no one in a horse and buggy along a country road would refuse to stop and pick up someone walking. Today few automobiles stop to give lifts to those on the highway, mostly because too many hitch-hikers have made hospitality impossible by their unhospitable conduct. Despite this, it is wrong to think the world is not fit to be trusted and that everyone is a rogue until he proves himself honest.

Granted the changing ways, the necessity of the virtue of hospitality still remains. Nor is it satisfied by identifying hospitality with the offer of a highball. The essence of hospitality is sympathy and kindness; it is selfishness which makes us think that the opportunities for hospitality are past.

> *"I thought the house across the way*
> *Was empty; but since yesterday*
> *Crepe on the door makes me aware*
> *That someone has been living there."*

The age of discovery is not yet over and the greatest discovery yet remains to be made by every individual, namely, there are other people in the world besides oneself. As a former Prince of Wales once said: "Number Ten Downing Street can never be a substitute for the good neighbor"; neither can the Community Chest nor the Social Agency. Immediate personal contact, courageous embracing of the worries and burdens involved in full personal and intimate relationships — these are the bloodstream of a healthy society.

On the Last Day, Our Blessed Lord said that He will judge us by our attitude to hospitality: "When did we see Thee a stranger and take Thee in?" Hospitality, therefore, not only has the duties of which we are aware, but also the more terrible awareness that it is Christ Who is the Stranger. In all our dealings, we are dealing with the Lord Himself, though we know it not. Maybe if we could see our wars aright, in between two trenches of the enemies, or between a plane in the sky and the Hiroshima beneath, there is Christ's Body being shot full of holes. What men do to one another, they do to Him, whether the act be of kindness or bitterness, and out of those acts will come our judgment.

The bold knight of the Round Table traveled far over mountain and desert in search of the Holy Grail, the Cup of Life from which the Saviour drank the night of the Last Supper. His journeys proved fruitless. Depressed in spirit and fatigued in body, he returned to Arthur's Hall. On the way he saw a poor man writhing in the ditch. Moved with compassion, he dismounted, gave a cup of water to the suffering man, and the cup glowed with fire as if it were alive with the joys of the new Covenant of Love. The Knight found the Holy Grail, not in deeds of prowess, but in hospitality to the needy.

Wells are made sweeter for the drawing. Those from which no man draws water for beast and fellowman become polluted. Riches too become more peaceful when used as fuel for charity. The poor cannot reward us for hospitality; therefore God will have to do so. It was these He asked us to invite to our dinners, and it is interesting to note that He always called them, not a meal but a "banquet."

Part 3

Happiness

Chapter 11
Joy And Sadness

THE wise man said: "Cast sadness far from thee, because it has killed many, and is good for nothing." There is hardly anything as apt to bring our hearts to a state of irksome disgust as sadness. Those who have made a psychological study of sadness tell us that one of its principal effects is to disturb our judgments, making us take a darker view of life than the facts justify. Thus, sadness leads to pessimism, and the reverse effect is also true; all pessimists are necessarily sad: disaster, for them, is just around the corner. A second effect of sadness is to make us rude to others and severe towards them, suspicious and ready to put the worst interpretation on the actions of everyone around us.

There are different ways of trying to overcome the sense of sadness. Some people take recourse to alcohol to make them forget. Others fling themselves into carnal pleasures, hoping that the intensity of a momentary thrill will compensate them for a want of a goal and a purpose in life. But all sad people are alike in this: at some time, they say—perhaps scarcely conscious that they are saying it—" I do not love myself." This is not an "inferiority complex." It is rather the higher part of the self-looking down on the lower part and reprimanding it for its pitiable condition. Animals cannot reflect on themselves as man does; hence they cannot feel the same kind of disgust.

There is a remedy for sadness—the one suggested by the Scriptures. To some minds it may seem far-fetched, when it says: "If you are sad, pray!" Actually, these words touch on a profound psychological truth, for they imply that we must be reconciled to ourselves in order to be happy. So long as we are merely the battleground of a war between the lower self and the higher self within us, there can be no relaxation and no joy. But to resolve the conflict, to bring the battle to an end, we must see ourselves as we really are. It does no good to blame the golf club if our game is at fault, or the pitcher because we spill the milk; the fault must be seen as our own in little mishaps of this kind, and for our states of mind as well. The discovery that we are to blame for being the way we are is greater than the discovery made by any explorer—such a discovery of our own fault is impossible unless there be a higher standard outside ourselves, from whose love we know that we have fallen.

When our own responsibility for our sadness has once been faced, prayer next leads us on to hope, because it shows us the real basis for our discontent: the knowledge that we could be quite different from the way we are. As one writer put it: "I was told that I was the offspring of a father and a mother. I had thought that I was more." And one is more. The Saviour said that each one of us is of more worth than the whole visible universe!

We begin to act differently when we recognize the immensity of our possibilities. Our whole life changes then, like that of a farmer when he discovers oil on what he had previously believed to be just a poor farm. Prayer overcomes sadness by putting us in relation with the Eternal, and then the change occurs. Before, we had thought ourselves unloved by anyone; now, we know that we are loved by God.

Unless man puts God between himself and his previous life, he cannot stand himself. But God does not give Himself to a man until the man has begun to feel his own nothingness. By assenting to the poverty of our personality we open the flood gates of Divine riches. It has been said that no man is a hero to his valet. It would be truer to say that no man is a hero to himself. Plutarch may tell us that Cato was a great man; but to Cato, Cato was a weak man.

It is one thing to discover one's nothingness, and to rest there—that is sadness. It is quite another thing to discover that one is nothing, and from there to make use of the Divine Energies—that is joy. Mediocrity is a sin against ourselves, a kind of sacrilege. The ennui some hearts feel is nothing but the instinctive reaction of their great and undeveloped possibilities in the face of the triviality and mediocrity of their lives. All around us, birds are flying, musical in song, eager to enter into our souls. But until we are reconciled with the goal of life, they have to be content to perch on the top of our roof for a moment, and then fly away.

To pass from sadness to joy requires a birth, a moment of travail and labor, for no one ever mounts to a higher level of life without death to the lower. Before such an ascent, conscience, for a moment, has a hard, stern work to do. Pearls come from the bottom of the water, gold from the depths of the earth, and the great joys of life are to be found in the recesses of a contrite, broken heart.

Joy is the happiness of love—love aware of its own inner happiness. Pleasure comes from without, but joy comes from within, and it is, therefore, within the reach of everyone in the world. For if there is sadness in our hearts, it is because there is not enough love. But to be loved, we must be lovable; to be lovable, we must be good; to be good, we must know Goodness; and to know Goodness, is to love God, and neighbor, and everybody in the world.

Chapter 12

Our Moods

Our blessed lord advised us: "When you fast, do not be sad nor wear a long face." Then He cautioned His hearers to so dress themselves that no one would know they were fasting. Sadness is atheism, but it is not Christian. It is atheism not only because one has no invisible means of support, but also because there is less hope as day adds to day and the lease on life runs out. Many who have an empty stomach or a trial on the inside, placard it on their faces, register it in their voices and show it in their actions. Their disposition is either morose, sad, taciturn, moody, grouchy, bitter or sharp.

All has not gone well at the office, or in the factory. The husband returns and answers his wife in monosyllables, if he answers her at all. The phone rings and a customer is at the other end; all is sweetness and light. This disproves those who say that bad humor is really not our fault at all, it is due to getting up on the wrong side of the bed, or "my rheumatism is bothering me today," or "my corn hurts and I know it is going to rain." These excuses are the same as those given in universities for sins, such as blaming it on our grandparents, as do the Freudians, or on the Capitalists, as do the Marxists. The truth of the matter is, as Shakespeare says, the fault is not in the stars, but in ourselves. External circumstances do condition our mental outlook and our dispositions, but they do not cause them.

Just as there is a right and wrong theory about the sun and the earth, so there is a right and wrong theory about external circumstances. If we revolve about what happens on the outside, then the latter determines our moods and attitudes. But if we make what is external revolve around us, we can determine the amount of their influence. Either what is outside makes our moods, or our moods determine our outlook on what is outside us. The pot that overboils can boil over the temper, or the temper can see the pot overboil and not get mad. Continuing that figure, it may be said that there are some people who in a quarrel love to keep the "pot boiling."

Rainy days do make some people sad, but the author remembers saying once to a resident of Killarney: "Too bad it's raining." He answered: "But it's a good day to save your soul." Come to think about it, it may be easier to do that on rainy days than on sunny days. Our humor and disposition are not so much the reflection of the weather or the wrong side of the bed, as they are the reflections of the state of our soul. What is outside of us is beyond our control; but what is within us can be mastered and woven to any desired pattern. As Pascal once said: "Time and my moods have little relationship; I have my fogs and my bad weather within me." Our personal dispositions are as window panes through which we see the world either as rosy or dull. The way we color the glasses we wear is the way the world seems to us. To a great extent what we see is colored from the inside, rather than from the outside.

Two considerations are helpful in developing a good disposition. The first is to be mindful that a happy conscience makes a happy outlook on life, and an unhappy conscience makes us miserable on the inside and everyone else miserable on the outside. When our conscience bothers us, whether we admit it or not, we often try to justify it by correcting others, or by finding fault with them. The readiness to believe evil about others is in a large part ammunition for a thousand scandals in our own hearts. But by finding black spots in others, they believe they distract attention from their own miserable state. The good conscience, on the contrary, finds good in others even when there is some discontent with self.

The second aid to good humor is the spirit of joy. Joy is rejoicing in another's progress. This is one of the rarest virtues and the last to be won. Too often the progress of others is regarded as stolen from self. A man loses his good humor when he calls his wife "dear" when they are out and an "ox" when at home. The wife loses her joy when she would rather spend her time mending his ways than mending his socks. All have joy when they thank God that their friends have done good work, that they are loved by others, and that their virtues proclaim the joy of a good conscience.

Chapter 13

Melancholy

Melancholy is a strictly modern phenomenon, made by the wings of the soul beating against the bars of the cage of time. The greatest analyst on this subject, Soren Kierkegaard, once expressed his own personal melancholy as follows: "I have just returned from a party of which I was the life and soul. Wit poured from my lips, everyone laughed and admired me—but I left—and the dash should be as long as the earth's orbit—and wanted to shoot myself."

This type of melancholy is not so much due to the burdens of life as it is to a reaction from its pleasures. Nero, one of the greatest of all sensualists, was notoriously melancholic. In more religious days of the past the pleasure addict had remorse, which implied conscience. But melancholy, unlike remorse, is devoid of conscious ethical considerations; it is an emptiness that comes from having spent too riotously the honeyed pleasures of the body; it is a horrifying sense of barren activity, romantic nothingness, and the futility of life itself. The unhappy man begins trying to escape from himself by losing himself in excitements, stimulants and erotic experiences. But instead of any of these being a bed where he may feather his nest in repose, each turns out to be a rubber wall which makes him rebound upon himself. The very self from which he sought release is now the very self which tortures him. The more he tries to lose himself, the more he finds himself. He breathes in the same air he breathed out, and each time it becomes more corrupted and less bearable.

Melancholy thus produces what might be called "re-duplication." The self is confronted with self. A prisoner escaped one night from a prison, walked all night, swam a river twice, and at sun-up found himself back at the very prison from which he escaped. The melancholic is like this: he is always trying to "get away from himself," but all the roads he takes are circular and he meets himself coming back. It is not a pleasing sensation, any more than the first glance in the mirror on awakening. There is the inescapable "thou" and the "I," and there hardly seems to be room for both in the apartment of the soul. The man without a goal in life goes fishing for pleasure and on the hook, he catches himself not in enjoyment but in disillusionment and suffering.

At this point, one of two things may happen. First, he may become defiant about his despair, and if he is an author he will write a drama or a novel proving that melancholy is the lot of humanity. Because he burned his hand on the fires of egotism, he seeks relief by describing burns as normal and conflagrations as hearths where hearts may warm themselves. Evil is always easier to write about than goodness, because all people have some experience of evil, but not all have a major experience in virtue. The nightmares of despair and melancholy that provide themes for the stage and movies bear witness to the frustration in many modern souls and to their ineffectual attempts at purgation by spreading the epidemic.

But there is another possible reaction to melancholy than defiance, and that is realizing that one is locked in a combat with self. As soon as one sees that his mind is a battlefield in which the personality which is split is waging a war, one begins to look for a peacemaker. The "two have to get together," used so often in speaking of social and international disputes, is now applied to self. Obviously, peace cannot come from within, for that is the source of all the trouble. The mind is like a willow tree whose branches are already wet with tears. As the sun alone can dry the dampness of the tree, so now the melancholic mind looks outside self for help and deliverance.

And this is the way many a modern mind is finding God, through the emptiness of self and the despair within. It has always been known that man could come to God through a series of disgusts, but it remained for our day to form it into a pattern. The contradiction within, which drives the defiant melancholic individual to suicide, is the same force which drives the self-acknowledged melancholic to God. Sartre is the world's spokesman for the despair that prefaces hell, and Kierkegaard the spokesman for those who in the darkness of their self-sealed tombs cry for light. The modern mind has been closed to God for a long time, but it seems now that God is finding His way back as He did at the beginning of Christian history—coming once more through closed doors!

Chapter 14
Inner Life

THE more we look for happiness in the outer world, the more we endanger our inner peace. Only the man who is self-possessed is serene, for he alone has set up conditions for peace which are under his own control. The others are victims of circumstance, slaves of things which any moment may withhold. The drunkard is alcohol-possessed; the avaricious are money-possessed; the trifling are style-possessed ... the universe of any one of them can be rocked by somebody else's will. None of us can control the way in which others will act toward us; but we can always control our reaction to them.

Our relations with external things are all in terms of having or of not having; the inner life of the spirit centers, in contrast, on being, on what one is. Too often people spoil their whole lives in desires to have, when our main interests should be devoted to efforts to be. Since nothing in the material universe is greater than the spirit, the personality within each of us, every yielding of ourselves to some material craving or necessity is a loss. Having anything at all creates problems; the more keys a man carries on his keyring, the more numerous his problems. And not-having things we think we need can cause frustration, too. But the man who wants nothing is free; whatever happens to him is acceptable, and whatever is withheld from him is surrendered without a pang.

Refusal to value the external things as a goal is the pathway to self-possession. To be wholly integrated and happily simple, as we ought to be, demands that we flee from the chaotic, the multitudinous and conflicting objects that surround us. For if we allow these things to fill our souls, they will crowd out the Divine which ought to dwell there. The man who relies on outside satisfactions is in a constant state of civil war; he is the house divided against itself which cannot stand.

In this age many things solicit us to look for happiness among cheap and material satisfactions which require no inner effort, no use of the reason or the will. Even our magazines now tend more and more to use pictures instead of text: we do not even have to read or think to "keep up." Stimuli from stage and screen and bill-boards pull us in different directions, arouse in us a constant series of emotions, keep us living in a turmoil of surface experiences. This kind of living can make us the victims of our own sensations, which are cruel tyrants; men who surrender inner mastery are heading for a nervous breakdown.

To restore peace to the shattered, nervous man of today, all that is needed is for him to place a ring of silence between himself and the outer world ... to begin to place more importance on what he is than on what he has or what he feels. If we detach our attention from the ego and its selfish needs, we have made a start. The next step is to try to fulfill, down to the least detail, the Holy Will of God—for doing this affords our self-perfection and our peace. Clinical health and moral health are usually identical. A violation of the moral law always disturbs mind and body, but submission to God's will inevitably brings a greater health to the body and a deep peace to the soul.

For a while, the sacrifice of our selfish whims will demand an effort; but to the man who has once placed God's wishes ahead of his own, there is no further sacrifice involved. The early stages of the spiritual life are like the years of a musician's apprenticeship: he has to think in terms of effortful study, of finger-exercises and of missing parties in order to practice. But later, these things are willingly accepted, for the mature musician sees them as curtain raisers to his joy. The man who loves God with his whole mind and his whole heart sees all obedience to Him as a way to beauty and wonder. As lightning strikes the metal pole which is already full of electricity rather than the wooden shaft, so God's serenity strikes those creatures who are already best prepared for it through love of Him.

Such inner peace can be won only by making God the ruler of all that we do. Many people who believe in God refuse to go this far: they keep Him in a small compartment of their minds. Their plans are laid without consulting Him; their trials and sufferings are endured with no recollection of the fact that Love may hurt in order to cure; their days are passed in loneliness and weariness, although each hour might have been filled with sweetness.

To such hearts a single moment of grace may work the change. They suddenly become aware that "the Lord is in the house." Better still: the Lord is in our hearts. They are no longer self-centered, now, but they are God centered; outer events of their lives can no longer ruffle their peace. What they have has become unimportant; the only thing that matters is what they are, and what they are is His Children. At last they are able to hear His words: "Peace is my bequest to you, and the peace I give you is mine to give; I do not give peace as the world gives it. Do not let your heart be distressed."

Part 4

Virtue

Chapter 15

Selflessness

THERE are three ages of man: Youth, middle age, and maturity. Each has its corresponding passion, which would destroy or impair personality by making it a slave to something low or base. The passion of youth is sex; the passion of middle age is power or ambition; the passion of the mature is avarice. These passions are not base in themselves—no passion ever is. They become base only when consented to against right reason and the Law of God.

Those who consent to the deordinations of the flesh in youth often sublimate into the ambitious in the forties, and to avaricious in the sixties. The object of their passion has changed, but they have not. In one instance, the object is the body; in the other the ego or the proud mind; and in the last instance, things (wealth) outside both body and mind. The first excess of the flesh is generally recognized as wrong, but modern civilization does not regard pride or avarice as "dirty" sins, though they can be just as disastrous as lust.

Of the three, lust, egotism and greed, the first is the easiest for the spirit to master, because its excesses create its own emptiness. Sated flesh-love can create a desire for spirit-love. But egotism and greed are very difficult to cure, because they are inflationary sins. Excesses of flesh deflate, but pride and wealth swell the ego to a point where a man believes he is truly great, either because he thinks he is, or because he judges himself by what he has, rather than what he is.

Since egotism, pride and selfishness are so dominant in middle age, it is important to concentrate on their judgment. One day when the Apostles were quarreling among themselves as to who was the greatest among them, Our Lord placed a child in the midst of them, as an example that the littlest is the greatest. Later, He followed this act with the words: "He that is the greatest among you, let him be as the servant."

By the Divine standard, true greatness is indicated neither by the possession of great abilities nor the buzz of popular applause. Any talent a person has, such as a talent for singing, speaking, or writing, is a gift of God. He has done nothing more to merit it than a child with a beautiful face. "If then, thou has received, why dost thou glory, as if thou hadst not received." The richer the gifts, the greater the responsibilities on the day of Judgment.

When Our Divine Lord said that the great must be as the least, He made the measure of greatness usefulness and service to his neighbor in His Name. Service of others is necessary because it involves the constant repression of those egotistic tendencies in us which exalt us at the expense of others. Aristotle said that the two most degrading tendencies in man were towards bad temper and ill-regulated desire. Either one or the other is present in every egotist. He either gets mad at others because they do not praise him or do his will, or he seeks his own pleasure at the expense and shame of others.

Service corrects both of these evil tendencies. It removes ill-temper by making the person do good to others out of obedience to God's Will. A man in love with a woman conceals his ill-temper to win her love. A soul in love with God kills his ill-temper to be worthy of the love of God. Service also corrects ill-regulated desires by constantly putting the needs of the neighbor before the wishes of the ego. They are selfless because absorbed in other selves; happy because they have no needs except to bestow on their fellowman the overflowing goodness of their hearts. And such selfless souls are always the most popular in offices, schools, clubs, factories and playgrounds.

What a lesson nature teaches about selflessness! Clouds, playing like lambs in the pastures of the sky, never keep their treasures of moisture to themselves, but pour them out in the beautiful benediction of rain to a thirsty earth. No drop of water leads a selfish life. There is no breeze without its mission. Human lives were not sent into this world as ornaments. God has prettier things for that purpose. As the bird that sings for others gladdens its own heart with song, as the rivers flee the decay of stagnant self-content to service the mighty ocean, as the sun burns itself out to light a world, so does everything—man included—become good by doing good to others.

But if we are to do good to others, they must be loved for God's sake. No moral profit comes from doing good to another because "he can get it for us wholesale" or from giving gifts to others because of the pleasure they give us. There is not even great merit in doing good to those who love us. "You love those who love you. Do not the heathens this?" The greatest spiritual profit comes from loving those who hate us, and from giving gifts and dinners to those who cannot give anything in return, for then recompense will be made in the Kingdom of Heaven.

The inertia of selfish idleness and of greed will best be overcome by a man on his knees, praying for the entrance of the Spirit of Love. The millwheel stops when the rushing waters are stilled; the moving train stops when the hot embers cool; and charity vanishes as the love of God declines. If people only knew how happy they would make themselves if they really helped their neighbor for the love of God, we would soon become a nation with songs in our hearts, as well as on our lips.

Chapter 16

Insincerity

It is quite generally taken for granted that the way to be popular is to say things you do not mean, or to draw a veil between your mind and your lips, or divorce thoughts from actions. Their lips then carry honeyed speech; their hands carry stilettos; the speech is for other ears; the stilettos are for others' backs. Psychologically, those who manifestly are shams are generally known through three techniques: first they shake hands with you up to the elbow, and they thrust their face against your nose with a smile which seems to say, "See how nice I am," or they shout out their greeting in tones calculated to make volume substitute for honesty.

Children do not have this duplicity because they are natural and it is acquired. If their mother tells them to tell a stranger at the door that she is not at home, they will invariably say, "My mother told me to tell you that she is not at home." I know of a mother who, after an introduction to several ladies who had dropped in for tea, asked her child, "Now which one did I say was my best friend?" The child in the presence of all answered, "The one with the big teeth." It takes some falling away from the childlike simplicity that purchases heaven, before one develops the film of dishonesty.

There are moments when it is very difficult to express one's views, for example, when a husband is asked how he likes his wife's new hat, or how he likes her new Italian haircut—which to him resembles unstrung spaghetti. Women, when faced with something they do not like, generally go into ecstasies of praise in order to cover up their real mind. Men generally descend to monosyllables or a long grunt. When a man gets mad at his wife at cards, he generally calls her "dear" but with such a coolness as to make her think she is a "Frigidear." Tact, in such difficult moments, does not mean lying, nor smoothness at the expense of truth, but it does mean circumspection. Some women, on being asked how they like another woman's dress, will generally say that it is "lovely," but the tone of the voice betrays the suspicion that it is not.

The opposite form of insincerity is flattery. As we have said before, there are two kinds of flattery: blarney and baloney. Blarney is the varnished truth; baloney is the unvarnished lie. Blarney is flattery laid on so thin, you like it; baloney is flattery laid on so thick, you hate it. Shakespeare says, "it is laid on with a trowel." The amount of flattery one spreads on another depends on either how much one wishes to exalt his own ego, or how much one wishes to deceive the ego of the hearer. Rare are those who use such restraint in flattery in order to delude others into asking them to "say that again." A Bishop who was just consecrated was laughingly told, "From now on you will never hear the truth again."

Insincerity of a minor degree is that in which we constantly promise something that we never expect to fulfill. The "Yes Man" is Exhibit A of that group, who is always afraid to assert his own mind and who identifies agreement with agreeableness. Another form is the invitation to dinner, "Come up and have dinner with us sometime," brings the equally agreeable and insincere answer, "Yes, I will." The insincerity is in the indefiniteness; "sometime" can often mean, "We are not expecting you," and its answer sometimes means, "Nor do I expect to go."

At the opposite extreme of these forms of insincerity are those who identify insult, boorishness, contempt, scorn, loud-mouthing's with sincerity, candor and honesty. They boast that they are unafraid of public opinion or "what others think," or that they are always saying "what is best for you" or "what your best friends won't tell you." Little do they know that their readiness to criticize is a mask for their own egotism; afraid of having their own weakness pointed out, they keep others off guard by their poisoned attack.

The sincere are those who have an ensemble of virtues, who are equally good at speaking and listening; who have silences, as well as words; who are not opaque like curtains, but transparent like window panes. They speak, knowing that one day they will have to be judged by God and obliged to give "an account of every idle word." That makes them love the Truth and because they love it, they are always kind and charitable.

Chapter 17

When The Good People Do Wrong

THE good sometimes do wrong. Let us face it. And when they do wrong it is not the same as the evil who do wrong. Evil is an exception in the life of the good; it cuts across the long road of their life as a tangent. But with the evil, good is an exception. A master pianist may hit a wrong note, but everyone still knows him to be a good pianist. A beginner may hit a right note, but everyone knows that he is not a good player.

As a result the inner workings of the mind are quite different in the good doing wrong and the evil doing evil. In the latter, a hardening process sets in. Conscience first shouts, then after repeated chokings becomes so weak it can only whisper; finally its voice is stifled altogether. Since such people willed to have no moral law except of their own making, God leaves them alone. It is terrible for the soul when God pursues it and drives it to perfection; but it is more terrible still when He leaves the soul to its own conceits.

The psychological effect is entirely different when those who truly love God do wrong. The difference between them and others is like to that between a waif who steals and a devoted son who steals. The first does not feel the rupture of a relationship; the second does. The latter has hurt one whom he really loves. Furthermore, the waif does not feel the urge to restore the broken buds of love, but the ordinary good boy does. There is a mysterious magnet operating in the case of the good. As the steel filings fly to the attraction of the magnet, leaving the dirt behind, so the good are pulled back again to God, but only after having shaken the dust of evil from their lives.

Picture two men married to two old shrews. One man was married before to a beautiful, wise, devoted wife who died. The other was never married before. Which of the two suffers the more? Obviously, the man who once knew love and happiness. So, it is with doing evil. He who has known the inner peace of soul that comes from union with God, undergoes greater agony and torture in his sin than the one who never was ushered into such treasures. The rich who become poor suffer more than the poor who never were rich. The soul which offends God Whom he loves suffers more than the soul who willed not to have God in his life.

This does not mean that the evil do not experience an agony. In the good, the effect of doing evil is moral and leads to repentance. In the evil, the effect is physical and psychological. It shows less in the soul and more in the mind and the body. The moral effect is sorrow, contrition, repentance, which leads to a restoration of the fellowship with God and therefore peace. The physical or psychological effect is anxiety, fear, worry, psychoses and neuroses. The good take to their knees when they do wrong; the evil, if they have money enough, betake themselves to a couch. The good want their sins forgiven; the evil want them explained away. The good recover peace of soul; the evil have to be satisfied with peace of mind.

The explanation of this phenomenon is that the good have another principle of action in them than the evil. The evil are guided solely by the thought either of the satisfaction of the flesh or the spirit and that this world is all. But the good have another principle in them, entirely above nature which is called grace and by which they are united to God. This principle of grace is always rising up against their sin and generally triumphs over it with the slightest cooperation of the will. A man refrains from adultery because of the love he has for his wife. This principle of love militates against his carnal desires and if he falls, pulls him back again to fidelity. So, with grace. As St. Paul wrote to the pagan Romans: "My own actions bewilder me; what I do is not what I wish to do, but something I hate. Why then, if what I do is something I have no wish to do, I thereby admit that the law is worthy of all honor."

That is the point. The very regret one has is an admission that the law of God is right. A child told by his parents not to stick his finger in the fires does so. But he immediately discovers that their law was worthy of all honor.

There are two ways of knowing how good God is. One is never to lose Him; the other is to lose Him and find Him again.

Chapter 18
Wars And Rumors Of Wars

There are two great evils in the world: sin and suffering. Sin is moral, suffering is physical, and the latter is a result of the former. What happens to the body of man as pain, and to nature in the form of cyclones, earthquakes and floods, is ultimately an echo, a repercussion and effect of what has already happened in the moral universe. When the big wheel in a machine is cracked, all the little wheels get out of order. As man eliminates sin, he eliminates suffering; as he loves God, he ceases to hate his fellowman and therefore engages in fewer wars.

The more morality and decency and virtue there are in mankind, the more peace there will be in the world. Wars are consequences of a moral rebellion. The Scriptures boldly affirm that war is the result of egotism and selfishness. When civilization is made up of millions of men and women who are at war with themselves, it is not long until communities, classes, states and nations will be at war with one another. Every world war is a turbulent ocean made up of the confluent streams of millions of little wars inside the minds and hearts of unhappy people. War is the final logic of self-will.

War is not necessary, but it does become an inseparable ailment of any world that abandons the supremacy of the spirit. Nietzsche, after proclaiming the death of God in the nineteenth century, prophesied that the twentieth century would be a century of wars. There is a possible connection between the importance given to politics and the frequency of wars. In any era of history where politics is the major interest, war is the major consequence. This does not mean that one ought to subscribe to the dictum of Karl von Clausewitz that war is the prosecution of politics by other means. It does mean however, that since politics stresses expediency and pragmatism on a great scale that dedication to truth and morality are minimized. Since the latter are essential for peace, war becomes a greater possibility. When the people are interested in the raising of a family, the cultivation of virtues and the salvation of their souls, they act as a balance wheel against the power-motive of politics. But when both the state and the people give supremacy to politics, the stabilizing influence of society is lost, and with it come civil strife and discord and war.

There is much truth in the thesis of Pitirim Sorokin that as civilization in the modern sense of the term advances, there is an increase of war. There have always been more wars than peace. From 1496 B.C. to 1861 A.D. or in 3,358 years there were only 227 years of peace and 3,130 years of war; this makes 13 years of war for every year of peace. Within the last three centuries there have been 286 wars in Europe.

From 1500 B.C. to I860 A.D. there were 8,000 treaties of peace which were supposed to remain in force forever. The average length of these treaties was two years. It is likely that there was never a single year when the world did not have a war at least in one country or the other. Two other analyses have revealed that since the year 1100 England has spent half of its history fighting wars; France nearly half, and Russia three quarters.

It is not a very sweet pill for our civilized world to swallow, to realize that the false prophets of the last century who predicted an evolution of man into a god, and the necessary progress of humanity to a point where there would be no war or disease or death, were wrong, and we are now living in a century of war. It behooves humanity to admit that there is an evil tendency in man, and that this tendency when uncontrolled by morality and grace will devolve more rapidly than it will evolve. It is our views of man that have been wrong; by denying the possibility of sin and guilt, we have denied the very existence of perversity within us which makes war. Not all men will submit to this moral regeneration through self-discipline, but those few who will, will be the leaven in the mass of the world.

It is not our politics and our economics which have to be changed first; it is man. It is the wars within that have to be stopped. The remaking of the world is the remaking of man. The return of man to God is the condition of more peaceful times.

Part 5

Learning

Chapter 19

Pride And Humility

Man can set himself above his fellows, and feel superior to them, in either of two ways: by his knowledge, or by his power; by flaunting what he knows, or by using money and influence to make himself supreme. Such forms of behavior always spring from pride.

Now pride of the first kind—intellectual pride—changes its expression with the fashion of the age. In some periods of history (when the public idols were men of learning, esteemed for their scholarship) the proud man pretended to possess vast knowledge which was not really his. Intellectual bluffers were common. Phonies (who always wish to seem, rather than to be whatever kind of leader is applauded in their age) put on a pretense of scholarship which was not theirs.

Such intellectual bluffers are less common today: we do not, in our society, reward our men of learning with sufficient glamor or publicity to make it worth the phoney's while to try to seem to be one of them. Traces of the old snobbery of the intellect still remain in those circles of the intelligentsia where the question, "Have you read such and such a book?" is used as a test of whether one is intellectually on his toes.

Nowadays the commoner form of intellectual pride is negative. The proud man does not exalt himself; he tears the others down and thus accomplishes the same goal in the end—that of finding himself raised high above his fellows. The cynic and the scoffer are common examples of modern pride. They do not pretend to share the knowledge of the learned man; they simply tell us that his knowledge is untrue, that the great disciplines of the mind are a tangle of outworn absurdities, that nothing is worth learning because everything is obsolete. The ignorant man, boasting of his ignorance, thus tries to establish himself as the superior of all those who know more than he: for he knows what they do not know— that study "is a waste of time."

The new-fashioned egotist of this type—the man who scorns the knowledge others possess—is as guilty of pride as the old-fashioned intellectual snob who pretended to wisdom he had not taken the trouble to absorb.

Both errors, the old and the new, might be rarer if education stressed, more than it does, the quality of receptivity. The child is humble before a fact; he loses himself in admiration of it. The older man, too often, asks of every fact, "How can I use this to extend my ego, to make a bigger splash among my fellows, to induce people to admire me more?" Ambition to use knowledge for our selfish ends drives out the humility which is required of us before we can learn anything.

Intellectual pride destroys the mood in which we learn; it also places a film of self over our eyes, so that we cannot enjoy the life around us. When we are preoccupied with ourselves we do not give our full attention to any person or thing that comes our way, and so we do not get, from each experience, the enjoyment it could give to us. It is because the small child knows that he is small, and accepts the fact without pretending to be big, that his world is a world of wonders. To every little boy, his father is a giant.

The capacity for wonder is killed in many universities. Men emerge interested in the question of whether they are at the top of the class, or the foot, or somewhere in the middle, working their way higher. This interest in the self and its rating poisons the proud man's life—for self-centeredness is always a form of pride.

The willingness to learn, to change, to grow is a quality of self-forgetfulness, of real humility.

It is the pride of the show-off which makes it impossible for him to learn ... or, indeed, to teach the things he knows. For only the mind which humbles itself before the truth it wishes to impart can pass the knowledge on to other minds. The world has never known a humbler teacher than the Word of God Himself, who taught in simple parables and homely examples drawn from sheep and goats and lilies of the field, from patches on worn clothing and wine in new bottles.

Pride is a watchdog of the mind, which keeps out wisdom and the joy of life. Pride can reduce the whole vast universe to the compass of a single ego, self-contained, unwilling to expand.

Chapter 20
Entering Into Oneself

Most of us know our neighbors better than we know ourselves. We can tell all their faults, enumerate all the scandals about them and even add a few for good measure, but we are hardly conscious of any single fault of our own. And yet man is the only creature in the universe that has the power of being able to look at himself in a mirror; he can turn back on himself, judge his motives, see his faults and his good deeds, and thus either be pleased or angry with himself in the light of his conscience.

Most of us do not like to look inside ourselves for the same reason we do not like to open a letter that has bad news. Some try to get away from conscience by eliminating consciousness through alcoholism and drugs; others use the dubious technique of calling things by their wrong names, for example, calling darkness, light, bitter sweet, and sweet bitter. Thus they seek to escape the eternal distinction of right and wrong. Speak of evil in its true terms and you rob it of half its seductiveness. "Sex" is less appealing when called "lust"; "providing for the future" becomes vicious when labeled "avarice", and "asserting self" loses its glamor when called "egotism."

The great Greek historian, Lecky, said that the surest sign of utter degradation is when men speak of virtues as if they were vices, and of vices as if they were virtues. "They altered," he says, "the customary meaning of words in reference to actions. Men looked on deeds of infamy and were not shocked. The sin of the world and its moral corruption infected the air. Men were naked and not ashamed, not because they were innocent, but because no sense of guilt assailed them."

In our days when some politicians prostitute public office or else ally themselves with evil forces, they justify their wickedness on the ground that "they did nothing against the law." The only law for them becomes civil law, and their individual interpretation of it; never do they think of the moral law in their conscience, or the Ten Commandments. Even men who in their own personal lives are moral will nevertheless condone and even approve anything their party does even when manifestly dishonest or immoral. It is for such subservience to the trivialities of petty parties that the number of true patriots in public office steadily declines, leaving the real patriots to the battlefields.

This paralysis of conscience reaches its final stage in the mind when, as pure water becomes loathsome to the drunkard, so does justice and virtue to the depraved conscience. Then comes that mentality spoken of by the Roman satirist: "Virtutem videant, intabescantque relicta." "Let them see virtue and pine for it for now it is beyond their reach." No condition of the mind is worse than to forget the heavens from which we fall, for then we lose all aspirations for conversion.

This condition of a moral awakening is the same for all men as it was for the prodigal son who "entered into himself." Most people do not consider the state of their conscience until they are driven inside by the collapse of everything on the outside. As poverty, famine and disillusionment made the prodigal "come to himself," so it may be that some great catastrophe may be a necessary curtain raiser to a spiritual regeneration.

The earliest summons of a conscience is generally met with rebellion and resistance. The man who hates religion does so because of the evil in his life. When conscience begins to awaken, it exasperates into a more vicious rebellion. A man becomes a moral Laocoon, stung into a living martyrdom with the sting of the serpents of his guilt which lie in the bosom of conscience. When remorse scourges, the old ego becomes mad and even more violent than ever before. Temper flares, hatred of others multiplies as a projection of a disguised hatred of self, and a despondency seizes the soul from which no distraction gives relief. But all these violent outbursts against virtue are really nothing but the gathering of dark and angry clouds which one day will be dissolved in showers.

Those who have to counsel other people should therefore never take too seriously the seeming wrath against goodness and morality. It may be only the swathing grave cloths out of which the new man is to rise. He really does not hate goodness, but himself. But in his pride he will not admit it, until at last restlessness and uneasiness drive him to his knees for pardon and for light. When he begins to blame himself and not economic conditions, or his companions, or his grandmother, or his ductless glands, he find the key to happiness. There was more than fable in the old mythology which told of Pandora's box— a very receptacle of ills made tolerable only because there was hope at the bottom. Modern man is not coming to God from the goodness in the world; he is coming to God from the evil in his own heart.

Chapter 21

Goodness In Others

There are three different ways in which we may judge others: with our passions, our reason and our faith. Our passions induce us to love those who love us; our reason makes us love all people within certain limits; our faith makes us love everyone, including those who do us harm and who are our enemies. The greatest drama in life takes place when the other person is wrong from our point of view. Almost every quarrel has its basis in a mutual misunderstanding. Each of us is really an open book, but some who know us do not read the book well. We speak with great sympathy of those who understand us or who read us aright, and with some diffidence of those who do not understand.

Perhaps no one understands us better than saints, not only because they correct their bad judgment of us through their own weakness, but also because they see us as souls precious in the sight of God. St. Francis de Sales used to say: "O the beautiful souls of sinners." It was not their sins he loved, but their souls. The Cure of Ars used to walk two or three blocks alongside his country Church where there was a long line of penitents waiting to see him. He would pick out the great sinners and reserve for them the greatest sympathy. When one is in trouble, one should never go for advice to one who never says prayers or who has not passed through suffering.

There is much more goodness in most people than shows on the surface. Underneath the dross of every human there is some gold. When the sinful woman came into Simon's house, he continued to regard her as a sinner, even after she had repented. He would not give any one a chance to be different. It was no wonder the Divine Saviour had to say to Simon: "Dost thou see this woman?" Simon did not see her as she was, but only as he wanted to think of her. He thought he know all the facts, but as one of the professors of the College of France once said to his students: "Seek the facts above all else, but remember that the facts can be wrong." What he meant was that false conclusions are too often drawn from the facts, and particularly about people.

The good are not always good in all things, and the wicked are not always wicked in all things. As it has been said, "There is so much good in the worst of us and so much bad in the best of us," that it ill behooves us to talk of our neighbor. We often carry our faults in sacks behind our backs and the faults of our neighbors in open baskets in front of us. The separation of people into sheep and goats will take place only at the last day. Until then we are forbidden to make the classification. It is very likely that there will be many surprises in heaven. Many people will be there that we never expected to find, and many will not be there whom we expected to see; and finally, we probably will be most surprised to find ourselves there.

Our Divine Lord said: "Judge not and you will not be judged." By the mere fact that we judge someone else, we have already judged ourselves. How do some women know that other women are catty, unless they themselves know how it feels to be catty. The evil that is said of others is often because one is jealous of what they have. Some believe that the good qualities of others have been stolen from them. Jealousy is the tribute which mediocrity pays to genius.

One day in a group of girls, there was much admiration expressed for the dimples in the cheek of one of them. But another of them said sneeringly: "Weak face muscles." She felt that to praise another meant to condemn her.

A good rule to follow is always to judge the neighbor by his best moments rather than by his worst; not to call him a poor piano player because he hits one poor note in an entire evening, but to judge him because of all the right notes he hit. Nothing so much encourages a merciful judgment of others as the Divine warning that as we judge others, so shall we be judged. As we show mercy, we shall receive mercy. We harvest what we sow. Most people demand of their neighbor much more than God demands of them. God is more merciful to the men who mock Him, than men are merciful to the gods they make. When David sinned, God gave him the choice of being punished either by Him or by man. David chose God—His Mercy is greater.

Chapter 22

Age

As medical science increases life expectancy it has also brought to the fore the problem of growing old. The average age when life's lease runs out is, in France 61 years, in Sweden 65, in the Low Countries 68, in the United States 64 and in India 27.

Cicero wrote on old age and enumerated several of its advantages. Horace spoke of the elders as "praisers of things that are past." St. Peter in his Pentecost Sermon said the "young men will see visions, and the old men will dream dreams." Youth is full of hope and sees visions in the future; age is retrospect and recalls the glories of the past. Our Blessed Lord told Peter that old age is a restriction of liberty: "But when thou shalt be old, thou shalt stretch forth thy hands and another shall gird thee, and lead thee whither thou wouldst not."

Each age has its compensations and also a particular vice against which it must battle. Youth has to struggle against the uncontrolled impulses of the flesh. As dirt is matter in the wrong place, so lust is flesh in the wrong place. In the middle age, the passion that has to be watched is egotism or the unbridled craving for power. Here the unregulated impulse moves from the flesh to the mind, from sex to selfishness, from carnality to pride. In the third stage of life, the tendency to avarice supplants the other two. Here it is not what is within man, namely his body or his mind which distracts him, but what is outside him—the world, riches and possessions. As if conscious of his life passing, he would give a security to his mortality by filling up his barns even to the night the angel requires his soul of him.

Where there is a sense of dependence on God, a consciousness that this life is a stewardship, and a firm conviction that what we do here determines our eternity, old age does not bring sorrow or regret, but rather a joy as it did to Simon. But where life is empty there are several dangers, the first of which is alcoholism. The medical profession today is alarmed at those who have passed middle age who would dull with stimulants the little of life that still remains. The cause is very often both moral and physical. It is moral when they attempt to drown either an unrequited sense of guilt or else escape responsibility for the emptiness of their lives. It is physical when they try to excite new strength to compensate for what they know is passing, or else give themselves an illusory world with its false sense of power. St. Paul had this in mind when he said: "Let the aged men be sober."

Modern civilization has little respect for the aged for the same reason it has little for tradition. There is a love for the antique but not for the ancient. Yet the aged are to culture what memory is to the mind. Just as one cannot think without going into the storehouse of memory for the foundation stones of thought, so neither can a civilization progress without its memory which is tradition. The ancients surrounded their elders with great respect. The Greek word "presbus" was used not only to indicate an old man, but also an important and respectable ambassador chosen because of his experience. From this word has also come not only the word "presbyter" or "priest" but also "presbyope" which indicates one who is far-sighted rather than near-sighted—which is one of the qualities associated with old age.

Those who have a philosophy of life are not troubled with age. Our last days should be the best days. The evening praises the day; the last scene commands the act; and the music reserves its sweetest strains for the end. Simeon, when he saw the Divine Babe sang: "Now Thou canst dismiss Thy servant, O Lord." He speaks like a merchant who has got all his goods on shipboard, and now desires the master of the ship to hoist sail and be homeward bound.

Happy old age which uses this life to purchase the next has an outer and an inner contentment. The outward work is the spreading of charity, the using of experience to help others. The inward work is the rounding of the soul into as great a perfection as possible to meet its God.

The secret of growing old is in this counsel an old man once gave a youth: "Repent on your last day." But the youth answered: "But who knows when is my last day?" For that reason, said the Saint: "Repent today for it would be tomorrow."

Part 6

Wisdom

Chapter 23
Stick Out
Your Tongue

Ours is the most talkative age in history, not only because we can multiply words a million-fold through radio and print, but also because there are few who like to be listeners. Even youth is called upon to give its views before it has had time to learn principles. If you just put your head between your hands today to think out something, you are asked if you have a headache. What we say is a revelation of the heart.

Scripture says: "It is from the heart's overflow the mouth speaks." Modern psychology has just begun to discover that what is in the heart sooner or later makes its report on the tongue. Socrates well said: "Speak that I may see thee." When a doctor would ascertain the condition of the health of his patient, he says: "Stick out your tongue." As on that member is registered to a great extent the physical state, so also is registered there the moral condition. If there is a skunk in the cellar it will not be long until it makes itself known in every room in the house. If jealousy, hate, evil and resentment are in the heart, it will not be long until they find utterance on the tongue;

Science tells us that the vibrations of speech are recorded through the centuries. Some have even spoken of the possibility of picking up in the universe the great voices of the past, even that of the Word Himself. The spoken word is like the spent arrow; it cannot be recalled in its flight but its responsibilities endure forever. Alpine climbers bid travelers at certain points not to shout too loudly, lest the vibrations of the voice precipitate a terrible avalanche. The hasty or intemperate word, or the whispered slander has often provoked great crises in history which have drowned thousands in their misery.

It is interesting how through history law has recognized the dangers of the unbridled tongue. In China, excessive talkativeness on the part of a woman was regarded as sufficient grounds for putting her away. Menu, the legislator of the Hindus, wrote: "Whatever places are reserved for the slayer of a priest or the murderer of a woman or child, are reserved for those who give false evidence." Augustus Caesar ordered that the authors of all libels were to be punished by death. The art of speech has been studied with great competency from Aristotle onward, but few there are who regard the morals of speech. If a moral man sat down to decide for himself the one secular profession he would approach with the greatest reluctance, because of the responsibility it involved, that profession would be the publishing of a newspaper. An unskilled doctor could kill the body, but he who would use the printed word either to kill a soul, or deprive it of a single grain of divine truth, or put into it a single germ of evil would be guilty of the greater crime.

As Christ is the Word Incarnate, so every spoken word is the thought incarnate. As Hawthorne said: "Nothing is more unaccountable than the spell that often lurks in the spoken word."

A kind word gives encouragement to the despondent heart, and a cruel word makes others sob their way to the grave. There are not sufficient apostles of encouragement in the world today. The great tragedy is that so many people are unloved in the right sort of way. Instead of trying to find out what is worst in people, everyone would be happier if there were a search for even just one good point.

Streetcleaners were one day discussing a companion who had died and who indeed had few good points. But one stood up for him, scraped the bottom of the barrel for something good to say about him, and came up with the praise: "But whatever you say about him, he did sweep well around the corners." There is good in everything if we but distil it out.

Chapter 24

Patience

THE opposite of "flying off the handle" is patience—another virtue forgotten by our modern world, although Our Blessed Lord said: "In your patience you shall possess your souls" (Luke 21:19). The Greek origin of the word patience suggests two ideas: one continuance, the other submission. Combined, they mean submissive waiting; a frame of mind which is willing to wait because it knows it thus serves God and His Holy purposes. A person who believes in nothing beyond this world is very impatient, because he has only a limited time in which to satisfy his sordid wants. The more materialistic a civilization is, the more it is in a hurry. Douglas Woodruff, the English essayist, said that "Americans do not like Rome; they heard it was not built in a day." The Chinese, on the other hand, can wait for centuries, for their wants are not compassed in a generation.

Patience is not something one is born with; it is something that is achieved, such as seeing. A baby has to learn to see—to distinguish objects, and to learn distances. Sight is a gift of nature, but seeing has to be won. When Our Lord healed the blind man, he had still to learn seeing, for he said that to him the "men were as trees walking." So it is with self-possession and patience; but such a virtue is developed by resistance and control. The big problem every man has to face is whether he will, under difficulties, ride out the storm to port. Of course, if he does not know why he is living, then he must substitute tiny little wishes for one great consuming purpose; and this makes his life miserable and unhappy.

To us, often, the principal thing is the frustration, the war, the dislocation, the chaos, and the confusion. But it ought to be the destiny of the soul in the midst of this "confusion worse confounded." The winning of the battle of life is nothing but the winning of our souls, and souls are won by patience under tribulation.

Patience is not a virtue to be practiced only by the sick and by those in prison. Actually, few virtues are more essential for peace of soul, for there are hardly any circumstances of life where it cannot be practiced. There are four great areas of life in which patience can be learned. First, in the midst of provocations, that is, the indifference of others, the incivility and haughtiness of those with whom we work, the vexations at home, office, and on the highway. One of the reasons why people who are calm at home are impatient behind the steering wheel is because they know, as they shout at other drivers, that they are unknown. They regard anonymity as a protection of their character. Second, in disappointments; the rain on the day of the picnic, the late dinner guest, the cancelled visit, and the honor that never came through test us. Giving way to violence under these circumstances is a loss of self-possession. Third, restraints. No man can always be his own master. The tin can that will not open, the key that will not turn, the zipper that refuses to zip—all these are circumstances under which losing one's temper is to lose inner calm. It does no good to blame the club when the golfer is at fault. To be impatient is to aggravate the evils we must endure, and thus postpone their solution. Fourth, injuries and wrongs. No station is so high as to be immune from unjust criticism. The higher we climb, the better the target we make for sticks and stones! It is well to remember under such circumstances what Walter Winchell once said: "No man will ever get ahead of you as long as he is kicking you in the seat of your pants."

There are many who excuse themselves, saying that if they were in other circumstances, they would be much more patient. This is a grave mistake, for it assumes that virtue is a matter of geography, and not of moral effort. It makes little difference where we are; it all depends on what we are thinking about. What happens to us is not so important, but rather how we react to what happens. Judas and Peter both sinned against the Lord, and He called them both devils. But one became a Saint, because he overcame his weakness with the help of God's grace.

It is the winds and the winters which try the herbs, the flowers, and the trees, and only the strongest survive. So tribulation tries the soul, and in the strong it develops patience, and patience, in its turn, hope, and hope finally begets love.

Patience is the great remedy against becoming panicky. To be able to use reason and good judgment when everyone else goes to pieces not only saves self, but also neighbor. Men use reason better when they are calm; women use reason best at the point where man loses it. Passion impairs reason in a man; in a woman it does not. But, regardless of these differences, the patient soul can use judgment and counsel when all others are agitated and disturbed. Patience is power. As an Eastern proverb put it: "With time and patience the mulberry leaf becomes satin." Patience is not absence of action; rather it is "timing"; it waits on the right time to act, for the right principles and in the right way. The yoke sits easiest on the neck of the patient ox, and he feels his chain the lightest who does not drag, but carries it.

Chapter 25

How We Judge Anything

It is quite easy to calculate what will be the judgment of different groups of people on any moral issue which attracts public attention such as betraying the Government, using a military or political post for self-aggrandizement, or stealing another man's wife. One can predict the reaction on any moral problem with amazing exactness. Little do people realize how much they reveal their own character by the judgment they make on these moral issues.

The principle by which one predicts is the old Latin one which rendered literally is "whatever is received is received according to the manner of the one receiving it." If water is poured into a ditch, a glass and a bonfire, the reaction will be quite different. Even if a truth is poured into a mind that is sincere, a mind that is indifferent and a mind that is evil, the reception will be quite different. Why is it that children who receive exactly the same education vary so much? It is because they have a disposition or pattern made up of their choices, decisions and desires which makes them act as differently as stomachs receiving the same food.

Actually, it is not so much the knowledge that people have which determines their reaction, but their behavior; not the way they think, but the way they live. That is what Our Lord meant when He said: "Everyone that doeth evil hateth the light, but he that doeth the truth cometh to the light." Here is the reason for every assault against morality and truth. "The carnal mind is in enmity with God." Is it wrong for students to cheat, to break a sworn code? Your answer depends on whether you do evil or whether you do good. In the text, Christ charges the want of faith to immorality. Men prefer darkness; therefore they hate the light.

No man hates the Gospel so long as he keeps it; but when it rebukes his evil deeds, then he hates it. He who murders does not believe in the Fifth Commandment. The wicked can endure the Word so long as it does not gall their conscience and dig into their hearts. The drunkard does not cavil at a condemnation of hypocrisy, nor a profligate at one against avarice. The evil are in constant fear lest their actions be discovered to themselves, because that creates anxiety, guilt and trouble. The truth robs men of the good opinion they had of themselves, so they are offended by it. A sluttish housemaid, when scolded at the untidiness of the rooms said: "I am sure the rooms would be clean enough were it not for the sun which is always showing the dirty places." The good man on his way home at night wants the street well lighted; the robber or the foot-pad hates the light because it reveals his evil. Religion is loved or hated for the same reason. It all depends on what we are bent on, goodness or evil. There is a blindness which is a result of evil passion, which, if continued, can make us odious of all truth. Agnosticism is not an intellectual position, but a moral position, or better still, an intellectual defense for a life which is afraid of the light.

He, however, who lives the truth has new horizons of truth constantly opening up before him. There are many who like to boast that they are looking for the truth, but they'd drop dead if they ever found it. They like to knock at its door, but they do not want the door opened, because truth creates responsibilities. Truth is not only objective, but subjective. It is objective because independent of us. Two plus two makes four whether we like it or not. It is subjective when we are so possessed by it that we do not cheat our neighbor by adding two and two to make three. As doctrine is the intellectual phase of Divine Truth, so obedience to it is its practical phase. Truth is not just something to be believed in, but to be acted out. Once man possesses it, and it possesses man, he becomes something very different than he was before. The true life therefore is one which responds faithfully to all God's influences and which says in its joy: "My soul waiteth on the Lord."

Chapter 26

Right Attitude Toward Those Who Differ With Us

Everyone believes in the absoluteness of the multiplication table, and agrees that two and two make four. Ibsen, however, once said: "Maybe two and two make five in the fixed stars." To this, G. K. Chesterton retorted: "How do you know there are any such things as fixed stars, unless you keep adding over and over again, two and two make four?" Many persons adhere to certain causes with the same energy as they believe in the multiplication table, e. g., labor leaders, chambers of commerce, staunch Democrats, strong Republicans, etc. The greatest convictions are in the field of religion, though these actually in modern society provoke less social disturbance than economic conflicts among economic groups.

Why is it, on the one hand, when people firmly believe some religious truth, that they often consider others who refuse to accept that same truth as either stupid or bigoted? Why is it too, on the other hand, that others who have no compass or map in life, and who deny there is any truth or goodness, other than that which they decide for themselves, take a position of cynicism and ridicule in face of the believer?

Here we are concerned not with deciding which group is right but what attitude one ought to take toward, first, his own convictions, and, second, to the convictions of others. The best answer to the first problem was offered over 1,500 years ago by St. Augustine: *"Sic ergo quaeramus tanquam inventuri, et sic inveniamus tanquam quaesituri."* "Seek for the truth as one about to find it, and find it with the intention of always seeking it." Those who already have a philosophy are not to rest in idle adherence, but to keep on studying to deepen the knowledge one has, or else to discover that what he thought were profound truths were mere emotional adhesions or inherited prejudices without foundation either in history or in reason.

The second problem is the attitude to take toward those who differ with us. The answer is charity, love, benevolence and a recognition of the sincerity of motives and honesty of purposes of others. Sometimes this is called tolerance, but tolerance can be bad as well as good.

Tolerance is not right when its basic principle is a denial of truth and goodness and when it asserts that it makes no difference whether murder is a blessing or a crime, or whether a child should be taught to steal or to respect the rights of others.

But there can be another form of tolerance which is right, such as one inspired by true charity or love of God. Even though a virtuous man may hold absolutely to his philosophy of life, he does so, not because he looks down on the views of others as not as good as his own, but because his own beliefs are so real to him that he would not have anyone else hold them with less reason, less love and less devotion.

He then becomes like a mother who is very "intolerant" about the love of her child. It is not because she believes her child is prettier than any other child, or more wise, but because she would have no other mother love her child less than she loves her. She would not want that mother to believe that her child was no different from a wolf, or that it was purely a matter of opinion whether the child should have love or not. Rather her love is so deep for her child, she wants others to love just as much, and in that bond of love they will be one.

There is too often a tendency to condemn any opinion of a group or a race or class, simply because it belongs to them. A spirit of charity would suggest a willingness to search for the truth in their position, or at least to give it as kindly an interpretation as possible. There is something good in everything. Evil has no capital of its own; it lives in goodness as a parasite. But loving the partial goodness in others we bring them more quickly to the circle of Goodness which is God. This was the tactic of Our Lord when He spoke to an adulteress at the well. There was nothing in common between His Divine Goodness and her sinful life, except a love of a drink of cold water. So, He started there ... and led her on to a declaration that He was Love and Saviour of the world.

Chapter 27

Silence

WE live in the most talkative age in the history of the world. It would take ten or fifteen million men in previous ages to communicate to others the same information which one person today gives in a single broadcast. The love of noise and excitement in modern civilization is due in part to the fact that people are unhappy on the inside. Noise exteriorizes them, distracts them, and makes them forget their worries at least for the moment. There is an unmistakable connection between an empty life and a hectic pace. To make progress the world must have action, but it must also know why it is acting and that requires thought, contemplation and silence.

The world is in danger of becoming like a turnstile that is in everybody's way but stops nobody; it is a place where we look into everything but see nothing. Felix Frankfurter tells the effect of excessive talkativeness on government; everything is done under blare and noise, the deliberative process is impaired and government becomes too susceptible to quick thinking. It is, I believe, of deep significance that the Constitution of the United States was written behind closed doors, and it is well to remember that earth was thrown on the streets of Philadelphia to protect the Convention from the noise of traffic. It might also be added that when the Apostles received the Holy Spirit it was behind closed doors too, and after they kept nine days of silence awaiting the coming of heavenly Wisdom.

Action is the great need of the Eastern World; silence the need of the Western. The East with its fatalism does not believe that man does anything; the West with its actionism believes that man does everything. Somewhere in between is the golden mean wherein silence prepares for action. He who holds his tongue for a day will speak much more wisely tomorrow. Even friendships are matured in silence. Friends are made by words; love is preserved in silence. The best friends are those who know how to keep the same silences. As Maeterlinck wrote: "Speech is too often not, as the Frenchman defined it, the art of concealing Thought, but a quiet stifling and suspending Thought, so that there is none to conceal.... Speech is of time; Silence of Eternity."

The Ancient Spartans used to say that "a fool cannot be silent" and the Scriptures say that "a fool's voice is known by a flutter of words." It is all very well to plaster our Church lawn with placards saying: "Leave the world better than you find it," but no man will ever leave the world better until through silence, contemplation and prayer he improves himself. He must leave the world to help the world. That life is most effectively lived which every now and then withdraws from the scene of action to contemplation where one learns the terrible defeat and futility which come from excessive absorption in detail and action.

Throughout the United States there is growing what is known as the "Retreat Movement" in which busy men betake themselves over a week-end to a quiet place in the country where they spend time in silence, prayer and purging their consciences. The ancient Romans used to keep a bowl outside the business house, and whenever they left it at the close of day they washed their hands as if to imply that they even washed their hands of their business.

In silence, there is humility of spirit or what might be called a "wise passiveness." In such the ear is more important than the tongue. God speaks, but not in cyclones—only in the zephyrs and gentle breezes. As the scientist learns by sitting passively before nature, so the soul learns wisdom by being responsive to His Will. The scientist does not tell nature its laws; nature tells the scientist. Man does not tell or impose his will on God; in silence like Mary, he awaits an Annunciation.

From this learn the lesson that he who would become wise must become silent. A mirror is silent, yet it reflects forests, sunsets, flowers and faces. Great ascetic souls, given to years of meditation, have taken on a radiance and a beauty which are beyond the outlines of face. They seem to reflect, like the mirror on the outside, the Christ they bear within. What is really important is what happens within us, not outside us. The rapidity of communication, the hourly news broadcasts, tomorrow's news the night before—all these make people live on the surface of their souls. The result is very few live inside themselves. They have their moods determined by the world. Instead of carrying their own atmosphere with them, as the earth does as it revolves around the sun, they are like barometers that register every change in the world outside. Silence alone can give them an inner sanctuary into which they may retire for repose; as hidden gardens wherein like man before the Fall they walk with God in the cool of evening.

Only in solitariness is true spirituality born, when the soul stands naked before its God. In that moment these are the only two realities in the universe. In this discovery is born love of neighbor, for then one loves his fellowman, not because of what he can do for us, but because one sees that he too is a real or potential child of God. Though truth is not personal, we make it personal by contemplation.

Part 7

You

Chapter 28

The Spirit Of Forgiveness

THE alarming amount of hatred loose in the modem world is largely caused by guilt: the man who hates himself soon begins to hate his fellowmen. Unconfessed, and sometimes unadmitted sins create a deep unease within the personality ... the balance has to be, somehow, restored; the self must somehow be placed in a more favorable light. The right way to do this is to admit, confess and do penance for our sins. The wrong way ... which many unhappy people take today ... is to make the self-seem better, sins and all, by detracting from someone else. The individual who has injured someone he loves often discovers that the act has turned his love to hate: he can now appear innocent in his own eyes only if he accuses the other of grave faults to justify the injury done him. To pass thus from love to hatred is all too easy; but to turn hatred into love is hard, for it can be done only if the self-deception is punctured, the injury confessed.

A second cause of hatred is fear: men who have ceased to fear the Lord soon begin to fear one another. Feeling themselves weak ... as they are ... men tremble before the dangers of a "hostile world" they cannot placate or conquer. Fear of God is a very different thing: it is not a servile fear, such as a slave feels toward his tyrant, but a reverential fear, such as a child may have for a loving father. The proper fear of God relieves us from all temporal fears: we trust Him to protect us and to befriend us through all dangers. But those who lack this belief in God direct their fears towards other men and grow to hate their neighbors as so many threats to their security.

Hatred is a dangerous emotion to encourage. It can even become a physical poison: an English medical journal reported the case of a mother whose hatred of her husband affected her milk and poisoned the baby she was nursing. Anger and hatred can also affect the digestive processes, causing dyspepsia and ulcers.

Hatred is hard to stop, for, if let alone, it sets off a chain-reaction. One man's animosity arouses anger in another, who, in turn, creates rage in someone else. That is why Our Lord told us when we are struck on one cheek, to turn the other; thus, by an interior effort of the will, we bring the chain of anger to an end. The only way to destroy hate is for an individual to absorb it and, in his own heart, convert it into love.

Such a course is difficult for us: we men have so small a reservoir of love within us that, if we draw on it, it soon runs dry. We have then to find another source of love in order to forgive ... a new and added quota of potential mercy.

There are two considerations which make it easier for us to ask God to help us to forgive others. We can remember how many faults of our own He has forgiven us. And we can try to help God in His own perpetual efforts to save the erring soul.

The first consideration is a matter of plain fact: each of us has done worse things to God than any neighbor has ever done to us. That is why Our Lord warns against seeing the speck in our neighbor's eyes and ignoring the great beam in our own: when we recall the offenses we have had forgiven us, then we realize that we are in no position to withhold forgiveness from a neighbor. As our Divine Lord has told us, "I remitted all that debt of thine at thy entreaty; was it not thy duty to have mercy on thy fellowman, as I have mercy on thee?"

The second consideration moving us towards forgiveness can be reduced to earthly terms: suppose that some enemy has done us a very serious injury. But suppose that the father of our enemy comes to us and says that, for years, he has tried to make his son kind and good, but without success. Yet he has not abandoned hope, and he pleads with us that we, too, shall join his efforts to save the son. Such an appeal would soften our hearts.

God is, in fact, such a father. He, Who is long-suffering with His rebellious children, wishes us to be patient with them, too—to try to help Him bring them to an area of love. This point is brought out in the story told of Abraham in the desert: one night a stranger is said to have approached his tent and implored his hospitality. Abraham gave him the best of food, surrendered his own bed, waited on him ... but the stranger complained and upbraided and found fault. Abraham was about to turn him out, in anger at his ingratitude, when God spoke to him: "Abraham," he said, "I have put up with that man for forty years. Can't you stand him for one night?"

The ability to forgive others their offenses comes to us only from God, but He will not withhold the power if we ask for it. His own words tell us, "Be merciful then as your Heavenly Father is merciful. Judge nobody, and you will not be judged; condemn nobody, and you will not be condemned; forgive, and you will be forgiven. The measure you award to others is the measure that will be awarded to you."

Chapter 29

The Divine Psychology of Gossip

TRADITIONALLY, all gossips are women; but men are often guilty of the same offense. They call it "judging."

Our Divine Lord, in speaking of gossips, said: "Do not judge others, or you yourselves will be judged." His admonition not to "judge" demands that we make no wicked evaluations, do not look for the worst in others. God alone sees our neighbor's heart; we see only his face. In England the judges wear wigs in court, to show that it is the law which is passing judgment, and not their own personal views. This is done in recognition of the truth all men suspect—that there is something impudent in allowing even the wisest among us to engage in pigeon-holing our friends or cataloguing our enemies.

When we judge others, we also judge ourselves. Our Lord asked us not to judge, lest we be judged; and sometimes the judgment we make of others is in itself a condemnation of our own faults. When one woman calls another "catty," she reveals that she knows what cattiness involves. Jealousy can be a tribute paid by mediocrity to genius: the jealous person then admits the superiority of his rival but since he cannot reach that level himself, he drags the other down to his. Other forms of criticism are equally revealing of the one who criticizes.

Our Lord told us that the gossip's faults are often greater than those he criticizes in his neighbor. "How is it that thou canst see the speck of dust which is in thy brother's eye, and are not aware of the beam that is in thy own? By what right wilt thou say to thy brother, Brother, let me rid thy eye of that speck, when thou canst not see the beam that is in thy own? Thou hypocrite, take the beam out of thy own eye first, and so thou shalt have clear sight to rid thy brother's of the speck."

The "speck" was only a bit of chaff, a splinter of wood. But the beam was a sizable piece of timber. To set ourselves up as worthy of judging others is already to see ourselves as their superiors, to be guilty of the sin of pride, the huge "beam" that obscures our vision. We cannot gossip without either over-rating ourselves or under-rating our neighbors ... and frequently we do both. For the gossip is prone to project onto another the fault he suspects within himself. No one gets angrier at being told a lie than an habitual liar. The incurable gossip flies into a rage when he hears that he, in turn, has been talked about behind his back.

Our Lord asked the gossips to examine their own right to condemn the faults of others. "He that is without sin among you, let him cast the first stone." The implication is clear: innocence alone has the right to condemn. But innocence will always wish to take on the guilt of the other, to atone for his failings as if they were his own. Love recognizes the sin, but love also dies for it.

We instinctively feel that the abuse of our neighbors is wrong, and we show it by the words we use when we are about to cut somebody's throat. For they are words of self-apology: "One doesn't like to be uncharitable, but ... or, "Of course, we mustn't criticize, but ...," or "I always prefer not to judge anyone, but ... These words presage the knife ... and the effect on him who has wielded it is always psychological darkness. "He that loveth his brother abideth in light ... But he that hateth his brother is in darkness."

God has offered a beautiful reward to those who do not "judge": they themselves shall not be "judged" when they are brought before the heavenly court. Yet God's "judgment"—which they will escape—is sure to be more merciful than any that we make. David, when he had sinned, was asked whether he would rather receive his punishment from God or from man; and he wisely chose God's judgment as offering the greater mercy.

We men and women are not wise enough nor innocent enough to judge each other. And the only decision we can rightly make about our brother who is doing wrong is to admit it and to say, "We will leave him to God."

Chapter 30

The Dark Side
Of Good

BECAUSE of cold wars, high taxes, threats of Communism, and general insecurity, we have become accustomed to take a dark view of the world. There is some justification for this, for never before in the history of Christian civilization was there ever such a mass attack on decency, honor, personal rights and freedom as there is at the present hour. While there is justification for looking on the dark side because of evil, there is, however, no justification for the present tendency to look upon the dark side of good. It is one thing to be gloomy about starvation, but it is quite another matter to be gloomy about good health; disease has its shadows, but why see shadows in health? In a word, why is it that so many see the dark side of virtue, goodness, honesty, purity and honor?

In other ages, though men lost virtue, they still admired it; though they ran from the battlefield at the first need of courage, they still admired the hero who fought and suffered; though they threw away the map of the roadway of life, they never denied the need of a map. But, in our generation, men look for shadow in the radiance of every virtue. Love of truth is called harshness and intolerance; purity is called abnormality or fear of totems or myths; humility is termed weakness; the meek are made to appear as lacking in force and strength; those who pray and believe in God are labeled "escapists"; the generous are accused of seeking acclaim; the contemplative are sneered at as "useless"; the husband of one wife and a devoted father of a family is "in a rut."

A civilization can be forgiven for seeing the dark side of evil, but should it not examine its conscience when it begins to fear the dark side of the good? The right and normal reaction when one sees a shadow is to think of the light; in fact, the darker the shadow the brighter the light. Goodness needs but little explanation, for good is self-propagating and self-explanatory; it is the evil, darkness and suffering which need explanation. One does not only conclude to the existence of God because there are good things in the world; but one argues that because there is evil in the world, therefore there must be a God, for evil is a parasite on goodness. It has no capital of its own. Darkness is not a positive entity; darkness is the absence of light and is intelligible only in terms of light. Most of the suffering of the world is intelligible in terms of the abuse of something that is so profoundly good that not even God will take it away for all eternity, and that is our freedom.

Whence then comes the tendency to see the bad in things, if it be not that our consciences are already so burdened with guilt and hidden distortions that to ease them, we have to minimize the good in others and drag them down to the level of the worst or else reduce heroism to mediocrity. Public officials are thought to be best described, when not the good that they do is recounted, but when some suspicion or slur is cast upon their characters. The kettles are unhappy unless they call the pots black.

How our outlook on the world would change if the makers of public opinion, instead of seeing the dark side of the evil alone, would see the bright side of the good; if they would single out politicians, business men, labor leaders, parents and others who mirror forth great virtues and moral integrity, then the evil of the world would be more quickly overcome. When pestilence is abroad, it is encouraging to know that there are recoveries and there are many who are not stricken. But if our doctors are accused of being diseased and our teachers are accused of ignorance; if our public officials are all crooks, then who shall hope?

We do not make children give up writing because they spill the ink. The world is discouraged enough; it needs encouragement, inspiration, good example; above all, it will be happier when it sees a standard and a Redeemer Who invites us away from the dark side: "I am the Light of the world; he that followeth Me walketh not in darkness."

Chapter 31
Memory

Memory is one of the most neglected factors in modern education. In previous generations children had to memorize poetry, irregular verbs, and important historical dates, and such is still the case in many European schools. Perhaps the neglect of memory is in part due to the modern contempt of anything that implies effort, discipline and application. But the penalties are terrific as business men go madly searching for typists who can spell.

God has blessed some people with remarkable powers of retention. It is said that Themistocles knew by heart the names of twenty thousand citizens of Athens. History records that Cyrus knew the name of every soldier in his army. On the other hand, Aristotle held that people who have such vivid memories for details never have good judgment. This may be because images pile up with such rapidity as to destroy the relation between abstract ideas which are essential for judgment.

Lord Bacon and Coleridge both held that nothing that is impressed on the memory ever leaves it. This is evident in persons who in old age are brought before the scenes of their childhood, and immediately names, places and incidents come out from their storehouse of memory and the past is lived again. As old palimpsests bear the original writing under dust or new messages, so the memory retains all that we have seen and heard, said and done. Today is but the product of all our yesterdays, and our present is but the harvest of the past. The fragments of our memory are very much like islands for the moment unconnected. But it may be that they are continuous, as the solid earth itself is continuous if one did but drain off the water from the seas.

Hidden in this retentive power of memory may also be the basis of what will be our final judgment, for what is memory but an infallible autobiography? As at the end of the day the business man takes out of the cash register a record of all the debits and the credits, so at the end of life the memory offers the basis of how we shall be judged. As Coleridge put it: *"And this perchance is the dread book of judgment, in whose mysterious hieroglyphics every idle word is recorded. Yes, in the very nature of a living spirit, it may be more possible that heaven and earth should pass away than that a single act, a single thought, should be loosened from that living chain of causes, to all whose links, conscious or unconscious, the free will, our own absolute self, is coextensive and co-present."*

Memory is the source of unhappiness to many people today; hence their attempts to stifle it with alcohol. What is the explanation for the vast amount of sleeping tablets sold to the American public? It has been pointed out that enough are sold to put every person in the United States to sleep twenty-two nights a year, or to put nine million people to sleep three hundred and sixty-five nights a year. Undoubtedly, some of this is medically necessary for the easing of pain, but more likely most of the pills are taken in an effort to "forget" or "get away from it all." The memory has the peculiar trick of never asking our permission for anything it shoots up into consciousness; sometimes the more displeasing the ideas are, and the harder we try to forget them, the quicker and the more often they flash before our eyes. It is a psychological fact that the more the mind fears a thing, the more that fearful thing comes like a ghost out of the past to torture it. What we hate and dread we remember best, and nothing that we present to our mind can blot it out. No wonder Lady Macbeth asked: *"Who can blot from the mind a rooted sorrow?"*

What is driving people to sleeping tablets is to some extent driving them to psychoanalytical couches—they are in flight from what is distasteful and what cannot be blotted out—and most often it is unrequited guilt. We point out these sad facts to remind those who are full of fears and anxieties that there is another remedy besides sleeping tablets, and that is consciously confronting our guilt and asking the pardon of God. Another way is to live right, so we won't have to try to forget.

Chapter 32
What Makes Us Normal

Unless we have a clear idea of what it is to be normal, we shall never know when we have departed from the standard of mental and moral health. And so, an understanding of how a human being "works" ... and ought to "work" ... will help us to catch ourselves, in time, and put a stop to our tendencies towards abnormality.

Every single human movement passes through three stages. First, there is a thought. Next, an emotional response. Finally, an act.

The idea always comes before the emotion. A daughter's tears do not cause her mother's death; it is the death which occasions the tears. Thus the mind registers experience, as it becomes aware of events in the world about us; then, like a captain on the bridge of a ship, it signals the event to the body which is under its control, like orders going to a ship's engine-room. The body responds with the appropriate emotion.

We may think of our bodies (which include our emotions) as musical instruments upon which the mind of a man may play whatever tune he wishes. For the kind of thoughts we allow into our minds determine the kind of feelings we will later have. Worry can cause ulcers, and the thought of something fearful can drive blood to the active muscles, causing them to tense.

Emotions normally lead us to action, and so become discharged; for actions are the third or final stage, of which an idea was the first. In even the simplest actions the process is clear: a spectator at a football game may swerve his body towards an opening which the player does not see. The idea of the opening brought about a wish to see it filled (the emotion), and the body's action followed the wish and the idea!

When we once know this much about ourselves, we can use the facts in everyday life. We see, at once, the absurdity of saying, "It makes no difference how you think; all that matters is how you live." For we act on our beliefs, and if our ideas are wrong, so will our actions be. To desire evil is to prepare ourselves for evil deeds: "He who casts his eyes on a woman so as to lust after her has already committed adultery in his heart."

And if our creed is wrong, our behavior will err. If we have not discovered true answers to the question of why we are here and where we are going, we cannot feel or act with certainty or with consistency. The man who does not think straight will neither feel happy nor act rightly, for the idea is the source of all he feels and does.

Sometimes wrong ideas slip past our guard; they may even reach the second stage of emotional attraction before we are able to arrest them. But usually we can catch an idea in its first stage, and should, if it is a wrong or unhealthy idea, always try to banish it from our minds at once. It is always best to watch it early, before it begets an emotion: the mind must be as careful of the ideas on which it feeds as the stomach is of the food it absorbs. Yet many people who would never dream of serving garbage at their tables will welcome garbage-literature and garbage-moving-pictures into their minds.

Ideas and emotions should not be repressed ... that is, they should not be pushed out of consciousness through fear or guilt or an unwillingness to admit that "someone like me" could ever have such thoughts. Ideas that run counter to the moral law and the Christian ideal should be expelled from the mind calmly, and with no more flurry than we would use in rejecting an undigestible piece of food which is offered us.

If an idea which is evil reaches the emotional stage, we can still dispose of it, and without either repressing it (which is dangerous) or expressing it in action (which is usually worse). We can express the emotional energy the idea has given us, but in the opposite direction, so that it becomes a force of good.

Suppose, for instance, that a man employed by a bank has a strong temptation to effect a robbery, and that he finds his heart beating in anticipation of the pleasures such a theft would buy for him. If he dwells on the idea in morbid fear, he will paralyze all his normal actions. If he submits to the temptation, he will find stealing becoming a habit, for "appetite grows by what it feeds on". But there is a way out: he can channel his energy into a useful direction. Instead of letting his mind contrive methods of defrauding the bank, he can use the same mental energy to increase his efficiency and, eventually, win for his honest own the money he had begun to covet.

Evil thoughts are best destroyed by good thoughts that crowd them, evil loves by stronger loves of the good. St. Paul says, "Be not overcome by evil, but overcome evil by good." Evil is not to be fought, head-on, by mere brute will-power; it is better for us to flank it, to drive it from the field by a greater intensity of goodness, a greater love for God. A mind filled with ideas of love and beauty has little room for evil notions.

Part 8

Faith

Chapter 33

For Those Who Work For God

Those who are working for the acquiring of a fortune, or to enjoy life, or maybe to exist, will approach work from an entirely different point of view than the man who works for God. The peculiar characteristic of the latter is that when he has rendered it all he may not indulge in any self-complacency as if he had done anything extraordinary or deserved any special commendation, for everything that is done belongs to God. There will be no whimpering over his lot or complaining that it is tremendously hard as if he were undergoing a species of martyrdom. On the other hand, he will not be looking for any extraordinary reward as if it were that which was sought rather than the service of the One we love.

The difference between those who labor for themselves and those who labor for God is the difference between a hired servant in the house and a son or a daughter who works out of love for his or her parents. When the life of a mother is hanging in the balance no one can persuade a daughter or a son to take rest. All standards of duty and "enoughness" and legalism are destroyed and transcended by love. A love transforms work to such an extent that it almost ceases to be work where there is love. So long as a man's work is merely the carrying out of another's orders it will tend to become mechanical and methodical. But the moment a man becomes identified in spirit with his work, the moment the work becomes the expression of the great idea and the instrument of sympathy and affection, above all, when it takes on the character of a passion or an enthusiasm, it overlaps all mechanical bounds.

Sick patients always feel very differently toward the physician when he visits and charges for it, than when he visits saying: "I just dropped in to see how you were." Our Blessed Lord had no word of thanks for the grumbling slave who grudges the service at table after the day's ploughing. Those who love the master never even think of sacrifice. Nothing can be called a sacrifice which is simply paid back as a small part of a debt which is owed to God and which never can be repaid. The very moment we grow complacent about our work, our work spoils in our hands. We begin to think of ourselves instead of our work, of the wonders that we have achieved instead of the toils that lie before us and how best we can discharge them. As soon as complaint about our lot and our task begins, as soon as we protest that our burdens are too heavy, we immediately unfit ourselves for them, make them more formidable than before and ourselves less competent to do them.

Honesty of intention, purity and sincerity of motives, the cheerfulness with which we address ourselves to our work counts more before God than the amount of work that we do. He said that we should be content even to wait at the Master's table after we had ploughed the soil and fed the cattle. Though the time of our eating and drinking may come later, we shall work then for His Glory, thus eating our bread with gladness and singleness of heart, not for enjoyment alone but that we may gain new strength for serving Him. Creation alone, not to speak of Redemption, places us under a debt to God which our most accurate creditors can never discharge. If our best services cannot discount His past favors, much less can we plead them for the future. Whatever encouragement He gives as an annex to our obedience will be acknowledged as a pure bounty of grace and love.

There is a beautiful story told about the great Spartan Brasidas. When he complained that Sparta was a small state, his mother said to him: "Son, Sparta has fallen to your lot and it is your duty to adorn it." We are all workers of this world and regardless of the lot in which we are cast, the duty is ever the same—to adorn it.

Chapter 34

Cares

THE world and modern man are learning the same lesson in the present crisis, namely, the helplessness of either to save self. A century and a half of pride has made modern man feel that the burden is on himself alone, and that if he steps from under it there must be a crash. This kind of pride begets the greatest despair, for in a crisis it can appeal to nothing outside itself.

It may well be that the world at the present time is being humbled that we may learn that trusting in God is something else besides an inscription on a penny. God, of course, does not hold out His arms to our burden without our cooperation. Casting all our care on God is casting self on God, for self is our worst care. As a parent will not for a time help his son with his studies, if he in the beginning said he could learn them by himself, so God sometimes shuts Himself up from man until man is sorely in need of help. Even then God does not force man's will, but He wills that he should look squarely at the importance of self and acknowledge that he has used up all his capital, that the world cannot help him, and that he has nothing in heaven or on earth but God. The bitterest draught man can ever drink is the confession of his utter inadequacy. The world says that at this moment man is at his worst; actually he is at his best. Man is at his worst if he falls into despair; but he is at his best if humbled he cries to God for help.

The words of Our Divine Lord: "He that humbleth himself shall be exalted, and he that exalteth himself shall be humbled" express sound psychology insights as well as a spiritual fact. How often we see a man endowed with more conceit than ability, more self-confidence than resources conducting some important business. His very exaltation brings out his humiliation, his height accentuates his nothingness.

On the other hand, those who have swallowed their pride, confessed their inability to perform great tasks, from that moment on grow in the esteem of men. The sporting world traditionally loves the "underdog." In the boxing world the little fighter with the small odds wins the crowd by his courage. Comedians too "exalt" themselves by being "humbled" by their "straight man" or by the guest star. The humble violet that grows close to the earth is more praised by poets than the sunflower that always turns its head to the spotlight.

The humble man casts his cares upon God—such cares as business and family cares, frequent misunderstandings with fellowmen and the culture of his own soul. There would be much less anxiety in the world if souls would see that trials are often permitted by an all-loving Providence to purify us from sin, to detach us from what is harmful. Fellow creatures generally do not want our cares, for they have enough of their own. Only God is left to be solicitous of our cares. Throwing them upon Him is done in two ways: by prayers and by faith. Prayer tells God what care is; faith believes that God can and will lift it. No man can cast his cares upon an "it." If there is ever to be a relief for the burdens of the human heart, there must be behind the universe something more than a vague Power, namely, a loving Father. He who careth for the sparrows, the lilies of the field and knows even the fall of the hair from the head, will not indeed be unmindful of us toward whom He made the greatest act of love this world has ever seen.

Some wrongly believe the proper thing to do with cares is to try to banish them from our mind and to seek pleasures in order to forget our cares. But it is not easy to ignore anxieties. Dr. Johnson's cure for toothache —to treat it with contempt—is all right for those who have no toothache. Then, too, pleasures indulged in too much beget their own cares. The greatest care of all, which is a feeling of personal guilt the denial of which has produced so many mental upsets, can be relieved only by throwing ourselves on an all-loving God. Aristotle said men would laugh if they were told to cast their cares on Jupiter, for his work was only to shake the heavens as a thunderer, not to draw men to him in their woes.

To solve our cares God must not only be Personal, He must also be in the dust of human cares. That is why He with full understanding of our troubles can say: "Come to Me, all ye who labor and are heavily burdened and find rest for your souls."

Chapter 35

How To Overcome Bad Habits

"I have a bad temper," or "I drink too much" — "I am always criticizing," or "I am lazy" are familiar complaints from those who still believe that nobility of character is an important goal. They would not make such admissions if they did not have a strong desire to break the chain of evil habits. They can realize this desire—any bad habit can be broken. But getting free of it requires four things:

Introspection is necessary in order that we shall isolate the habit and see it clearly as a sin. The surprise we feel when others criticize some fault in us proves that we have not practiced introspection sufficiently to know ourselves. Some people are afraid ever to look into their consciences, for fear of what they might find; they are like the other cowards who dare not open telegrams because they dread bad news. But introspection is to the soul what diagnosis is to the body—the first necessary step toward health. The Prodigal Son "entered into himself" before he was able to resolve to admit his mistakes to his father. Turning the search-light of attention upon ourselves shows us the vice or evil habit which requires correction; it makes us see ourselves not as we wish we were, but as we really are.

Avoiding the occasions of sin is the easiest way of avoiding sin itself. The way to keep out of trouble is to keep out of the situations that lead up to trouble: the man who gets burned whenever he is near a fire had better eschew fires. The alcoholic must avoid the first sip of the first drink; the libertine must keep away from pretty women, the evil-minded must flee the company of those who degrade him. Our Lord said, "He that loveth the danger will perish therein." Temptation is hard to overcome at the last moment, when the sin is within our reach; it is easy to overcome if we act decisively to avoid a situation in which we might be tempted. Environments can make sin repulsive or attractive to us, for our surroundings affect us all. But we can choose the environment we wish and can ruthlessly reject the one that leads to trouble. Our Lord told us, "If thy right eye is the occasion of thy falling into sin, pluck it out and cast it away from thee." This means that if the books we read, the homes we visit, the games we play cause us to stumble morally, then we should cut them out and cast them from us.

Chapter 36

God Is Self-Preserving

If our wills are on the side of God, we cannot be discouraged, for the side which we have chosen is always victorious, is never flouted. God is self-preserving, and evil is self-defeating. The reality of things is ever on the side of God.

Evil is necessarily unstable, because it runs counter to the nature of things as they were made. All the laws of our human nature nudge us toward our proper destiny of holiness, as of health. If we attend to our bodies properly, obeying the rules of health, we are healthy; if we break these laws, our rebellion brings sickness ... and few of us would take proper care of ourselves if the violation of the laws of health did not carry some penalty, as a reminder.

We are free in this and other fields to break the laws God has set down, but we are not free to escape the penalty that breaking His laws entails. To jump from a window does not destroy the law of gravitation; but it may destroy our lives. Nature is on God's side, always; it will betray our wants, but never His commands. And this is as true in the moral sphere as in the physical.

When men sin, there is no need for God to intervene to see that they are punished: our natures are so made that we cannot oppose Him without being in opposition to ourselves. If we break the law of temperance, a headache follows. God did not send that headache by a special Act; He had already made us in such a way that our evil deeds result in evil effects. The poet Francis Thompson describes how even things turn against us when we do not use them for God's purposes. He calls created objects "servitors":

> *"I tempted all His servitors, but to find*
> *My own betrayal in their constancy*
> *In faith to Him, in fickleness to me,*
> *Their traitorous trueness, and their loyal deceit."*

When Peter denied our Lord, the cock crowed, causing him great pain. The very barnyard had turned on Peter, for Nature belongs to God.

When we reject the moral law, we suffer ... not because we intended evil, but simply because we defied a force stronger than ourselves: the reality of things. In sinning, we thus produce an effect which we did not intend; this never happens as a result of our good actions. If I use a pencil to write with, the pencil is unharmed; if I try to open a tin can with it, I break it in two. I have used the pencil in a way contrary to its purpose, and so destroyed it.

If I live my life according to its highest purpose ... and that is the attainment of Truth and Love ... I will perfect it. If I live according to my animal impulses, I frustrate myself as surely as I would frustrate a razor by using it to hew a stone.

Evil is always mutilation of the self. If I live as I ought to live, I become a man; if I live as my whims dictate, I become a beast, and an unhappy beast. This is not a result I ever planned, but it is still unavoidable. The man who wills to over-drink does not intend to ruin his health, but he does just that. The man who overeats does not count on indigestion, but he gets it. The man who wills to steal has not aimed at prison, yet that is where he lands.

When a traveller refuses to follow the guide-posts showing him the right way, he may still, eventually, reach his goal by finding disappointment at the end of every false trail. Disorder is a stern teacher, and a slow one, but a certain one. The Spanish have a proverb: "He who spits against Heaven spits in his own face." Evil may triumph for a little while. It can win the first battle, but it loses the booty and the reward.

Caesar built roads to carry the screaming eagles of Rome across the world in military triumph; but over those roads Peter and Paul carried the Gospels, instead. Thus the end of this very century will see scientists and philosophers picking out of the wastebasket of the universities all the Sacred and Divine Truths which the Eighteenth and Nineteenth Centuries threw away.

For good is self-preserving. Evil defeats itself.

www.ingramcontent.com/pod-product-compliance
Lightning Source LLC
Chambersburg PA
CBHW030230100526
44583CB00013BA/639